Positioning
Pooh

Children's Literature Association Series

Positioning Pooh

Edward Bear after 100 Years

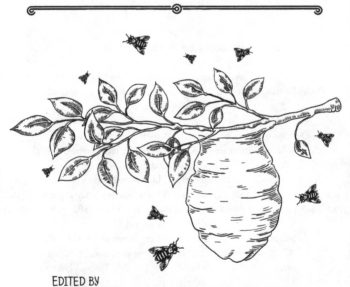

EDITED BY

JENNIFER HARRISON

University Press of Mississippi / Jackson

The University Press of Mississippi is the scholarly publishing agency of
the Mississippi Institutions of Higher Learning: Alcorn State University,
Delta State University, Jackson State University, Mississippi State University,
Mississippi University for Women, Mississippi Valley State University,
University of Mississippi, and University of Southern Mississippi.

www.upress.state.ms.us

The University Press of Mississippi is a member
of the Association of University Presses.

First printing 2021
∞

Library of Congress Cataloging-in-Publication Data

Names: Harrison, Jennifer, 1983– editor.
Title: Positioning Pooh: Edward Bear after one hundred years / edited by
Jennifer Harrison.
Other titles: Children's Literature Association series.
Description: Jackson: University Press of Mississippi, 2021. | Series:
Children's Literature Association series | Includes bibliographical
references and index.
Identifiers: LCCN 2021010551 (print) | LCCN 2021010552 (ebook) | ISBN
978-1-4968-3410-2 (hardback) | ISBN 978-1-4968-3411-9 (trade paperback) | ISBN
978-1-4968-3412-6 (epub) | ISBN 978-1-4968-3413-3 (epub) | ISBN 978-1-4968-3414-0
(pdf) | ISBN 978-1-4968-3415-7 (pdf)
Subjects: LCSH: Milne, A. A. (Alan Alexander), 1882–1956.
Winnie-the-Pooh—Criticism and interpretation. | Children's
literature—History and criticism. | LCGFT: Essays. | Literary
criticism.
Classification: LCC PR6025.I65 Z84 2021 (print) | LCC PR6025.I65 (ebook)
| DDC 823/.912—dc23
LC record available at https://lccn.loc.gov/2021010551
LC ebook record available at https://lccn.loc.gov/2021010552

British Library Cataloging-in-Publication Data available

Contents

Introduction

Jennifer Harrison

A Brief History of Pooh

One hundred years ago, in August 1920, a baby boy was born whose name would soon become known throughout the length and breadth of the English-speaking world—and beyond (Connolly 1995, xiii). Christopher Robin Milne, known to his family as "Moon," was the only child of A. A. Milne, a respected playwright, *Punch* columnist, and soon-to-be author of *Winnie-the-Pooh* and *The House at Pooh Corner*.[1] In the same year, a young Canadian bear named Winnie was settling into her new home in London Zoo. She had been donated to that institution in December 1919 by Canadian soldier Harry Colebourn, who had bought her from a trapper in 1914 for twenty dollars but was forced to leave her behind when his regiment departed England for the battlefields of Europe (Mattick 46–47). In 1920, a further piece of the puzzle that would later become the Winnie-the-Pooh canon was falling into place: production was underway on a small stuffed bear toy, one of many that would soon grace the shelves of Harrods Department Store in London. This bear would be purchased in 1921 as a birthday present for the one-year-old Billy Moon and would become one of his most beloved toys, as well as a muse for his literary father. Close comparison of pictures from the New York Public Library (New York Public Library n.d.) and from Harrods' designer pages suggest that the bear was one of Harrods' now-famous Steiff bears, originally conceived by designer Margarete Steiff in 1880, and redesigned and rereleased by Harrods and Steiff periodically ever since (Harrods n.d.). At this early point, boy, bear, and toy were yet to become acquainted; nevertheless—seemingly independent of the agency of the author who would later make them famous—all three were already contributing the Pooh phenomenon as we know it today. This culmination of disparate events would make 1920 one of the most momentous for the history of children's literature.

Pooh has, perhaps more than any other classic character in children's literature (although Alice and Peter Pan may well come close), suffered from a multiplicity of existence, as will be further described by contributors throughout this volume. Ann Thwaite, in her 2014 biography of Milne, identifies the "real" Winnie as the Canadian black bear residing at London Zoo who was a particular favorite of Christopher Milne; she states that "Milne could not remember whether Winnie at the zoo was called after Pooh or Pooh after Winnie, but we know that that large American bear was Winnie long before Christopher Robin was born" (Thwaite 2014, 285), a story that is corroborated by the 2015 children's book *Finding Winnie*, written by Lindsay Mattick, a descendent of the Canadian soldier Harry Colebourn who had brought Winnie to London. The "Pooh" portion of the famous bear's name is identified variously in *When We Were Very Young* and the introduction to *Winnie-the-Pooh* as being a swan, also befriended by the young Christopher Milne (Thwaite 1994, 58).

The collaboration originally begun by the Milnes, illustrator Ernest Howard Shepard and his family, Winnie herself, and the many toys and personalities who fed into the Pooh legend would continue to metamorphose throughout the twentieth and twenty-first centuries to become the phenomenon known across the globe today. However, an equally strong argument can be made for the "real" Pooh being identified with the toy bear, bought from Harrods in London, that Christopher Milne was given by his grandparents on his first birthday in 1921 (Connolly 1995, xiii); this bear would, according to Christopher himself, become his constant and inseparable companion as well as the basis for the famous stories written by his father (Milne 2016, 76). That bear, however, despite being the bear to whom the name "Winnie-the-Pooh" was first given, was not the bear most readers would identify; Thwaite explains that the bear drawn by Shepard, which would become the iconic "classic" image of Winnie-the-Pooh, was in fact modeled on his own, older son Graham's bear, Growler, and appeared first in the pages of *Punch* in 1913, long before Christopher Milne was even born (Thwaite 1994, 31). The

Pooh who appears twice in *When We Were Very Young* is still known as (and named as) Edward Bear, modeled on Growler but reflecting the personality of Christopher Milne's Winnie-the-Pooh (Thwaite 1994, 58).

As the Pooh franchise grew, this initially murky ontological start would become more convoluted still. As early as the 1930s, the popularity of Pooh had spawned a number of spin-off toy products, resulting in "real" Pooh toys ranging from plush dolls to china figurines (Thwaite 1994, 138), a marketing phenomenon that would explode even further with the Disney acquisition of the franchise in the 1960s. Daphne Kutzer writes that Milne "is as beloved today as he was in the twenties, and in fact, Pooh has become an emperor of sorts in the commercial kingdom: there is a plethora of *Pooh*-related merchandise available to consumers, everything from bubble bath to videos" (Kutzer 2000, 80). Pooh products, which give tangibility to the literary figures (which are themselves modeled on a tangible reality), have become further complicated by the proliferation of different versions that followed from Disney's involvement in the franchise. Aaron Taylor's incisive exploration of the effects of Disney's marketing campaign on the ontology of Pooh, for example, highlights the way in which identity has become an integral concern for the franchise: "The invention of a 'Classic Pooh' has led to issues of a problematic authenticity with which other Disney characters have not had to contend. Which is the true Pooh?" (Taylor 2005, 182). Paula Connolly writes regretfully that for many modern fans, Pooh is identified solely with the Disney character(s)[2] and the products associated with him (Connolly 1995, 111). Even more extreme is the 1981 case cited by H. Peter Steeves, in which "the family of a nine-year-old girl took Winnie-the-Pooh to court, claiming he had slapped her across the face"; according to Steeves, not only was the actor inside the costume required to give his testimony, but Winnie-the-Pooh made a second appearance in the courtroom as himself and answered cross-examination "only by nodding his head or stomping his feet" before being acquitted (Steeves 2003, 176). Clearly, the fractured identity of Pooh in this example indicates the extent to which his "reality" has become problematic in modern American culture.

What becomes clear after only a brief examination of this evolutionary history is that the Pooh phenomenon has been marked from the beginning by a complexity belied by the seeming simplicity and innocence of the stories themselves. This volume, which hopes to fill a decades-long leanness in concentrated Pooh scholarship, seeks to offer insight highlighting the plurality of perspectives, modes, and interpretations these stories offer, especially after the insinuation of the Walt Disney Company into the canon in the 1950s.

A Brief History of Pooh Scholarship

Hindered perhaps by the publication of Frederick Crews's *The Pooh Perplex* in 1963 (Yarbrough 2011, 16),[3] Pooh scholarship is sparse compared to other classics from the "golden age" of children's literature. The stories were traditionally considered simplistic and datedly nostalgic; painting a classic picture of childhood innocence, they seemed to many readers to gloss over issues of conflict, inequality, privilege, and prejudice in support of an idealized fantasy world, leading Peter Hunt to ask in 1992, "[W]hat makes them survive despite the fact that they encapsulate so many of the central dilemmas of children's books?" (Hunt 1992, 112). This question is of fundamental critical importance, because the Pooh stories continue to be both popular and relevant, and deeply entrenched in popular culture.

In the wake of *The Pooh Perplex*, Pooh criticism followed three distinct patterns. The first was in biographical approaches to the books, with Milne's own *Autobiography*, published by Dutton in 1939, and Christopher Milne's autobiography, *The Enchanted Places*, published in 1974, providing an important foundation. Biographies such as Thomas Burnett Swann's in 1971 and Ann Thwaite's in 2014, and biographical criticism such as Anita Wilson's (1985), Humphrey Carpenter's (1985), and Robert Hemmings's (2007), have emphasized the varied influences on the form and narrative of the stories, including Milne's close relationship to his brother, his experiences as a soldier in World War I, and his rejection of organized religion. Some examinations of the texts have also focused on the semibiographical approach of scholars themselves, as they have attempted to reconcile their own critical perspectives to their childhood impressions of the books: Roger Sale (1972) and Wendy Smith (2005), for example, criticized the books for failing to live up to their childhood memories. Paula Connolly's work represents the most extensive body of Pooh scholarship, with *Recovering Arcadia* in 1995 providing a detailed critical exploration of both Milne's life and his writing. Fascinating as such approaches are, however, they only scratch the surface of the full critical complexities of the Pooh stories.

A second pattern of Pooh scholarship has been that which seeks to uncover hidden meanings, agendas, or usages for the stories. Carol Stanger (1987) has argued for feminist readings of the stories, writing that they "are about the difficulty of coming to terms with a patriarchal society" (35), while Claudia Nelson (1990) makes the tongue-in-cheek claim that "Pooh ... is that rarest of creatures, the true androgyne" in her feminist parody "The Beast Within" (17).⁴ William Wynn Yarbrough's 2011 analysis, in contrast, examines the construction of masculine identities within the stories. Daphne Kutzer (2000) analyzes the texts from a postcolonial perspective, finding hidden imperialist agendas in the power relationships between the different animals represented. Focusing on how the stories play with language and character, Elliott Gose (1988), Paul Wake (2009), Ella Wehrmeyer (2010), and Sean Ferrier-Watson (2011) all provide analyses from the perspectives of psychoanalysis and child development, exploring how Winnie-the-Pooh "functions as a testing of physical and psychological realities from which the listening child can learn" (Gose 1988, 29); "dramatize[s] the resistance of, and final entry into, the symbolic order of a shared language" (Wake 2009, 28); allows educators to explore "behavioral characteristics" with readers (Wehrmeyer 2010, 86); and helps child readers learn about free will and choice (Ferrier-Watson 2011, 33).

The most recent Pooh scholarship has focused not on the plurality of perspectives, modes, and interpretations these stories offer to readers but on the way in which Pooh's image and identity have changed as a result of the involvement of the Disney Company; Aaron Taylor (2005) and Paula Connolly (1995; 2015) have both provided insightful explorations of the way in which the Pooh franchise and Disney adaptations and merchandising have problematized the image, reception, and identity of Winnie-the-Pooh. Lorna Wood (2013) has explored the ethical perspectives offered by the Pooh books as part of a wider discussion of the ethics and philosophy of Emmanuel Levinas, and Niall Nance-Carroll (2014; 2015) has explored the prosaic ethics of Milne as expressed with these stories, emphasizing the multiple perspectives, viewpoints, and ethical approaches the stories model for readers. As Nance-Carroll argues: "[T]he narrative structure of the Pooh stories offers readers—children as well as adults—a number of potential viewpoints, including that of Pooh (and occasionally the other toys), of Christopher Robin (the listening child), or the narrator, or of a reader fully external to the text" (Nance-Carroll 2015, 64). A number of critics over the years have also explored the elements of language play within the Pooh books. David Rudd, for example, writes that "[t]ying signs to their referents is a perennial problem in the Pooh books: the relation of names to things, which can shift with alacrity" (2013, 66–67), while Karín Lesnik-Oberstein suggests that "Winnie-the-Pooh's nonsense seriously reveals the inherent instabilities of language while depending on the drive to make sense that is language" (1999, 200). Both writers indicate how the Pooh stories play not only with language but with the notion of identity itself. This approach is more fully articulated in Zoe Jaques's 2015 volume on posthumanism in children's literature, in which she states that Winnie-the-Pooh, as an animated toy, "aligns with just the types of interplay between the organic and inorganic that . . . is central to much posthuman discourse" (2015, 209). Finally, anthropologist Layla AbdelRahim's 2015 monograph on wildness and domestication in children's literature explores how language and narrative both work to complicate humanist perspectives and positions in the Pooh stories: "Milne does not use language to reveal its absurdity, arbitrariness, or unreliability like Lewis Carroll does with Alice. Rather, he explores its un-logic through the lens of childhood, that not fully domesticated stage of life imbued with revolutionary potential due to the child's uncrystallized relationship to social norms" (2015, 42). What these new approaches reveal is the way in which the Pooh stories remain relevant not only because of their enduring place in popular culture but also because they encourage and present diverse, unstable, and flexible perspectives, interpretations, and modes of being in keeping with the global, postmodern, posthuman ethos of the twenty-first century.

In keeping with this new thrust in Pooh scholarship, this volume seeks to further contribute to the debate about Pooh and add to the currently sparse field of critical Pooh research. It will present a central argument that the Pooh stories remain relevant for readers in a posthuman, information-centric, media-saturated, globalized age because of the ways in which they destabilize social certainties on all levels—linguistic, ontological, legal, narrative, political, and so on. Through essays that focus on geography, language, narrative, characterization, history, politics, economics, and a host of other social and cultural facets that have shaped the Pooh phenomenon, this volume will explore how the stories open up discourses about identity, ethics, social relations, and notions of belonging. It brings together some of the most cutting-edge approaches in children's literature theory, both from key established scholars in the field and from the currently unfolding scholarship of new researchers. Crucially, this will be the first volume to offer multiple perspectives from multiple authors on the Winnie-the-Pooh books all within a single collection, drawing together all three strands of previous scholarship but also focusing on and developing those approaches, which bring this classic of children's literature into the current era. The essays included in this volume will not only be of relevance to those scholars with an interest in Pooh, Milne, and the "golden age" of children's literature but will also showcase the development of children's literature scholarship in step with exciting innovations in literary theory.

Positioning Pooh Today

It is fitting that this collection begins with David Rudd recalling two critical moments in Pooh scholarship: the enshrinement of Christopher Milne's stuffed toys in the New York Public Library and Frederick Crews's use of Pooh to parody postmodernism. The first—the appearance of the stuffed toys as part of the New York Public Library's permanent display, simultaneously creating a popular tourist attraction—symbolizes Pooh's movement from children's literary character to public cultural icon. The second—the publication of Crews's *The Pooh Perplex*—marks the moment when Pooh became a contentious figure in serious literary criticism. Tacking both of these shifts in the Pooh phenomenon head-on, chapter 1 provides a Derridean reading of the language and symbolism of the Pooh books. Looking at the slippage between sign and signifier in personal names and personal dwellings within the books, Rudd introduces many of the key themes of this volume: the way in which the Pooh books complicate notions of identity, embodiment, stability, unity, and meaning. His chapter argues that the Pooh books demonstrate the instability of language as a signifier for the "real" world, particularly within the context of childish play.

In chapter 2, Donna Varga uses the lens of critical animal studies to explore the transformation of the real Canadian bear, Winnie, into an anthropomorphized toy and cartoon character, effectively erasing her identity and value divorced from her human connections. This chapter serves as a poignant reminder that our children's stories, however fantastic, remain grounded in an undeniable and not always comfortable material reality.

Zoe Jaques, in chapter 3, examines the spectral quality of nostalgia in two recent biographically influenced film adaptations: *Goodbye, Christopher Robin* and *Christopher Robin*. Her exploration indicates the extent to which the Pooh phenomenon is haunted by its future as well its past, troubling adult-child relationships across time and generations. In chapter 4, Niall Nance-Carroll provides a reading of two recent official Pooh sequels, *Return to the Hundred Acre Wood* and *The Best Bear in All the World*, through the lens of literary nostalgia. His analysis of these two additions to the Winnie-the-Pooh canon speculates on the intersection between revisionism and social responsibility. Taken together, these two chapters address important questions about the enduring and yet changing place of Pooh in modern children's culture.

In chapter 5, Jonathan Chun Ngai Tsang provides a close analysis of the Hong Kong Disneyland theme-park ride *The Many Adventures of Winnie-the-Pooh*. Providing a comparison of the mimetic and diegetic modes of narration in both the Disney ride and the original Milne source texts, Tsang demonstrates the deliberate positioning of the ride participant in the role of Christopher Robin. Moreover, through analysis of the extratextual setting of the park, Tsang makes a convincing argument for the role of the ride and this form of immersive narrative more generally in promoting the translation of East-meets-West, which is central to the colonial Chinese identity of Hong Kong. Megan De Roover, Nada Kujundžić and Ivana Milković, and Sarah Jackson all offer further insightful explorations of Pooh's dissemination across the globe. In chapter 6, De Roover takes us once again back to Canada, to describe how the reappropriation of Pooh's origin story via the narrative of Winnie the Bear has impacted Canadian nationalism as well as the Canadian ethos of stewardship toward nature. Reflecting on many of the same issues as Varga in chapter 2, De Roover provides an alternative perspective for understanding the intersections between the "real" Winnie and the fictional Pooh. Kujundžić and Milković move the discussion in chapter 7 beyond the English-speaking world to discuss the reception of Croatian translations of the Milne texts, particularly within the context of school-focused adaptations. Examining in detail the didacticism that has increasingly characterized translations and adaptations for Croatian readers, this chapter raises important questions about the value of English-language classics such as Milne's books within non-English speaking contexts. At the same time, Kujundžić and Milković identify the influence of Disney and the availability of Disney-related alternative texts as a significant factor in the poor reception of Milne translations and adaptations in Croatia; these observations suggest that simplification and universalism as a result of globalization may be complicating issues concerning the dissemination of English-language classics. Overall, their chapter raises a number of thought-provoking questions about translation, globalization, and commodification. Finally, Jackson in chapter 8 provides an alternative to previous postcolonial readings of Milne's work by critics such as Daphne Kutzer and Donald Hall. Examining the intricacies of colonial rhetoric within the texts, and especially the linguistic process of categorization, Jackson argues that rather than being straightforward proponents of colonial attitudes, these texts offer a space in which both colonialism and anticolonialism can be practiced.

In chapter 9, Perry Nodelman takes readers on quest through the layers of narrative in the Pooh books, in search of the boundaries of childhood. Examining the intersections of childlike and adult qualities in characters that are hybrids of humans, toys, and animals, he discovers that the childish arcadia of the forest has been contaminated by that which it seeks to exclude even from the moment of its inception. Chapter 10 concludes by reasserting the centrality of humanism to the Pooh books, and to animated toy narratives in general. Tim Wadham compares the animated toys of the original Pooh stories of Milne's books to other animated toys in the history of children's literature, from classics such as Raggedy Ann and the Velveteen Rabbit to iterations postdating the ascension of AI and "smart" toys, such as Brian Aldiss's "Super-Toy" teddy and the Lots-o'-Huggin' Bear from Pixar's *Toy Story 3*. Through these comparisons, Wadham argues that it is only through the introduction of a human child with the agency to imagine, narrate, and interact that these toys can offer posthuman "magic" to the reader: the posthuman exists only in opposition to the human, and neither can exist without the other.

The volume concludes on a light note with a bonus chapter from Nick Tucker. Taking the always present yet rarely discussed double entendre embedded in Pooh's name as a starting place, Tucker uses the concept of cognitive dissonance to take us on a journey through the many verbal "time bombs" of classic children's literature. Tucker's exploration of the cognitive dissonance, which affects readers of not just classics such as *Pooh* but a wide range of children's texts, asks deeper questions about the adult-child divide, which, as the essays in this volume indicate, continues to be a central theme of children's literature studies. Why is this chapter included in this volume? Well, because even when we have put on our serious academic faces to ask serious questions about these texts, we are all still (I hope) children enough at heart to be giggling quietly inside about what we are all thinking, and not talking about. With its insistence on laughter, this final chapter is a reminder that Pooh scholarship can (and should) be playful without being irrelevant.

Notes

1. For a detailed discussion of Milne's writing career, see either Ann Thwaite's biography, *A. A. Milne: His Life* (2014), or Christopher Milne's autobiography, *The Enchanted Places: A Childhood Memoir* (2016). Other good sources include Tori Haring-Smith's *A. A. Milne: A Critical Bibliography* (1982), Thomas Burnett Swann's *A. A. Milne* (1971), and A. A. Milne's own *Autobiography* (1939).

2. There are two characters: the classic Pooh, which so closely resembles Shepard's illustrations, which appears on merchandising but which never actually appears in any of the Disney films; and the better-known Pooh Bear with the bright red T-shirt from the animated films.

3. *The Pooh Perplex* is a parody; intending to poke fun at the seriousness of academia, Crews's book has served to devalue serious Pooh scholarship for decades, rendering the idea of analyzing Pooh ridiculous. A second foray by Crews into Pooh parody, *Postmodern Pooh* in 2001, certainly has not helped matters.

4. While editing this collection, I received a note from Claudia Nelson, explaining that "The Beast Within" had been written as a parody, in the spirit of the *Pooh Perplex*, and not as serious feminist criticism. It seems that when the article was published, the publisher failed to flag the piece as parody, occasioning a certain amount of confusion over the years.

Bibliography

AbdelRahim, Layla. 2015. *Children's Literature, Domestication, and Social Foundation: Narratives of Civilization and Wilderness*. London: Routledge.

Carpenter, Humphrey. 1985. *Secret Gardens: The Golden Age of Children's Literature from "Alice's Adventures in Wonderland" to "Winnie-the-Pooh."* Boston: Houghton Mifflin.

Connolly, Paula T. 1995. *"Winnie-the-Pooh" and "The House at Pooh Corner": Recovering Arcadia*. Woodbridge, CT: Twayne Publishers.

Connolly, Paula T. 2015. "The Metafictive Playgrounds of Disney's *Winnie the Pooh*: The Movie Is a Book." In *Walt Disney, from Reader to Storyteller: Essays on the Literary Inspirations*, edited by Kathy Merlock Jackson and Mark I. West, 179–94. Jefferson, NC: McFarland.

Crews, Frederick. 1963. *The Pooh Perplex: A Freshman Casebook*. Chicago: University of Chicago Press.

Crews, Frederick. 2001. *Postmodern Pooh*. New York: North Point Press.

Ferrier-Watson, Sean. 2011. "A Bear and His Choices: Rebellion, Questioning and Existentialism in *Winnie-the-Pooh*." *Journal of Children's Literature Studies* 8, no. 2 (July): 33–44.

Gose, Elliott. 1988. *Mere Creatures: A Study of Modern Fantasy Tales for Children*. Toronto: University of Toronto Press.

Haring-Smith, Tori. 1982. *A. A. Milne: A Critical Bibliography*. New York: Garland.

Harrods. n.d. "Steiff." https://www.harrods.com/en-gb/designers/steiff. Accessed May 13, 2019.

Hemmings, Robert. 2007. "A Taste of Nostalgia: Children's Books from the Golden Age— Carroll, Grahame, and Milne." *Children's Literature* 35, no. 1 (January): 54–79.

Hunt, Peter. 1992. "*Winnie-the-Pooh* and Domestic Fantasy." In *Stories and Society: Children's Literature in Its Social Context*, edited by Dennis Butts, 112–24. New York: Palgrave Macmillan.

Jaques, Zoe. 2015. *Children's Literature and the Posthuman*. London: Routledge.

Kutzer, M. Daphne. 2000. *Empire's Children: Empire and Imperialism in Classic British Children's Books*. New York: Garland.

Lesnik-Oberstein, Karín. 1999. "Fantasy, Childhood and Literature: In Pursuit of Wonderlands." In *Writing and Fantasy*, edited by Ceri Sullivan and Barbara White, 197–206. Harlow, Essex, England: Longman.

Mattick, Lindsay. 2015. *Finding Winnie: The True Story of the World's Most Famous Bear*. New York: Little, Brown.

Milne, A. A. 1939. *Autobiography*. New York: E. P. Dutton.

Milne, Christopher. 2016. *The Enchanted Places: A Childhood Memoir*. London: Pan Books.

Nance-Carroll, Niall. 2014. "A Prosaics of the Hundred Acre Wood: Ethics in A. A. Milne's *Winnie-the-Pooh* and *The House at Pooh Corner*." In *Ethics and Children's Literature*, edited by Claudia Mills, 89–100. Farnham, Surrey, England: Ashgate.

Nance-Carroll, Niall. 2015. "Not Only, But Also: Entwined Modes and the Fantastic in A. A. Milne's *Pooh* Stories." *Lion and the Unicorn* 39, no. 1 (January): 63–81.

Nelson, Claudia. 1990. "The Beast Within: *Winnie-the-Pooh* Reassessed." *Children's Literature in Education* 21, no. 1 (March): 17–22.

New York Public Library. n.d. "The Adventures of the REAL Winnie-the-Pooh." https://www.nypl.org/about/locations/schwarzman/childrens-center-42nd-street/pooh. Accessed May 13, 2019.

Rudd, David. 2013. *Reading the Child in Children's Literature: An Heretical Approach*. London: Palgrave Macmillan.

Sale, Roger. 1972. "Child Reading and Man Reading: Oz, *Babar*, and *Pooh*." *Children's Literature* 1: 162–72.

Smith, Wendy. 2005. "The Abuses of Enchantment: Why Some Children's Classics Give Parents the Creeps." *American Scholar* 74, no. 4 (Autumn): 126–31.

Stanger, Carol A. 1987. "*Winnie the Pooh* through a Feminist Lens." *Lion and the Unicorn* 11, no. 2 (April): 34–50.

Steeves, H. Peter. 2003. "Becoming Disney: Perception and Being at the Happiest Place on Earth." *Midwest Quarterly* 44, no. 2 (Winter): 176–95.

Swann, Thomas Burnett. 1971. *A. A. Milne*. Woodbridge, CT: Twayne Publishers.

Taylor, Aaron. 2005. "Everybody Wants a Piece of Pooh: Winnie, from Adaptation to Market Saturation." In *Rethinking Disney: Private Control, Public Dimensions*, edited by Mike Budd and Max H. Kirsch, 181–98. Middletown, CT: Wesleyan University Press.

Thwaite, Ann. 1994. *The Brilliant Career of Winnie-the-Pooh: The Definitive History of the Best Bear in All the World*. New York: E. P. Dutton.

Thwaite, Ann. 2014. *A. A. Milne: His Life*. Basingstoke, Hants., England: Bello.

Wake, Paul. 2009. "Waiting in the Hundred Acre Wood: Childhood, Narrative and Time in A. A. Milne's Works for Children." *Lion and the Unicorn* 33, no. 1 (January): 26–43.

Wehrmeyer, Ella. 2010. "Animal Characteristics in Children's Literature: Friends or Scoundrels?" *Mousaion* 28, no. 2 (January): 85–100.

Wilson, Anita. 1985. "Milne's *Pooh* Books: The Benevolent Forest." In *Touchstones: Reflections on the Best in Children's Literature*, vol. 1, edited by Perry Nodelman, 163–72. West Lafayette, IN: Children's Literature Association.

Wood, Lorna. 2013. "Milne and the Tonstant Weaders: A Levinasian Case for *Winnie-the-Pooh* and *The House at Pooh Corner*." In *Levinas and Twentieth-Century Literature: Ethics and the Reconstruction of Subjectivity*, edited by Donald R. Wehrs, 67–90. Newark: University of Delaware Press.

Yarbrough, Wynn William. 2011. *Masculinity in Children's Animal Stories, 1888–1928: A Critical Study of Anthropomorphic Tales by Wilde, Kipling, Potter, Grahame and Milne*. Jefferson, NC: McFarland.

Positioning
Pooh

CHAPTER 1

How Pooh Sticks . . . and Comes Unstuck
Derrida in the Hundred Acre Wood

David Rudd

On its website, the New York Public Library (2017) has a section entitled "The Adventures of the REAL Winnie-the-Pooh," implying that this rather threadbare teddy bear, along with his companions, somehow instantiates the authenticity of the Pooh tales. Such attempts to ground our favorite books in some tangible reality—to make Pooh stick, in fact—are undoubtedly seductive. There is the notion that through such artifacts we come closer to that "enchanted place," that Edenic space of childhood with its associated qualities of innocence, purity, and sensual richness. Such ideas are not only personally seductive but also economically lucrative, as literary tourism attests. I have no wish to decry such attempts, to pooh-pooh them in effect, but I do want to explore such "home truths," drawing chiefly on the work of Jacques Derrida. However, this is by no means an attempt to parody postmodernist approaches, as does Frederick Crews in "(P)ooh La La! Kiddie Lit Gets the Jacques of Its Life," with its rather desperate homophones. This is a more straightforward exploration of how the Pooh books chime with some of Derrida's key ideas. I do hope that readers will appreciate the "*différance.*"

If there is one constant in Derrida's work, it is his concern with borders, which I shall use to frame this chapter. Borders are necessary, of course, to establish meaning, whether it is in assigning things to basic, binary categories (e.g., living/dead; child/not-child) or making more nuanced distinctions (e.g., childish vs childlike). However, as Derrida continually points out, borders are provisional and permeable, such that each side of a divide depends on the other for its meaningfulness. The implications of this are what flesh out Derrida's neologism, *différance*; for, in naming anything, there are always such categorical decisions to be made. Meaning per se is never a given, regardless of whether language is written or spoken. Hence, for Derrida, textuality, or what he terms "arche-writing," always intervenes in our engagement with the world. It is in this sense only that Derrida states that "there is nothing out-side the text" (1976, 158), in that language always interposes itself.[1] Complete meaningfulness is, thereby, always deferred, although we hope to attain it at some point "to come" (Derrida 1992b, 38). The neologism *différance*, then, captures this slippage in two senses: first, in the notion that full meaning is forever *deferred*, and second, in that any meaning arises only out of a prior sense of *difference*. Finally, whatever sense is secured sticks only as a result of a word's repetition, though even then shifts occur because contexts of usage also change (what Derrida terms *iterability*).

Will the "Real" Pooh Please Stand Up

Let's now leaven this Owlish jargon with some of Pooh's more tangible "Crustimoney Proseedcake" by returning to the question of "the REAL Winnie-the-Pooh." Do his origins really lie in the purchase of that teddy bear in 1920? Or was it after encountering the "real" bear, Winnie, at London Zoo? Or was it only with the purchase of Cotchford Farm in 1925? The New York Library's website is less than helpful on this matter, stating only that "[t]he real Winnie-the-Pooh won't be found on a video, in a movie, on a T-shirt, or a lunchbox," suggesting that these web authors themselves have short memories, and ones heavily influenced by Disney.

Personally, I'd argue that the two slim texts take priority, there being no extant "adventures" of Pooh prior to their publication, however much the stories might subsequently have been repackaged and reimagined.[2] In fact, this is the only way to explain Rabbit and Owl's absence from the New York archive, as they never had any prior, corporeal existence. But even though Pooh is physically there, the extent to which he is the same bear as the one that features in those arguably less "real" adventures is also problematic as, although E. H. Shepard had been introduced to Christopher's nursery toys, this was only after the illustrator had already established an image of the bear from Milne's first collection of verse, *When We Were Very Young* (hereafter *WWWVY*), and this earlier bear had been based on that of his own son, Growler—that's the bear, of course, not the son (Thwaite 1994, 31).

However, even if it is accepted that Milne's texts take precedence, each and every signifier therein still carries its own history, along with its etymological heritage, its homophones, and the like. Proper names are no exception: no more than other signifiers can they capture the essence of someone or thing (Derrida 1976, 109; 1995b). Milne seems quite aware of the complexity and fickleness of names as he not only presents us with the etymology of "Pooh" but, just as readily, both overdetermines and, thereby, undermines it. Hence we are informed that the name of that original bear at London Zoo derives not from a person but a place: Winnipeg. Through this metonymy, a formerly anonymous stuffed toy, once standing alongside others in Harrods store, was elevated into something special that has links with a "real" bear. The name "Pooh" is also linked to a living creature, a swan (*WWWVY*, ix) and a royal bird at that. Pooh's desire, we are informed, had been to have "an exciting name all to himself" (*Winnie-the-Pooh* [hereafter *WP*], ix), together with stories also "[a]bout himself" (2), so it is appropriate that we witness "Edward Bear" (another royal, metonymic link) being transformed from inert teddy at the top of the stairs into Winnie-the-Pooh "at the bottom, and ready to be introduced to you" (1), as though he were formally "coming out" in fashionable society. Pooh's name is certainly privileged in these books, not merely because of his eponymous status but also because the names of the other characters are simply variations on everyday species names: Tigger, Kanga, Roo, and so forth.

But Pooh's desire for "an exciting name all to himself" (*WP*, ix) is not so simple for, as noted earlier, signifiers, always transferable, cannot express uniqueness; they can only ever open up the world of signification. Pooh seems to suffer this slippage from the outset, when we hear that he "lived in a forest all by himself under the name of Sanders" (2), and we are confronted with some basic semiosis: a picture of a signifier (the name "Sanders"), beneath which sits what appears to be the signified—the bear formerly known as Winnie. But Pooh does not "bear" this other name (Sanders) at all; he simply "*had the name over the door in gold letters and lived under it*" (2). Once this idiom is explained, though, we might ask in what sense these "real" names, whether "Winnie" or "Pooh," can be said to capture this bear in any more essential way, especially as we've already been told that each element derives from elsewhere. Clearly, as again noted, it is only through reiteration that names "stick" (and this itself is a word to cleave to), but in that very process, they also slide into fresh contexts (they are "iterable") and lose any seeming transparency.

As if in recognition of the fact that his name does not uniquely nominate him, we are tentatively offered a further etymological explanation, as though this might bolster Pooh's ownership of said name: "I think—but I am not sure" that, because his arms were stiff, he could only remove flies from his nose by blowing on them, and "*that* is why he was always called Pooh" (*WP*, 17). Apart from being blatantly post hoc, this explanation does try to give his name a more personal resonance, linking it to a physical idiosyncrasy. However, going back to the problem of *différance*, this explanation cannot account for why this particular noise might be alighted upon, rather than the various other sounds Pooh might make, or indeed, his attendant peculiarity at this moment: his upraised arms ("Hans Arp"?); nor can it account for why this fly-removing noise is rendered as "Pooh," rather than "Poof" or "Phew" (etc.). In short, this signifier still cannot uniquely identify him.

The nearest he comes to such distinction occurs when the narrator insists that he is "Winnie-ther-Pooh," taunting readers for not knowing what "*ther*" means (*WP*, 1). Of course, like Derrida's neologism *différance*, the distinction between "*ther*" and "the" will generally not be heard (the word "the" is often slurred). Its distinctness will reveal itself only in writing. However, given that Pooh and some of his friends are illiterate, and that this subtle marker of difference is quickly forgotten, its distinctiveness (or iterability) is soon abandoned.

Pooh's name continues its dissemination throughout the two volumes, and it pulls in opposing directions. On the one hand, as Gayatri Spivak notes, there is an "oedipal desire to preserve one's proper name, to see it as the analogon of the name of the father," and, on the other, there is a "narcissistic desire to make one's own 'proper' name 'common,'" part of "the mother-tongue." Spivak is interpreting Derrida here and illustrates the latter desire by quoting Derrida's own reflections on the French pronunciation of Hegel's name, which homophonically becomes "eagle," giving Hegel's work an unavoidably avian inflection (Spivak 1976, lxxxiv). One can see these competing desires in

Pooh's name, too. The oedipal side is apparent in his name's own avian links: to that royal bird, the swan, suggesting an aristocratic, patriarchal lineage. But equally, such avian pretensions are deflated (literally, following his airborne adventure), demoting his name precisely to the demotic as he sees himself "simply poohing / Like a bird" (*The House at Pooh Corner* [hereafter *HPC*], 79). We will move on, swift and fecal-free.[3]

The tension between these two tendencies of names reaches its apogee when Pooh is knighted, again emphasizing his patrimony, especially as this process seems to result in the dropping of the slightly androgynous-sounding "Winnie": he is now "Sir Pooh de Bear" (*HPC*, 173). However, the knighting itself is performed with a common stick, and his given name, despite the title, points more overtly to his animal roots and "common" ancestry. While this tension is never overcome, that famous, final sentence of the second book, celebrating "that enchanted place on the top of the Forest" where "a little boy and his Bear will always be playing" (*HPC*, 176),[4] effectively removes their individuality. In this understated un-naming, both the Bear formerly known as Pooh and the boy (whether Billy Moon or Christopher) attain a more mythical sense of presence as they become, to borrow again from Derrida, "messianic without messianism." This phrase comes from *Specters of Marx* (1994, 65), where, in line with his general wariness of essences, of ever attaining full presence, Derrida suggests the term "hauntology" in preference to "ontology," in that the former captures this idea that we only ever possess traces of things. But, as it is also important to note, such spectral elements (a boy and his Bear) are more abiding, continuing to haunt us down the years.

Playing at Home and Away

It is particularly important to grasp this messianic aspect, for Derrida's deconstructive approach is often seen in destructive and negative terms. Whereas, as Derrida repeatedly explains, it is precisely "the dream of a unity, or finally of a place" that motivates him. So, while "this dream is forever destined to disappointment" and "remains inaccessible," this "does not mean that the dream is but a fantasy, imaginary, a secondary moment" (Derrida 1995c, 136). In other words, it is this dream of unity, or of a place—one where the very categories of "human" and "beast" might be rethought (Derrida 2002)—that animates us. So, such an "enchanted place" is not located in any Edenic past. As his son Christopher makes plain, A. A. Milne interpreted that Wordsworthian line, "Heaven lies about us in our infancy," as being concerned not with how a child actually sees the world but with "how it seemed to the *onlooker*" (C. Milne 1974, 29).

In short, A. A. Milne scrupulously avoids the standard Romantic trope of the child figure, recognizing that this is nothing but an adult construction, and bringing to mind Jacqueline Rose's *The Case of Peter Pan* (1984). Milne pulls no punches about this: from the outset it is made clear that the adult narrator brings Pooh to life. When in the company of the child, the bear remains inert, being dragged "bump, bump, bump" downstairs "on the back of his head" (*WP*, 1). It is the father who animates Pooh, initially surmising that he might prefer another way of descending the stairs but can't "think of it" because of the relentless "bumping" (1). It is also Milne senior who provides the boy and Bear with stories/memories of their lives together, putting the very words into their mouths:

> "Good morning, Christopher Robin," he said.
> "Good morning, Winnie-ther-Pooh," said you. (*WP*, 8)

The child is certainly set up "as an outsider to its own process" in these fictions, then taken in, as Rose expresses it (1984, 2), albeit Milne is quite open about what he is doing, drawing attention to his narratorial intrusiveness. Such interventions are most overt in the first book, where the story is delayed and deferred as a result of the narrator's metafictional presence. But the process continues playfully throughout, confounding what would otherwise be a more straightforward children's story. And, once again, that final sentence confirms this view, as it is through the messianic imagination of the "*onlooker*" that the boy and Bear are seen to be playing forever, in a realm where even the categories of human and beast are reconceived.

Most of this playfulness is conveyed through Milne's witty disruption of language. We have already sampled his "Crustimoney Proseedcake" (*WP*, 45) and perhaps smelled those "mastershalums" (*HPC*, 58). But beyond these neologisms Milne seems generally attuned to the nature of signs and what can be "captured" within the various arrangements of glyphs and their phonic equivalents. So, aside from Pooh's inadvertent coinages (e.g., "Expotition" [*WP*, 101]), we have Owl's adventurous orthography ("HIPY PAPY BTHUTHDTH THUTHDA BTHUTHDY" [*WP*, 74]), Tigger's onomatopoeia ("*Worraworraworraworraworra*" [*HPC*, 18]), and the concrete poetry of Kanga's bouncing text (*WP*, 93). Yet more interesting still are Pooh's "Hums" (*HPC*, 5), which seem to gesture toward the inadequacy of language, attempting to reach beyond signification; to utter sounds (i.e., signifiers) untroubled by semantic baggage: "*Rum-tum-tiddle-um-tum*" (*HPC*, 20), "*Cottleston, Cottleston, Cottleston Pie*" (*WP*, 68), "tiddely pom" (*HPC*, 5), and even "*ther.*"

As noted before, for meaningfulness to occur, signifiers must have iterability (Derrida 1977); that is, signification can only "stick" if signifiers are repeated, even though slippage and, therefore, indeterminacy are unavoidable. A stick that is used in the process of naming (more specifically, of "knighting") is thus highly unstable and likely to revert to meaninglessness. Play, then, is an excellent vehicle for making the signifying process explicit while also showing how conventional it is, as the game of Poohsticks demonstrates. Originally, it might be recalled, pinecones had been used, but then sticks replaced them, being "easier to mark" (*HPC*, 92). Hence, by the time these sticks (i.e., signifiers) pass beneath that famous bridge—evocative of the Saussurean bar—they have become identifiable as Poohsticks (signifieds), only later to revert, just like the knighting swordstick, to arbitrary twigs. In other words, two sticks floating down a river would not function in a Poohsticky way for other people, even though someone upriver might have used them thus. Indeed, these sticks might just as well have been floating down the appropriately named Styx, to an oblivion as secure as that provided by another of Greek mythology's infamous rivers, the Lethe: their Poohstickiness would have been erased; they would have become unstuck (unless, of course, the archive marked their existence, of which more later).

Eeyore's house, also made of sticks, suffers a similar fate. Although meaningful to him, this "heap . . . on the other side of the wood. . . . Lots and Lots. All piled up" does not function as a legible signifier for others; according to Pooh, Eeyore "has nothing" (*HPC*, 7), simply living in that "damp bit down on the right which nobody wants" (155). His house lacks iterability, only gaining this quality after Pooh and Piglet first dismantle it (I won't use that now overworked term, "deconstruct"), then reconstruct it as a more publicly recognizable structure, most importantly one that is witnessed by Christopher Robin, such that Eeyore can proudly declare, "*That's* the way to build a house" (*HPC*, 16).

Although I want to concentrate on the centrality of houses, it is worth pondering the way that Eeyore, too (like Pooh with his hums), challenges signification. As a tangential, solipsistic figure who, as noted above, "has nothing," Eeyore is even more dismissive of the ability of signifiers to capture the world. This is made quite explicit in the scene where Eeyore closely considers what sticks signify, as we witness him gazing at three twigs arranged in the shape of an uppercase *A*, only to violently smash them up when he discovers that literacy is a "thing that *Rabbit* knows! Ha!" (*HPC*, 87). As Piglet had earlier surmised, these sticks are like "a Trap of some kind" (84).

But let me return to the question of houses, which are thematically central to the second volume, *The House at Pooh Corner*, its title taken from the tale of Eeyore's house (as opposed to the tale of Eeyore's tail, which relates to someone else's house). The map that is provided of the "100 AKER WOOD" and environs, "DRAWN BY ME AND MR SHEPARD HELPD" (*WP*, xii–xiii), features many of these domiciles: "MY HOUSE" (where Christopher proudly stands at his tree-trunk door, suggesting that he might feel more at home when he is away, playing), POOH BEARS, PIGLETS, RABBITS, KANGAS, OWLS, and, of course, Eeyore's "GLOOMY PLACE" (*HPC*, 7).

Two things are notable about these houses. First, how insubstantial they are. This has just been noted with Eeyore's "place," but Owl's house is also lost, such that Owl takes over the house of Piglet, who is in turn rehoused by Pooh, both Owl and Piglet having found themselves flooded out of their own houses in an earlier story. Second, that the word "house" is used in preference to "home," as though this latter space were more problematic. The point is humorously made by Rabbit when Pooh visits and asks, "Is anybody home?" The response is "No!," despite Pooh's persistence:

> "Bother!" said Pooh. "Isn't there anybody here at all?"
> "Nobody." (*WP*, 21)

Rabbit's reply is reminiscent of Odysseus's to the Cyclops, and Pooh, likewise, is also prevented from returning home, albeit the latter's punishment is self-inflicted. Nonetheless, Rabbit's lack of homeliness—treating Pooh's mooning rear end as a washstand—is indicative.

The chapter where that more emotive word, home, features most is the one where Kanga and Roo arrive at the Forest like refugees, only to have Rabbit contrive to oust them by kidnapping Roo and threatening not to return him unless the two "promise to go away from the Forest and never come back" (*WP*, 84). Kanga's revenge on the changeling Piglet, which involves a regime of cleanliness and medicine superintended by an intimidating mother figure, does little to render home a more attractive space.

But a lack of homeliness is present from the outset, even in Christopher's decidedly middle-class residence (it has a bathroom, after all). Where, for example, is his family? There is that retiring, first-person narrator, whom we presume to be Christopher's father, but there is no mother in evidence, even at bath time. As he ascends the stairs, Christopher most closely resembles his intertextual offspring, Bernard (who also drags a teddy after him [McKee 1980]). "Coming to see me have my bath?," Christopher prompts his father, who replies, "I might" (*WP*, 18). One is reminded of the "real" Christopher's biographical comment about his father, that "it was precisely because he was not able to play with his small son that his longings sought and found satisfaction in another direction. He wrote about him instead" (C. Milne 1974, 36); not only that, but he wrote about him living away from home, alone.

This setup would seem to have implications for what is regarded as the defining narrative arc of children's books: Home-Away-Home, as Perry Nodelman (1992) frames it, which is also what Derrida terms an "Odyssean structure," involving "the—circular—return to the point of departure, to the origin . . . to the home" (Derrida 1992a, 6–7). And yet, terms like "home" never have such full presence for Derrida. Home is always compromised, its borders troubled by absence. In naming "home," one is already displaced from its immediacy, its intimacy, haunted by a sense of otherness. Home and Away always rub shoulders, then, such that, instead of an Odyssean cycle, we find ourselves more in exile, like Abraham: "*destin-errant*," as Derrida puts it (1987a, 201).

It might be thought that I am being unfair here, for we all know that Christopher never really stirs from home; that, of course, these are just bedtime stories about an imaginary space that Milne's son, Christopher, is envisaged inhabiting with his nursery toys, albeit based on Christopher's own play in Ashdown Forest, climbing trees and hanging over bridges. But the way that Milne has rendered home is surely significant, especially in the framing of that first adventure, where domestic life is very coolly depicted. I have already mentioned the father's offhand comment about possibly coming to see his solitary son take his bath (the remark is repeated at the end of the first volume), perhaps to check that he hasn't drowned; but elsewhere the father sounds equally distant, as when he peremptorily declares, in the manner of Rabbit, "it is all the explanation you are going to get" (*WP*, 1). Beyond this, there is an air of abstraction about Milne's whole narratorial style, with its unnecessarily disembodied and ambiguous pronouns, avoiding more concrete referents. Over the first few pages, for instance, four different owners of the first person are mentioned: "When I first heard his name, I said, just as you are going to say, 'But I thought he was a boy?'" (*WP*, 1). The first two "I"s in this sentence refer to the narrator, but the third is meant to be a question that the implied reader might ask, which then becomes a different "I" in the following line—"So did I"—this one being Christopher Robin. And finally, on the next page, a fourth "I" is added, as "a growly voice" says, "Now I am" (3).

It is perhaps worth pointing out that, although I have referred to the narrator as Christopher's father, such a relationship is not explicit in the book, any more than we know that the author is a "he"; for those initials, "A. A.," are equally empty of signification. They might as readily indicate that Milne is an Automobile Association patrolman, or a member of Alcoholics Anonymous. Even that first book's dedication, "To Her," is impersonal, and, but for the gendered pronoun, the declaration that "Christopher Robin and I" come to "lay this book in your lap" might as readily refer to a male figure, especially given that Milne originally conceived Kanga as a male, despite the giveaway pouch (Thwaite 1994, 317, cf. note 7).

One should, though, note that this first story does at least end with a return to the hearth, just as the whole of the first volume concludes with Christopher going upstairs for yet another bath, rather than to be tucked up in bed by a parent. In the second volume there is not even this. There is no home in sight; no sense, say, of returning from some fantasy land to a meal that is "still hot," or even of being sent to bed without any supper. (One could speculate that if the bath were "still hot," like Max's supper in Maurice Sendak's tale, it might be metonymic of parental love but, personally, it seems too big an ask.)

To return to my main point, then, Christopher and friends have more in common with Abraham than Odysseus, being *destin-errant* (even the soft toys ended up in exile, in New York Public Library). This starker, Home-and-Away narrative is something that D. W. Winnicott seemed to recognize when he pronounced on "the central position of Winnie the Pooh [*sic*]" (1974, xi). An object-relations psychoanalyst, Winnicott saw Pooh as the perfect example of a transitional object; that is, as something like a security blanket, helping the child adjust to the outside world after he has foregone his sense of oneness with his mother. In the complete absence of such a maternal presence in these books, Pooh instantiates her, epitomizing that feeling of security that characterizes this whole "enchanted place":

> "Oh, Bear!" said Christopher Robin. "How I do love you!"
> "So do I," said Pooh. (*WP*, 64)

Pooh, in fact, is the one who provides hospitality unconditionally, exhibiting what Derrida saw as a key feature of an ethical society. It is Pooh who, we recall, woken in the night, welcomes the stranger, Tigger, by giving him shelter. It is Pooh, too, who offers to house Piglet after the latter has lost his own home to Owl:

> Piglet squeezed his paw.
> "Thank you, Pooh," he said, "I should love to." (*HPC*, 158)

Following Émile Benveniste, Derrida notes that the root of the word "hospitality" comes from *hostis*, which, like so many words when probed, encodes an ambivalence, meaning both guest and enemy. Milne dramatizes this incongruity by contrasting Pooh with Rabbit, the latter seeing all callers, whether strangers or not, as a threat, whereas Pooh treats everyone as a guest, adopting that openness to the stranger that Derrida avowed as an ethical imperative:

> Let us say yes *to who or what turns up*, before any determination, before any anticipation, before any *identification*, whether or not it has to do with a foreigner, an immigrant, an invited guest, or an unexpected visitor, whether or not the new arrival is the citizen of another country, a human, animal, or divine creature, a living or dead thing, male or female. (Derrida 2000, 77)

Just as the word "hospitality" troubles borders (a guest always being a potential enemy), there is a similar tension with the notion of the gift, also explored by Derrida (1992a, 30). For, although such an offering is meant to be freely given, a gift always instantiates the expectation of reciprocity, of some sort of exchange. Yet one could argue that the gifts presented to Eeyore by Pooh and Piglet—an empty honey jar and a burst balloon—are free of such allegiance: they are simply tokens of love.

Conclusion: "The Dream of a Unity, or Finally of a Place"

At this point it is worth recapitulating where my argument is heading, as it might otherwise be seen to emulate the cyclic path of Pooh and Piglet searching for a Woozle. Basically, we have seen how borders waiver (homes drafty with absence, hospitality threatening invasion, gifts courting obligation); for, as Derrida argues, such is the nature of language: meaning is always troubled by *différance* (i.e., by difference and deferral), with absence haunting presence. Through repetition we seek to secure meaning, but, like Pooh and Piglet circumambulating that tree, traces will multiply and slippage occur. Pooh's "Hums" are most overt in attempting to escape this signifying process, but here too dissemination occurs, such that even a "tiddely pom" can morph into "a *different* tiddely pom" (*HPC*, 5). But it is not merely inside the text that questions of the border are raised, for Milne's books also confound what it means to talk about the "inside" and "outside" of texts (remembering Derrida's pronouncement that "there is no outside-text"; cf. note 1 of this chapter).

Derrida explores this last idea in terms of the *parergon*; literally, that which is "around the work," supplementing it (1987b, 9). But where does a text begin (we've already pointed to problems here) and where does it end (isn't it continuing its dissemination even now, as this archive continues to swell?)?

Conventionally, the paratext is regarded as being more factual, grounded in truth through such devices as dates, places, signatures, and proper names. It is therefore a useful demarcation device, guiding our approach to the text "proper" (e.g., as a children's book). Yet, as has been argued, Milne deliberately problematizes this divide, such that we witness the inside of the text leaking out (and vice versa). On the title page, there is that initial image of Pooh, who at this point appears "under the name of," not Sanders, but E. H. Shepard. He (Pooh, that is, not Shepard—nor Sanders either) is brushing his hair, long before he is officially brought to life within the main text, suggesting that he might have an extraliterary existence and that he is merely preparing for his entrance in the role of a dumb, stuffed bear, bumping down stairs. Likewise, the other characters are heard complaining, "What about *Us*?" (*WP*, x) in the introduction, suggesting that they, too, have an animate existence beyond the main text. So, while on the one hand there is an attempt to ground the book in external reality (through the dedication and our introduction to a "real" Christopher Robin), this is undercut by having the fictional creations exceed their storybook frame, playing in the paratextual space. Text and context are thereby conflated, and this fusion is pursued into the first chapter, where we find both narrator and narratee discussing the story's progress. In *The House at Pooh Corner*, Milne makes the hybrid nature of the parergon even more overt, calling the introduction a "Contradiction," which is a term that Derrida himself might have deployed.

This brings me to Derrida's conception of the special nature of literature. For, as he argues, "literality" has nothing to do with either the language used or with the subject matter; rather, it is to do with the way that literature frees itself from the normal consequences of what it says: it can go anywhere, say anything, break any rules. In J. Hillis Miller's words: "Literature depends on the possibility of detaching language from its firm embeddedness in a social or biographical context and allowing it to play freely as fiction" (2001, 60). Literature, then, makes explicit what Derrida sees as characteristic of all language, once one fathoms its logocentric arrogance; namely "the limitlessness of play" (1976, 50), play itself being concerned with the "disruption of presence" (369).

However, Derrida does not examine the way that play is explicitly linked to children, given their facility for detaching behavior from its consequences, whether that involves mimicking adult ways (discovering North Poles, being knighted, going hunting) or, indeed, upending such ways entirely. As mentioned before, the Pooh books exploit this notion without falling into the trap of essentializing the child as a fey Romantic creature. "Ontology," as Derrida remarked, "is a conjuration" (1994, 202), and play is precisely that space where ontology parades its hauntology. Play, in short, concerns itself with what is not; with specters that will "always be playing" in enchanted spaces.

Once again, it is important to emphasize that these specters emanate from Milne's pen, which is something with which his son, Christopher, grapples, perhaps most overtly when he writes about Poohsticks: "It is difficult to be sure which came first. Did I do something and did my father then write a story around it? Or was it the other way about, and did the story come first?" But, as though appreciating that their exploits were always subject to inscription, at the mercy of the play of the signifier, Christopher goes on to say:

[I]n the end it was all the same: the stories became a part of our lives; we lived them, thought them, spoke them. And so, possibly before, but certainly after that particular story, we used to stand on Pooh-sticks [*sic*] Bridge throwing sticks into the water and watching them float away out of sight until they re-emerged on the other side. (C. Milne 1974, 58)

This declaration, of course, is quoted with an awareness that autobiographies are no more privileged than proper names in capturing the reality of the archive, which brings me to my final topic—which, in turn, takes us back to the beginning, where I first reflected on the glass-encased soft toys in New York Public Library.

In Derrida's meditation on the archive, he speaks about the ambivalence it elicits, which he captures in his title, *Archive Fever*. For, while archives certainly excite us, making us hot and agitated, at the same time they point to absence, to what is lost. The French "mal d'archive" makes this latter connotation more explicit, hinting not only at malady but at mourning and, ultimately, death. However, as Derrida also makes clear, and as this chapter has argued, it was ever thus: absence and *différance* will shadow us, but the excitement of the archive, to which we continually contribute, persists.

The "real" Winnie-the-Pooh therefore remains a haunted and spectral presence, despite our continued "desire for identity, completion and conservation" (Derrida 1996, 101). And yet it is this prospect of that future, enchanted place—"the dream of a unity, or finally of a place"—that will always orient us toward what is, in one of Derrida's favorite phrases, "to come" (*à venir* [1992b, 38]), however *destin-errant* or unhomely is that elusive, posthuman space. Tiddely Pom!

Notes

1. Beyond this, as most scholars accept, this famous sentence is a mistranslation of Derrida's French, which would be more correctly rendered as, "there is no outside-text" (Merquior 1986, 220).

2. This is not quite correct. The first story appeared in the *London Evening News*, Christmas Eve 1925. Pooh's publishers, Methuen, have also cheekily promoted the two earlier volumes of verse as "Other Pooh Paperbacks."

3. For those Freudians awaiting the anal interpretation, associating Pooh with, well, with "poo" (cf. Crews's Karl Anschauung chapter in *The Pooh Perplex*), this association did not exist till the 1930s (according to Eric Partridge's *Dictionary of Slang* [1937]).

4. While patriarchy might be seen to triumph, it is at the expense of the oedipal proper name and with the ascension of what Spivak terms "the mother-tongue." It is also worth noting other evidence: Christopher's remarkably androgynous appearance and the fact that his mother, Daphne, had always wanted a girl (to be named "Rosemary"), such that, for Christopher's first years, he was treated as female. Pooh, too, has androgynous qualities, and it seems of note that his "first" first name, Winnie, is regarded as inappropriate for a boy (". . . you can't call him Winnie?" [*WP*, 1]).

Bibliography

Crews, Frederick. 1963. *The Pooh Perplex: A Student's Casebook*. London: Arthur Barker.

Crews, Frederick. 2001. *Postmodern Pooh*. New York: North Point Press.

Derrida, Jacques. 1976. *Of Grammatology*. Translated by Gayatri Chakravorty Spivak. Baltimore: Johns Hopkins University Press.

Derrida, Jacques. 1977. *Limited Inc*. Translated by Jeffrey Mehlman and Samuel Weber. Evanston, IL: Northwestern University Press.

Derrida, Jacques. 1982. "Différance." In *Margins of Philosophy*, translated by Alan Bass, 3–27. Chicago: University of Chicago Press.

Derrida, Jacques. 1987a. *The Post Card: From Socrates to Freud and Beyond*. Translated by Alan Bass. Chicago: University of Chicago Press.

Derrida, Jacques. 1987b. *The Truth in Painting*. Translated by Geoffrey Bennington and Ian McLeod. Chicago: University of Chicago Press.

Derrida, Jacques. 1992a. *Given Time: 1. Counterfeit Money*. Translated by Peggy Kamuf. Chicago: University of Chicago Press.

Derrida, Jacques. 1992b. "This Strange Institution Called Literature." Translated by Geoffrey Bennington and Rachel Bowlby. In *Acts of Literature*. Edited by Derek Attridge, 33–75. London: Routledge.

Derrida, Jacques. 1994. *Specters of Marx*. London: Routledge.

Derrida, Jacques. 1995a. *The Gift of Death*. Translated by David Wills. Chicago: University of Chicago Press.

Derrida, Jacques. 1995b. *On the Name*. Edited by Thomas Dutoit. Translated by David Wood, John P. Leavey Jr., and Ian McLeod. Stanford, CA: Stanford University Press.

Derrida, Jacques. 1995c. *Points . . . : Interviews 1974–1994*. Edited by Elisabeth Weber. Translated by Peggy Kamuf. Stanford, CA: Stanford University Press.

Derrida, Jacques. 1996. *Archive Fever: A Freudian Impression*. Translated by Eric Prenowitz. Chicago: University of Chicago Press.

Derrida, Jacques. 2000. *On Hospitality*. Translated by Anne Dufourmantelle. Stanford, CA: Stanford University Press.

Derrida, Jacques. 2002. "The Animal That Therefore I Am (More to Follow)." Translated by David Wills. *Critical Inquiry* 28, no. 2 (Winter): 369–418.

Hillis Miller, J. 2001. "Derrida and Literature." In *Jacques Derrida and the Humanities: A Critical Reader*, edited by Tom Cohen, 58–81. Cambridge: Cambridge University Press.

McKee, David. 1980. *Not Now, Bernard*. London: Andersen Press.

Merquior, José Guilherme. 1986. *From Prague to Paris: A Critique of Structuralist and Post-Structuralist Thought*. London: Verso.

Milne, A. A. (1924) 1965. *When We Were Very Young*. London: Methuen.

Milne, A. A. (1926) 1965. *Winnie-the-Pooh*. London: Methuen.

Milne, A. A. (1927) 1965. *Now We Are Six*. London: Methuen.

Milne, A. A. (1928) 1965. *The House at Pooh Corner*. London: Methuen.

Milne, Christopher. 1974. *The Enchanted Places*. London: Eyre Methuen.

New York Public Library. 2017. "The Adventures of the REAL Winnie-the-Pooh." https://www.nypl.org/about/locations/schwarzman/childrens-center-42nd-street/pooh.

Nodelman, Perry. 1992. *The Pleasures of Children's Literature*. Harlow, Essex, England: Longman.

Partridge, Eric. 1937. *A Dictionary of Slang and Unconventional English*. London: Routledge.

Rose, Jacqueline. 1984. *The Case of Peter Pan; or, The Impossibility of Children's Fiction*. London: Macmillan.

Spivak, Gayatri Chakravorty. 1976. "Translator's Preface." In *Of Grammatology*, by Jacques Derrida, translated by Gayatri Chakravorty Spivak, ix–lxxxvii. Baltimore: Johns Hopkins University Press.

Thwaite, Ann. 1994. *The Brilliant Career of Winnie-the-Pooh: The Story of A. A. Milne and His Writing for Children*. London: Methuen.

Winnicott, D. W. 1974. *Playing and Reality*. London: Penguin.

CHAPTER 2

Winnie

Troubling the Idealization of the Bear as Childhood Innocent

Donna Varga

Twenty-eight seconds into the Historica Canada video *Winnie*, a bear is shown pacing and panting within a barred enclosure (Historica Canada. n.d.[b]).[1] A plaque identifies the site as London Zoo, and the inhabitant as WINNIE, an American black bear donated by "Captain Harry Coleborne [*sic*]" of the Second Infantry Brigade of Winnipeg, Canada. Over the bear's huffing we hear a child's high-pitched exclamation: "Oh, Daddy! I just love Winnie." The camera pans to the speaker, who viewers will know stands for Christopher Robin Milne figured as childhood innocent through his longish blond hair, blue eyes, rosebud-shaped pink lips, and translucence of skin that is heightened by the wearing of a white, wide-brimmed hat. Held in daddy's arms so as to have full view of the animal, he pleads: "Couldn't we take him home with us?" (00:00:30–00:00:32). The naïveté of the query guides viewers toward taking nostalgic delight in a longing that connects to earlier scenes of Colebourn's tender leave-taking from the bear when placing her in the care of zoo attendants. Audience and child are reassured that Winnie will be allowed entry to the Milne family home with the father's pledge: "Christopher Robin, I'll tell you what I'll do. I'll write some stories about Winnie, and Mr. Shepard here will draw some pictures" (00:00:33–00:00:39). The younger Milne then makes his declaration in the naming of the story character so promised, "Oh Daddy! Let's call him Winnie-the-Pooh." On query, "Why Pooh, son?," he answers, "I don't know," and reemphasizes the second and third parts of the name, "just Winnie-*the-Pooh*" (00:00:40–00:00:49).[2]

Throughout the exchange, viewers are allotted only a brief view of the real bear at the focus of their conversation, pushing her snout and tongue through the bars and nodding as if in agreement with the name assigned by the child to his father's creation. The usurping of her presence in favor of close-ups of the Milnes and Shepard conveys the contemporary devaluing of Winnie's animal-self that is explored in this chapter. As presented in the Heritage Minute, Winnie the bear is regarded as noteworthy because, in her coming under the gaze of Christopher Robin Milne, she contributed to the making of literary history. Since the 1980s, progressively exaggerated claims of her influence in this regard have been paralleled with diminishment of Winnie's bear-self.

Utilizing Judith Butler's concept of framing and the discourses of childhood innocence as expressed through the orientation of critical animal studies[3] (Malamud 2012; Varga 2009a, 196–203), this chapter provides a chronological tracing of the ways by which the animal essence of Winnie has, from the latter years of the twentieth century, been anthropomorphized in a manner that characterizes her as emblematic of Winnie-the-Pooh. In this merging of Winnie's selfhood with that of the literary character, the latter's childlike persona is reflected onto her.

The question might be asked: what harm is there, if any, in celebrating a real bear as if she were the one of the stories or films? After all, visualizing bears as having human characteristics has a long history, possibly arising from a similarity of features, and particularly in bears' ability to walk upright and with a heel-toe footfall (Brunner 2008, 103–11). Randy Malamud's exposition on how the visual depiction of animals, including through anthropomorphizing, can be acts of power that place limitations on how humans think about them (2012, 7, 27), draws on Judith Butler's interrogation of the conventions by which humans come to be recognized as living beings (Malamud 2012, 5; Butler 2010). Malamud contends that the "framing" of animals, that is, imposing identities on them suitable for human purposes, "delineates a boundary that defines the realm in which we allow the framed creatures to exist" (5). Through this process animals are transformed into cultural artifacts undifferentiated from material objects and as such are disallowed the agency of possessing their own narratives, their authentic-self being replaced by a script that "amuses or benefits or otherwise satisfies our natural cravings" (3). Such displacement makes it easier for humans to narrow the possibilities of animal lives, including even their having a life (see Varga and Dempsey 2016 for examples in children's literature). While Malamud limits his application of the concept of framing to visual representations of animals, its use in this chapter is expanded to other genres of communication to examine how the anthropomorphizing of Winnie has resulted in the substitution of her corporal and sentient being with cartoon imagery.

In Which Winnie's Arrival at London Zoo Causes Great Amusement

Initially, the public framing of Winnie does not begin with her purchase in Ontario by Harry Colebourn or her time spent with his army unit, but with her 1914 surrender to London Zoo. Commentary by the Zoological Society of London in the *Field*, a sporting magazine of distinction, about the zoo having accepted into its collection several black bears that had been mascots of various Canadian Forces regiments, highlights the one brought by Colebourn, scripting her as animal (Archives of Manitoba 1914, 1050). Prominence is given to Colebourn's bear not because she displayed particularly endearing qualities but because of the humorous juxtaposition between what seemed on the one hand to be a "perfectly tame" cub and, on the other, the wild behavior she was reported to have exuded during her attempts to escape from the automobile while on way to the zoo (1050). Additional evidence that Winnie was, at this time, visualized as fully bear is the story's denoting her recognition of, and enjoyment in, the company of other bears rather than the latter-day imagining of her as languishing on separation from Colebourn (Harrison 2004, 01:09:18–01:10:39). Also, while the report notes Colebourn as having brought the cub to the zoo, her origin is not presented as having arisen from his "rescue" of her (as has later come to be implied) but as issue of a living bear in the wild, having been "born somewhere about Christmas of last year while its mother was lying up in winter quarters" (Archives of Manitoba 1914, 1050).

Ten years on, and just prior to Milne's first Winnie-the-Pooh publication, the real bear had become broadly acclaimed for her dog-like behavior toward humans but was still coded as bear, with writers noting her instinctive seeking of refuge in "the darkest corner of her den" during the winter months—a time of black bear dormancy (qtd. in Shushkewich 2005, 47; Sidebotham 1925, 34). While the popularity of Milne's stories resulted in her being referred to by his bear's name (e.g., Bruce 1929, 386), she continued to be framed as animal. This included her having a potential for savagery, as provided in a 1931 story in which a zoo attendant declares that, given her strength, "[s]he could crush you to death if she would" (qtd. in Weatherhead 1989, 36). More generally, she remained depicted as pet-like, as evidenced in a 1933 remark on her behavior toward zoo visitors: "[S]he greets them all [admirers] in the same doggish manner—by rubbing her big black flanks against their legs" (qtd. in Shushkewich 2005, 49). Her compliance, and antics of opening her cage door and performing calisthenics on cue, were, from the viewpoint of a London Zoo attendant, attributed to kindliness in her early training (Alldis 1973, 10) rather than because of an *inherent* difference from other bears. Announcements of her death repeated mention of her docility and canine capers, including on-signal dropping to the ground and lying still (Graham 1987, 4), and even though called by the name of Milne's bear, her essence was remembered as being that of an "American black bear" (*Yorkshire Evening Post* 1934). Similarly, in a Winnipeg press report of her death, where credence was given to Winnie's having human-like intelligence through the anecdote of her assisting in her own care by "wrapping her feet up in blankets before lying down," she is nevertheless referred to as "a Canadian black bear" (Archives of Manitoba 1934, 10).[4]

Hence lingered the delineation of Winnie for the next fifty-plus years, valued for being a bear willing to carry children on her back and repeat tricks for food. Her link to the Milne stories endured, but even the London Zoo statue unveiled in 1981 presents her likeness as that of a wild bear. This changed when events of the late 1980s initiated a rewriting of her script, whereby Winnie came to be anthropomorphized through the nostalgic lens of childhood innocence.

In Which Winnie Returns to White River but Goes Unrecognized as a Bear

An appreciation for the sociocultural meaningfulness of Winnie's anthropomorphization is assisted with knowledge about the meaning of the term and its historical context. To speak of the anthropomorphizing of animals is not simply a reference to an imposing of human-like characteristics on them but "is about perceiving qualities in animals that we recognize in ourselves"

(Monteiro and Reis 2018, 4). John Berger argues that pre-nineteenth-century anthropomorphism "was integral to the relation between man and animal and was an expression of their proximity," which maintained that animals had a cultural significance equal to, but distinct from, humans (2009, 21). As animal life increasingly disappeared, perspectives toward the animal-human relationship changed, with humans considering themselves culturally superior to animal life. This ideological standpoint facilitated Descartes's proposition that animals are soulless and thereby machine-like in their lack of physical and cognitive sensibility. Over the next century, the anthropomorphizing of animals was embedded with a nostalgic longing that replaced animalness with an "invented innocence," which was, Berger explains, a means of spiritually transcending what was believed to be the human's problematic retention of animal mechanicalism (2009, 21). The outcome was a reduction of animal essence that strips them of being thought about as having (or needing) lives outside of that which is of interest to humans. Thus, restyled as innocents, they were allowed entry into human households as toys and characters in stories and movies (25). The prevalence of these types of representations, combined with our general lack of familiarity with how wild animals actually behave, can lead to incorrect assumptions about their behavior. The disappointment felt by humans when real animals do not match with the expectations created by their symbolic counterparts, or when animals indeed attack humans who have approached them because of a belief that all animals are interested in contact with humans, often ends badly for the animal.

Winnie's anthropomorphized reconfiguration occurred over a series of events that initially focused on commemorating Harry Colebourn's actions. It appears to have begun with a 1987 news story pointing out the confusion caused by the inscription on London Zoo's 1981 plaque (unveiled with the statue dedicated to the memory of Winnie) that reported her as having been a mascot for Princess Patricia's Canadian Light Infantry (Sharp 1987, A1). Even though the text of the plaque, in which a distinction is made between the bears, is included in the story: "She gave her name to Winnie the Pooh, and A. A. Milne and Ernest Shepard gave Winnie the Pooh to the world" (A1), assertions are made of her having had a more profound influence. The story reports that the Zoological Society of London was adamant that "the Winnie the Pooh character was inspired by the bear mascot" (A1), and that the zoo's press officer declared her as having been "inspiration for A. A. Milne's world-famous Winnie the Pooh" (A2).

While prior to this report Winnie might have been deemed as motivating Milne's stories, the report's avowal here seems to have initiated a concentrated anthropomorphizing of her *as* Winnie-the-Pooh. The story resulted in Fred Colebourn, Harry Colebourn's son, bringing attention to his father's role in the bear's life (Graham 1987, 1). At this juncture, Fred's pronouncements on the importance of the senior Colebourn's donation of the bear to London Zoo focus on the pleasure she provided its visitors. However, the newspaper's placing a Winnie and Colebourn photograph next to an illustration of Winnie-the-Pooh might have been the impetus for a more conclusive assertion broadcast the following month over Canada's national television network. In the introduction to its interview with Fred Colebourn, the narrator unequivocally declares that the London Zoo Winnie "inspired Milne to write his well-loved stories" (CBC 1987, 00:00:05–00:00:11). This enthusiastic assertion of Winnie's influence was not initially heeded by Fred Colebourn, whose focus remained on memorializing his father rather than celebrating Winnie by directing his efforts to having the zoo plaque amended so as to indicate Winnie's true regimental association and to include mention of his father's donation of her. He emphasized the latter as especially important because Winnie's popularity predated Milne's stories. Notably, throughout the interview both Fred and the interviewer conflate Winnie's gender with that of the literary character. It is a confusion repeated in the Heritage Minute production discussed at the beginning of this chapter, in which a London Zoo official advises an attendant: "You are noting that he is the official mascot of the Second Canadian Infantry Brigade?" even as this is followed by Colebourn's directive to the bear, "You be a good girl while I'm gone" (Historica Canada n.d.[b], 00:00:12–00:00:15). It is a reassignment that signifies another way that Winnie's bear-self has undergone transfiguration into Winnie-the-Pooh.

Although initially refraining from exploiting Winnie as the storybook character, by 1989 Fred Colebourn was also espousing the media scripting of Winnie as Milne inspiration, perhaps deciding that it was a more effective tactic for achieving the goal of a statue being erected in his father's honor. During a televised interview while campaigning to raise funds for its creation, the introduction of which restates the "inspiration" claim of the 1987 broadcast, he insists that Winnie was the basis for Milne's bear, proclaiming: "It would never have come into existence had father not taken that little cub with him to England" (CBC 1989, 00:01:05–00:01:11).

Later that year, a story in the *Beaver*, a Canadian magazine of long-standing cultural significance, published what seems to have been the most expansive account yet of the Winnie and Colebourn story (Weatherhead 1989). Its title, "In Which Pooh Joins the Army and Lands in the Zoo," and the inclusion of a Shepard illustration on its first page (35), demonstrate that by this time the bear was regarded as warm-up act to Milne's feature presentation. Nostalgic framing of her is carried out with Fred supposedly drawing on heretofore unmentioned childhood memories of a Winnie-the-Pooh connection: "Fred Colebourn says he enjoyed the Winnie-the-Pooh books as a child, and always knew the Pooh Bear was named after his father's real-life bear" (38), and through the author's concluding paragraph, which restyles the misery of the 1914 muddy slough that was Salisbury Plain into a dream sequence of boys at play:

> [W]hen the soldiers of today carry out manoeuvres on their Salisbury Plain exercise grounds, perhaps they at times sense about them ghostly sounds of their departed World War I comrades frolicking with a little bear that came all the way from Canada. (38)

The late 1980s anthropomorphizing of Winnie as the fictional bear was most fully realized in White River, Ontario. Megan De Roover's chapter in this collection points out the effort made by the town to exploit Winnie-the-Pooh fandom through its claim of being the real bear's original home. The town does not conceal its interest in profiting from Winnie's connection to the fictional bear, and it has done so by replacing her presence with that of the latter. On the town's webpage, the hyperlink leading to her history is labeled "Winnie the Pooh," and she is referred to by that designation in the history's paragraph headings. In the town, she has been displaced by an enormous Disney-approved Marbelite Winnie-the-Pooh, sitting on the limb of a massive tree constructed of the same material. The Walt Disney Company had initially denied the town permission to erect a Winnie-the-Pooh likeness but eventually consented, reportedly on the condition that it "it [resemble] the drawings in Milne's stories" (Vaughan 1989, par. 5).[5] The statue stands at the highway entrance to White River, and at the time this chapter was written, its image is displayed on the sidebar of the town's website (White River, Ontario n.d.). The Visitor Center sells Winnie-the-Pooh kitsch, including items marked with a (Disney-licensed) "Where It All Began" logo (Shushkewich 2005, 63), which encircles a drawing of Winnie-the-Pooh. The logo is ubiquitous on town signage and is even engraved on a replica of a commemorative plaque presented by the town's children to London Zoo in 1997.

In 1989, the town launched its "Winnie the Pooh's Hometown Festival," the year being noted as the seventy-fifth anniversary of Winnie's purchase by Colebourn ("History of Winnie the Pooh," par. 13, at White River, Ontario n.d.). While the festival is described as a commemoration of "a little black bear cub" ("Winnie Hometown Festival," par. 1, at White River, Ontario n.d.), there is marginal acknowledgment of her as real animal. Festival themes—Winnie the Pooh Looks to the Future, Winnie the Pooh Goes to Vegas, Winnie the Pooh goes Hawaiian—further remove the bear's wilderness origins from consideration. De Roover identifies the myriad of ways that activities typical of small-town celebratory events keep festival attendees entertained (see also "Winnie Hometown Festival," par. 3, at White River, Ontario n.d.). Festival amusements are likely selected based on commonsense knowledge of what visitors would enjoy, with education about black bears not among them. From the ecocentric perspective that all living beings are of intrinsic worth irrespective of similarity or usefulness to humans, it can be realized that the festival activities provide little opportunity to contemplate Winnie's life before or after the killing of her sow.

She does appear on the White River scene in a photograph showing her with Colebourn (included twice in the town's web pages, hung in the Visitor Centre, and appearing on the interpretive sign about the town—which also shows the iconic photograph of her alongside Christopher Robin Milne). Her other appearance is by way of a large cedar carving, created for the inaugural Hometown Festival (Shushkewich 2005, 63). It is an emotive piece, with the cub upright and facing Colebourn with her muzzle and his hand touching. The carving is not mentioned in the town's website information about Winnie or the festival (and a query regarding its status went unanswered). Further, in contrast to the ease with which an internet search located tourist photographs of Winnie-the-Pooh as displayed throughout White River, quite a bit of sleuthing was required to uncover those of the carving, and I found only two (see the trip blog Amy 2016 for the best-quality photograph).

De Roover's analysis reveals the complications that arise from the still-dominant perspective in northern Ontario (and elsewhere in North America) that black bears are nuisance animals, with extermination of their numbers thought to be an appropriate measure of control along with a lack of sympathy for any cubs that are indirect casualties as a result. This, along with the region's continuing dependence on trophy-hunting tourism (including black bear hunting), indicates that minimizing Winnie's presence would help prevent uncomfortable attention paid to her having been orphaned through the death of her sow by a hunter. Replacing her with the anthropomorphized bear through the use of Winnie-the-Pooh's name and likeness solves the problem of White River possibly having to confront the fact that the role it played in Winnie's contribution to children's fiction arose out of bloodshed, and it was the interloper Colebourn who, as De Roover explains, ensured her survival. This might also help illuminate why the carving of Winnie and Colebourn is screened out of the town's promotional materials. Its showing Colebourn with a grimace rather than a smile, while an authentic envisioning of difficulties experienced during military training, might be thought of not only as distracting from the festival's entertainment value but also as a reminder that Winnie's life was saved by his taking her away from the place now claiming her as its own. Given the lack of tourist photographs of the carving circulating on the internet, the strategy is plausibly an appropriate one as far as attracting visitors is concerned.

Back in Winnipeg, Fred Colebourn's effort to have a statue of his father erected was successful, and in 1992 a bronze sculpture that paired Harry Colebourn with Winnie was unveiled. It is similar to the White River cedar carving except that it depicts Winnie suckling from a bottle held by Colebourn and him smiling down at her. Its placement at the time was in the zoo area of the city's Assiniboine Park. While the setting symbolically retained her as captive, it was at least also a reminder that she was worthy of remembering because of her animal-being. As well, although the statue's plaque includes an image depicting Shepard's creation, it limits claims of Winnie's influence over Milne to the giving of her name, and enhances memory of her as animal by referring to her as Winnie-the-Bear.

The anthropomorphizing of Winnie as child-innocent came into broader material circulation with Canada Post's issuing of its "Winnie the Pooh at Walt Disney World, 1996" stamps (Canada Post Corporation 1996). The four stamps in the series are packaged in an order intended to convey the chronology of Winnie-the-Pooh's life story: first, Colebourn feeding Winnie from a bottle; followed by Christopher Robin holding his teddy bear; then, Winnie-the-Pooh waving goodbye to his Hundred Acre friends; and finally, Disney's Winnie-the-Pooh in sight of the Cinderella Castle of the Magic Kingdom theme park. In its brevity, the series is a succinct illumination of the late twentieth-century framing of Winnie as having "progressed" from real bear to anthropomorphized commodity.

In Which Winnie Arrives in Winnipeg but Is Mistaken for a Teddy Bear

The late twentieth-century scripting of Winnie's story as described above would seem to have completed the framing of her as a bear of some influence but little animal life. Still, there was more to come, with exaggerated imaginings that, although claiming to be real and true recitations of her biography, further devalue her animal-being. It is unclear what initiated these visualizations, which are alleged to be true. Maybe the 2004 television movie *A Bear Named Winnie* was a stimulus. The movie mostly presents Winnie as bearlike until the final scenes, in which she is depicted as the mystical healer of a war-traumatized Colebourn—although a hint of her as non-bearish is given in a London Zoo official's remark upon her looking toward him: "It's her eyes, wasn't like an animal at all. It was as if she could see what I was thinking" (Harrison 2004, 01:09:18–01:10:39). Perhaps the invention of a fictional breakdown for Colebourn, and of a deep friendship between him and poet John McCrae of "In Flanders Fields" renown, being broadcast in the ninetieth anniversary year of the start of the First World War as well as the month Winnie was given over to the zoo, ignited supposed correctives to the film. Or maybe, as Fred Colebourn was now deceased, it was thought that there would be no need to worry about his possible dismay at further misrepresentations produced under the guise of being the real story.

One of these is a 2005 biographical treatise about the bear by Val Shushkewich, *The Real Winnie: A One-of-a-Kind Bear* (2005), which expands on the 1989 suppositions published in the *Beaver*. Shushkewich accentuates earlier commentaries by zoo observers that had mused on Winnie's docility by visualizing her tractability as even *greater* than that of domesticated pets: "It was even possible to take whatever she was eating away from her and she would simply accept it. Generally, it would be foolish to attempt to do this, even with a tame dog!" (44). In this book's anthropomorphizing of her, Winnie is an archetype of nostalgic innocence:

The true story of this real bear—who faced life in an open, honest way, who never lost her temper or snapped at anyone—should be seen as just that: a true story, a real-life example of the potential goodness that lives in the hearts of humans and animals, which promotes love and respect and inspires imagination. The chain of goodness, set against dark moments in world history and put in motion by one kind-hearted soldier who rescued an orphaned bear, has not been broken. (70)

Such envisioning is expanded upon in M. A. Appleby's *Winnie the Bear: The True Story behind A. A. Milne's Famous Bear* (2011). Appleby uses her father's earlier friendship with Fred Colebourn as sufficient evidence of her authority over the claims she proffers, thus precluding the need for further evidence. The author blurs dates, misattributes quotations, and distorts events to create a biography of Winnie that defines her as Winnie-the-Pooh. Appleby argues that her inventions, termed as "creative intervention," have been done "only sparingly and in small ways" (105), but since all that is now known about Winnie's early days are the few brief entries in Colebourn's diary and the newspaper reports, "creative intervention" has been applied to the entirety of Winnie's story. This includes lengthy fictive descriptions of her playing with soldiers, incorporated for the explicit purpose of convincing readers that the bear had a personality similar to Winnie-the-Pooh's (11–12, 30, 35). Another is a fabrication of Colebourn in conversation with a London Zoo attendant that draws on material from a 1931 newspaper story in which the attendant remarks on the danger of bears (43–44). These deceits work toward establishing as indisputable Appleby's proclamation that Milne's bear was indeed Winnie, and thereby, Winnie *is* him, with reassignment of the bear's gender not impeding the assumption (75–76).

Appleby asserts that her claim of the two bears being one and the same is proven by two statements provided in Brian Sibley's *Three Cheers for Pooh* (1991) (which does not conflate the bears). The first is from Sibley's caption to a Shepard illustration of the fictional character: "A. A. Milne told a friend that his son's encounter at London Zoo with the American black bear, Winnie, had inspired him to write a couple of poems—and, possibly, even a story" (Sibley 1991, 35; qtd. in Appleby 2011, 100).[6] Following the presentation of this passage in her book, Appleby exclaims: "There it was—my big flash of insight right there in black and white! And all my ideas come together. I *knew* that Milne, with his creative ability to weave facts into fiction, would find Winnie the Bear irresistible" (100). However, the next statement in Sibley's caption, which Appleby does not include, begins with reservation toward the inspirational claim even while it recognizes that Milne's "Furry Bear" poem was about a real bear. He writes, "True or not, *Now We Are Six*, published in 1927, contained 'Furry Bear,' a verse in which the poet imagines what it would be like to *be* a bear" (Sibley 1991, 35). In addition to omitting mention of Sibley's hesitancy, and despite the verse excluding reference to either Winnie or Winnie-the-Pooh, Appleby relies on Sibley's remark that the illustration of the verse included both a Winnie-the-Pooh and a realistic bear, as substantiating her own perspective: "Thanks to E. H. Shepard, he [Pooh] is discovered coming face to face with his famous namesake at London Zoo in the illustrations to a remarkably Poohish 'Hum,' entitled 'Furry Bear'" (Sibley 1991, 75; qtd. in Appleby 2011, 100). Appleby further concludes that this statement establishes that Milne himself verified the claim, writing: "I believe I have found a critical piece of evidence—my ideas have some support, via Sibley, from Milne himself" (100).

Perhaps all this would little matter if the book received no notice, but its distortions have been legitimized with the publication being short-listed for the Manitoba Historical Society's Margaret McWilliams Award for popular history (Dominion Street 2020a). Although criteria for the prize is not listed on the society's website, the illusion is created that the book is historically accurate. Official sanctioning of its veracity is also suggested through Appleby's having presented copies to Prince Charles and Camilla, Duchess of Cornwall, during their 2015 visit to Canada (Dominion Street 2020b).

Furthering the diminishment of Winnie's animal essence as accomplished through these publications has been the application of what might be considered the ultimate of anthropomorphizing acts, being reconstructed in teddy-bear form. Soft cloth animal toys are a material synthesis of a late nineteenth- and early twentieth-century perspective that young children and animals share a natural kinship by both being in a state of uncivilized innocence (Varga 2009a, 187–90). Of such toys, the teddy bear is singular in denoting animal-child innocence through its having become representative of a 1902 Mississippi bear supposedly, but not actually, saved by Theodore Roosevelt from hunters (Varga 2009a, 199–201). The teddy bear has, therefore, come to stand for both childhood innocence and the protection of it (Varga 2009b, 75–78).

In 2012, Steiff, the luxury manufacturer of soft-cloth toys and famous for having inspired the early twentieth-century teddy bear craze, had available a nine-inch "Winnipeg" bear as a collector's item (see, e.g., Steiff n.d.[a]).[7]

Product advertising describes Winnie's purchase by Colebourn, journey to England, placement in London Zoo, and subsequent Christopher Robin Milne enthrallment (Steiff n.d.[a]).[8] In 2014, Steiff produced a fourteen-inch version, also named Winnipeg but no longer a grizzly (see, e.g., Steiff n.d.[b]), and one of ten inches designed to be hung as a Christmas tree decoration, with a retailer of the latter proclaiming the year officious because it marked "the 100th anniversary of the beginning of this magical story" (Bearly a Memory 2020).

The cultural normativity of animal stand-ins, whether as material goods or as characters in books and films, and their relationship to the idealization of childhood, can make their problematizing a challenge, with critique resisted by the overriding cultural ethos that these representations are innocent diversions. While casting Winnie in the form of a teddy bear can be thought a positive way of memorializing her, the marketing tactics that promote the primary value of her life as her role as a supposed influence over Milne's writing implies that, had her sow's killing not occurred, there might have been no Winnie-the-Pooh; and that, it is intimated, would be very sad indeed. As counterpoint, if Winnie or her sow could speak to the meaning 1914 had for their lives, it is unlikely that the experiences of killing and capture would be expressed as having been "magical."

The teddy-bearization of Winnie continued with Lindsay Mattick's children's picture book, *Finding Winnie: The True Story of the World's Most Famous Bear* (2015). On the book's cover jacket, Winnie is portrayed as a cub so tiny she fits atop a soldier's booted foot. The drawing employs strategies used in fanciful renderings of the bear supposedly (but, as mentioned earlier, not actually) saved by Theodore Roosevelt, which in some tellings is reduced to a cub of only eighteen inches in height (for an explanation, see Varga 2009c, 100), about the size of the average teddy bear. Winnie is further aligned to childhood innocence by being shown as having a broad forehead, oversize eyes (especially for a bear), and a round belly. All of this is in the style of a "baby schema" illustration, employed to convey an endearing infancy, the features of which have been identified as stimulating human caregiving responses (see Borgi et al. 2014 for examples). Winnie gazes toward the viewer with forelegs wrapped around the human's calf. It is a beguiling image of a child-bear afraid of the world-out-there finding protection through Colebourn as father. Notably, the soldier's boot and bear's fur are pristine, inviting a halcyon remembering of the relationship between Winnie and Colebourn as if it had occurred in a place and time free of First World War horrors.

On the train she is a babe-in-arms, cuddling on Colebourn's lap while nursing, her forepaws grasping the bottle and hind legs curling toward her belly. On the training grounds of Valcartier and during the trip to England, she reveals moments of bearness by climbing tent poles and the ship mast but returns to being depicted as a domestic pet when she sleeps under Colebourn's cot and poses with the soldiers for a group photograph. Otherwise, she is a roundish, teddy-like bear, paw in Colebourn's hand (with the book's back cover further augmenting the fashioning of Winnie as toy, through its image of Winnie-as-Teddy holding onto a child's hand). On the training fields, her eyes look toward Colebourn in adoration, but when he brings her to the zoo she deflects her gaze as if conscious of the forthcoming separation. However, her gloom is averted when Christopher Robin Milne enters her enclosure: "They became true friends."[9] Their supposed reciprocal bond is illustrated with a drawing of the boy embracing Winnie while astride her back, and Winnie gazing with satisfied look over her shoulder toward him as if she had an interest in ensuring his happiness and feeling love for him. The figuration of Winnie as desirous of this intimacy assigns to her emotions that we often demand animals hold toward ourselves. While on the surface it can be read as an empathetic depiction, this way of thinking about animals can result in our failure to understand, or meet, their real needs (Harfeld 2013, 693–96). John Berger puts it this way: "[W]hen animals are represented as synonymous with humans, the animal fades away" (2009, 29). Troubling the assumption that Winnie felt affection toward Christopher Robin Milne is not disregard of animal sentience but is intended to explain how such visualization frames her merit, and thus commercial value, as residing in her expression of behaviors uncommon to bears. The ecocentric concern is that veneration expressed about Winnie because she was an atypical bear can create an expectation that bears in general *should* behave in a similar manner, and if they do not, they are unworthy of consideration.[10]

The image also encourages acritical interpretation of Winnie's compliance with ferrying humans about during zoo events (Mainland 1925, 13; repeated in Appleby 2011, 64; CBC n.d.) as demonstration that she loved doing so in the same way that humans might have loved riding atop her. Perhaps her early taming and kind treatment made it possible for her to accept such activity, and maybe she found it enjoyable because it disrupted the ennui of her Mappin Terraces confinement. Nonetheless, as neither wild nor captive bears normally acquiesce to such employment, its affordance needs to be recognized as achieved through the erasure of Winnie's animal telos. Rather than Winnie's tolerance having been due to an inherent interest in humans, and thereby to her being a special kind of bear akin to Winnie-the-Pooh, it was most likely an outcome of her removal from the wild on the killing of her sow before having learned the ways of bears.[11] Mattick's dedication of the story to her son asserts a hope that it will "always remind you of the impact one small, loving gesture can have," a sentiment she repeats during interviews (see, e.g., Day 2015; CBC 2014, 00:02:32–00:02:38). The effect is a scripting of Winnie within a frame of maudlin childhood exceeding even that of Milne's bear.

Once again, the issue arises as to what relevance a children's picture book might have to considerations of Winnie as a fictional bear. In this case, even more concerns are raised than were brought up by Appleby's spurious historical publication, as Mattick and her book have been accorded greater prominence; and the fact that she is Harry Colebourn's granddaughter seemingly proffers on her an even weightier claim than Appleby to having provided an authorized version of Winnie's story.[12] Mattick was highlighted on a Canadian national television news report, which included the "Winnie" Minute, while accompanying Canada's National Arts Symphony on its First World War remembrance tour of England. During it, she is shown walking on Salisbury Plain while reminiscing about her great-grandfather's experiences there with Winnie, reading her 2015 book to a group of children, and invoking the dedication discussed later in the analysis of *Finding Winnie* (CBC 2014). *The Canadian Encyclopedia*, another Historica Canada product, has provided Mattick with three entries pertaining to Winnie, one featuring herself (Yarhi 2015) and another containing details about Colebourn's time with Winnie (Yarhi 2013). The third is an editorial (Historica Canada 2017) concerning Mattick's involvement with the Ryerson University (Toronto) exhibit *Remembering the Real Winnie*. The exhibit includes a Zoological Society of London video, *The Bear Who Inspired Winnie-the-Pooh* (ZSL 2014)—discussed later in this chapter in terms of its recharacterization of the bear. This media attention creates an impression that the contents of Mattick's storybook are as real as the historical events with which she has been associated.

In addition to authoring her 2015 picture book, Mattick was coauthor of a fictional story, *Winnie's Great War*, which added to the bear's anthropomorphizing (Mattick and Greenhut 2018). It is a chapter book that expands on the bear's biography as a wild cub and then with Colebourn, visualizing her as being of exceptional brawn and talent who accomplished splendid deeds.

While in these ways Winnie is decidedly not Milne's "bear of little brain," the use of elements from Milne's stories, such as a greediness for sweets that leads to her entrapment in tight places, reinforces consideration of their being one and the same. Although the authors note that this is a work of fiction, the cover promotes it as "based on the true story of the world's most famous bear." In an endorsement, Kallie George writes: "The spirit of Winnie-the-Pooh is captured beautifully in this retelling of the real bear's adventures" (Mattick and Greenhut 2018, back cover), further suggesting that the story causes confusion between reality and fantasy.

During the period that Mattick's 2015 teddy-bearization of Winnie was under production, this style of framing, with its continued diminishment of Winnie's animal-self, was reiterated with the manufacture of limited-edition teddy-Winnie-bears outfitted in camouflage jackets. Six were presented by Winnipeg's Fort Garry Horse Regiment, with which Harry Colebourn had been affiliated, to the same British royals who had been recipients of Appleby's book. As with all teddies, these are emblematic of childhood innocence even when clothed in military fashion, and they were in fact proffered as gifts for the royals' grandchildren (Fort Garry Horse Kit Shop 2020). At the time of this writing, several of the bears were still available from the regiment's kit shop. The item's expense (eighty-one Canadian dollars), lack of assertive promotion, limited opportunities for purchase due to the restricted opening hours of the regiment's physical shop, and costly shipping charges probably explain why several years following manufacture the bears had not sold out. Despite the seemingly minor consumer interest in this item, it might be that the one hundredth anniversary of Christopher Robin Milne's birth will result in Winnie-Teddy toys becoming a commonplace framing of Winnie as childhood innocent.[13]

In Which Winnie Finds Herself in a Gallery but Is Lost on the Way to London Zoo

Despite the excesses of the late twentieth century in the production of Winnie as anthropomorphized bear, in the twenty-first there have been a few instances of restraint. One example is Sally Walker's *Winnie: The True Story of the Bear Who Inspired Winnie-the-Pooh* (2015). This children's picture book repeats the story of Harry Colebourn as veterinarian-soldier who purchased the bear cub he subsequently named Winnie, depicting their time together prior to his deployment to France, Christopher Robin Milne's engagement with the bear at London Zoo, and the subsequent production of Winnie-the-Pooh stories. Throughout, Walker maintains Winnie as distinct from Milne's bear, and Jonathan Voss's illustrations show her as realistically animal-like. Bob Ross, writing in an environmental newsletter about the discovery of Winnie's skull in museum storage, also focuses on her as animal. While utilizing invented elements that first appeared in Ted Weatherhead's 1989 article, Ross's focus on her time with Colebourn retains her as a bear, and there is minimal explication of her as a Winnie-the-Pooh inspiration (Ross 2016).[14]

Winnipeg's Pooh Gallery, located in the city's Assiniboine Park Pavilion building, also maintains a separation between the two. Even though the gallery is designated with the name of Milne's bear and its web page banner features Winnie-the-Pooh imagery, its Colebourn exhibit, with images of Winnie and the story of her time with him, is in a room separate from that showcasing Winnie-the-Pooh (see Megan De Roover's description in chapter 6 of this volume). Visitors have to move through the one featuring Colebourn and Winnie to reach the other, in which the only visual relationship made between the real and fictional bears, as shown in a promotional video, is the inclusion of Mattick's 2015 book alongside some other books about Winnie-the-Pooh (HappyTravels 2018, 00:01:46–00:01:54). The demarcation works at the ideological level to at least somewhat sustain a memory of Winnie as animal.

Galleries, like museums, are positioned as authoritative institutions over matters of intellectual knowledge and artistic taste, and as such the perspectives being communicated can influence visitors' ideas and attitudes. Their features—exhibition site, items offered for viewing, presentation design, and content of interpretive information—encourage particular ways of seeing and thinking about the objects/subjects/topic under scrutiny (König 2016, 36). That the Pooh Gallery is situated in a Canadian provincial capital and in a building designated as historically significant (Canada's Historic Places n.d.) suggests that what is on offer is of noteworthy value. Although the "Pooh" appellation has lowbrow connotations through its focus on a character now better known through Disney than Milne, and with a coarse reference to bowel movements, the gallery's employment of aesthetics resembles the visual traditions of classical museums and galleries that encourage contemplation of, and reverence for, the materials on display.

Upon entry, visitors encounter framed brown-toned photographs of Colebourn with Winnie, hung on white painted walls. The emotive affect is that of a past time worthy of remembrance and urges appreciation of Colebourn as humanitarian icon and Winnie as pet-like animal. On moving into the Winnie-the-Pooh room, visitors enter a site composed, via its yellow-painted walls and child-size table and chairs, to evoke ideas of childhood delight. Still, the area is as spare in its contents as the previous room and maintains arms-length scrutiny of the archival materials exhibited, with early editions of Milne's Winnie-the-Pooh texts under protective cover. In these ways, the setting does not jostle for superiority over how visitors might have experienced Winnie as Bear in the previous room, and thereby does not tempt rejection of the more somber Colebourn/Winnie presentation in preference for a fantasy alternative.

All the same, these examples are outweighed by the preferred latter-day framing. Even the Zoological Society of London has rescripted Winnie through a 2014 video that declares her as Milne's inspiration (ZSL 2014, 00:00:09–00:00:12) and that includes a view of the society's 1995 statue of Winnie (donated by Winnipeg), which shows her being bottle fed by Colebourn (00:01:52–00:01:55), rather than the 1981 sculpture of a wild bear.

Claims that these ways of visualizing Winnie honor Colebourn's love for her and will encourage others to engage in kindly acts, necessitate revisiting commentary made earlier in this chapter regarding the problems with this manner of anthropomorphizing animals. While some argue that this form of representation is effective for teaching empathetic values toward animals (Hurt 2014), there is evidence that these intentions often miss their mark (Ganea et al. 2014, 6–8). This indicates that such ways of showcasing Winnie are unlikely to result in kindliness toward real bears or other animals, and De Roover's example of Ontario's reinstatement of the spring black bear hunt, resulting in the death of hundreds of cubs through starvation, is a case in point. Furthermore, as the anthropomorphized delineation of animals leads children to hold inaccurate understandings about them (Waxman et al. 2014, 5–7), those of Winnie are liable to promote erroneous knowledge about bears and unrealistic expectations of their behavior toward humans. From the paradigm of ecocentrism, such anthropomorphizing negates the animal's worth as "a fellow sentient being with a life of its own" (Hogan 2009, 156). Laying claim to Winnie's story but visualizing her essence as that of Winnie-the-Pooh, delineating her as more human than bear, or transmuting her into the object of a teddy bear toy are acts of degradation because they rob from her an inherent value in being *bear*. Bereft of her animalness, Winnie is commodified into whatever forms serve human commercial interests.

The Heritage Minute described at the opening of this chapter concludes with a depiction of Christopher Robin Milne as real child merging into the form of Christopher Robin as story character. In both, he is figured as the epitome of childhood innocence. Dressed in an Edwardian frock coat and high-buttoned leggings, he skips on the streetscape outside the zoo. It is an enactment of Milne's 1924 "Lines and Squares," which begins:

Whenever I walk in a London street,
I'm ever so careful to watch my feet;
And I keep in the squares,
And the masses of bears . . . (Milne 1948, 12)

As the publication of this verse predates Milne's Winnie-the-Pooh stories, the scene is ostensibly included because of its bear theme. The child's frolic occurs at the point of a voice-over benediction of the visit's literary outcome: "And that's how a young Canadian bear inspired four volumes of stories and verse that still sell millions of copies around the world" (Historica Canada. n.d.[b], 00:51–00:57), encouraging the symbolic transformation of Winnie's bearish presence into Milne's fictional character. The displacement of Winnie's animalness in favor of childhood innocence is settled with the Minute's thumbnail featuring the child's beguiling face, rather than the bear's visage.

Substitution of the bear for blond-haired childhood innocence is an expression of the revisualization of Winnie from animal-bear to barely-animal. While it is the case that during her life at London Zoo she was favored because of non-bear-like behaviors, she remained scripted as animal. Late twentieth-century anthropomorphizing emphasized those characteristics as well but extended their meaning to being evidence of Winnie as something other than a bear. This reframing calculates her worthiness as residing in her similarity to the character first imagined by A. A. Milne and Ernest Shepard, and later recast by the Walt Disney Company. This is most evident in White River's promotion of its connection to her capture, sale, and zoo life through visualizing her as a monstrously sized fantasy character, but also as manifested in publications that, in claiming to be truthful representations of her life, stress her importance as having contributed to the production of the fictional bear. With the memory of Winnie stripped of animal essence, her value is now determined by the extent to which she replicates an imaginary character, and additionally by the pleasure she brings to humans through such framing.[15]

When a cartoon is judged as more real and true than the actual animal, the animal is denied recognition as having had or indeed of having needed a life (see Butler 2010 on "frames of recognition," 4–12).

Turning back to the earlier question as to whether such depictions should be thought problematic, Randy Malamud proposes that we need only ascertain, "[D]o they do more good than harm?" (2012, 6). An anthropocentric response would be that, lacking evidence of violence done to Winnie (disregarding the violent loss of her mother, removal from her natural habitat, and life spent in an artificial and confined space), they do no injury because the animal is not affected.[16] From an ecocentric standpoint, harm is done because the preponderance of anthropomorphized images supplants a more authentic consideration of Winnie herself, and because of her anthropomorphized fame the resulting lack of animal recognizability becomes extended to bears and animals in general, with the usual outcome being a prioritizing of human interests over animal needs. It is a legacy that Harry Colebourn would not likely have favored.

Notes

1. The Heritage Minutes are sixty-second video documentaries produced by Historica Canada, a private corporation helmed by members of Canada's political and economic elite, that are broadcast during program breaks on the country's television networks. They are intended to convey the essence of a Canadian "culture" by highlighting the positive contributions its peoples have made to the nation-state (Historica Canada n.d.[a]). Peter Hodgins has identified how misrepresentation of events has been purposefully woven into the stories to support the hegemonic function of manufacturing a Canadian "grand narrative" (Hodgins 2003, 15), with those set in the twentieth century designed to "approximate Hollywood standards of 'excitement' and 'significance'" (572). He includes *Winnie* in this category, as an example of an event presented as if momentous to Canadians but actually having minimal impact on the Canadian state or national identity (348). Historica Canada uploaded *Winnie* to YouTube on March 2, 2016, but it is an undated production, with its creation occurring around the year 2000. The 22 Minutes comedy team has had great fun with the scatological inference of Christopher Robin Milne's preferred naming of his father's literary bear (CBC 2015).

2. While Milne's introduction to his 1926 and 1928 books gives credit to the real bear as explanation for the first part of the character's name, his Winnie-the-Pooh was an imagined enlivening of his son's teddy (Thwaite 1990, 293). Notwithstanding inclusion of Ernest H. Shepard in the Heritage Minute scene outside the bear's enclosure engaged in drawing a likeness of her, it was a teddy bear toy that stood as the model for his illustrations (Thwaite 1990, 294–95). Inaccuracies additional to this and the misspelling of Harry Colebourn's name on the plaque pictured in the video include Colebourn leaving Winnie in the care of zoo personnel at what looks like a street-side pub; the zoo official referring to Winnie

as "he"; Colebourn speaking without a trace of a British accent despite his only having left England nine years previously when he was eighteen; and Christopher Robin Milne sporting Edwardian-era leggings, coat, and hat—a facsimile of the child who appears in the decorations for the first two poems of Milne's *When We Were Very Young* ("Corner-of-the-Street" and "Buckingham Palace").

3. Critical animal studies is an interdisciplinary perspective that challenges anthropocentric attitudes about and behaviors toward animals, including their being anthropomorphized in ways that present their having humanlike attributes as resulting in their being "better" animals because they are more like "us."

4. The source is a newspaper article clipped from the top left half of its broadsheet original, including the page number and *Free Press* title on its folio but inscribed with a hand-written date of "July 13, 1934." A search of microfilmed issues of the *Winnipeg Free Press* for the dates spanning May 14, 1934–July 31, 1934 did not locate the article. Furthermore, the folio on all the newspaper's pages over this time period have *Winnipeg Free Press* as the title. As the article's contents confirm that the publication is Winnipeg based, it was likely published in the *Winnipeg Free Press*, but probably in an evening edition that was not preserved through microfilming.

5. Val Shushkewich writes that the statue was "[b]ased on a design provided through Walt Disney Co. (Canada) Ltd" (2005, 63).

6. It is not clear if the remark originates with Sibley or if it was reproduced from another source. The book has illustrations and photographs throughout, but citations are not always provided. A list of sources included in the book's front matter does not identify the pages from which material was utilized, or to which materials in the book they refer.

7. The date of its release was established from a promotional video posted by a Steiff retailer (Paul Seven Lewis 2012).

8. As other shops retailing the item used the "grizzly bear" reference and provided descriptors similar to this one, it can be assumed that they were of Steiff origin. While 2012 was the one-hundredth anniversary of Steiff's first toy bear design, no explanation is provided as to why "Winnipeg" was made available in that year; conceivably, it was motivated by Disney's 2011 animated *Winnie the Pooh* film.

9. At the point in the story, when child and bear meet, the child's name is kept a mystery. He is referred as "the boy" who attends the zoo with his also nameless father, and as "the boy" who becomes "true friends" with Winnie. He is then revealed as being "Christopher Robin Milne" and immediately afterward is called "Christopher Robin."

10. For a discussion of the animal-toward-human gaze from an ecocentric paradigm, see Armstrong 2011. Winnie's loving look toward the child on her back also encourages the transposition of Winnie as Bear into a Winnie-the-Poohish play companion through its inference to a 1926 tale told by A. A. Milne, in an interview conducted by Enid Blyton, that his son and Winnie engaged in wrestling tussles (newspaper reproduction in Thwaite 1992, 97; Appleby 2011, 64, 74). Brian Sibley labels the story as "highly romanticised" (1991, 36), and it has elsewhere been discounted as myth (Frost 2011).

11. It might also be the case that Winnie's docility was the outcome of a cerebral impairment caused by injuries inflicted during her capture or retention. This would not have been unusual. It was the slamming of a rifle butt onto a bear's head that enabled the one encountered during Theodore Roosevelt's 1902 Mississippi hunt to be captured and then killed by knife. Illustrating Winnie and Christopher Robin Milne in happy gambol while observed from above by A. A. Milne is also a romanticizing of the long-realized deleterious effects on animals of zoo

enclosure, including that of Mappin Terraces, with its concrete artifice, lack of stimulation, inadequate space for roaming, and limited means of retreat from human observation.

12. That the attention is disproportionate to what has been accorded to other Canadian children's authors, especially given the book's minimal literary merit (despite what being a Caldecott Medal winner might imply, for that award honors illustrators), speaks to Lindsay Mattick's personal influence as a public relations expert and former journalist in the communications industry.

13. Winnie-the-Pooh teddy-type bears had been produced under Disney license since 1966 (see, e.g., Sears, Roebuck and Company 1966, 173), the year Disney's animated short *Winnie the Pooh and the Honey Tree* was released, with these being more Winnie-the-Pooh rather than "teddy" in appearance.

14. Ross erroneously reports that Milne's writing success only came after his observations of Winnie at London Zoo and the subsequent publication of his Winnie-the-Pooh books.

15. Serendipitously, while taking a break from constructing these concluding remarks, I opened my Facebook newsfeed and what should appear but a posting on the Meanwhile in Canada page that reads: "102 years ago [*sic*], a Canadian soldier found an orphaned bear and adopted her, brought her to England and inspired a classic book." Below this commentary are two side-by-side images. Their positioning is indicative of Winnie's refiguration as discussed in this chapter. On the left is a photograph of Christopher Robin Milne feeding her, while on the right is an image of Winnie-the-Pooh. Beneath the images is a summary of her story, apparently copied and pasted from a text source. It concludes with the statement: "A young boy named Christopher Robin adored the bear and urged his father to take her home. Instead, his father A. A. Milne transformed Winnipeg into the hero of a classic childhood story, 'Winnie-the-Pooh.'" That Winnie's life is thought notable because of this supposed outcome is affirmed by a commentator who enthuses, "Thank you Canada again, for another great contribution to the world" (Zavatsky 2019). The creators of Meanwhile in Canada describe their page as a satirical look at events (Meanwhile in Canada n.d.), but much of its content, like that of Historica Canada, is directed toward affirming positive myths of Canadian distinctiveness albeit with a light touch.

16. Details about the harm done to animals through breeding practices that attempt to re-create anthropomorphized imagery are described by James Serpell (2003, 92–93). For a troubling example of how animals are presented in the belief that their anthropomorphized counterparts are more worthy models of emulation than those that are real, see the story reported in Disneyland Paris (2018).

Bibliography

Alldis, Jim. 1973. *Animals as Friends: A Head Keeper Remembers London Zoo*. Exeter, Devon, England: David and Charles.

Amy. 2016. "White River and Winnie the Pooh Story." Our Journey, July 11. www.aboutour-journey.com/2016/07/white-river-and-winnie-pooh-story.html. Accessed December 15, 2018.

Appleby, M. A. 2011. *Winnie the Bear: The True Story behind A. A. Milne's Famous Bear*. Winnipeg: Dominion Street.

Archives of Manitoba. 1914. "Mascots at the Garden." *The Field*, ca. December, 1050. Harry Colebourn Collection, Microfilm #M62.

Archives of Manitoba. 1934. "Winnie, Noted Canadian Black Bear Who Amused Londoners at Zoo Passes." [*Winnipeg*] *Free Press*, ca. July 13, 10. Harry Colebourn Collection, Microfilm #M62.

Armstrong, Philip. 2011. "The Gaze of Animals." In *Theorizing Animals: Re-Thinking Humanimal Relations*, edited by Nik Taylor and Tania Signal, 175–99. Leiden: Brill.

Bearly a Memory. 2020. "Steiff Mohair Winnipeg Ornament." www.bearlyamemory.com /steiff-specials/usa/ean-682711-steiff-mohair-winnipeg-ornament-black/. Accessed October 19, 2020.

Berger, John. 2009. *Why Look at Animals?* London: Penguin.

Borgi, Marta, Irene Cogliati-Dezza, Victoria Brelsford, Kerstin Meints, and Francesca Cirulli. 2014. "Baby Schema in Human and Animal Faces Induces Cuteness Perception and Gaze Allocation in Children." *Frontiers in Psychology* 5, no. 411 (May 7). doi:10.3389/fpsyg.2014.00411.

Bruce, Kate Mary. 1929. "Taking the Children to the 'Zoo'; or, True Altruism." *The Sketch*, February 27, 386–87.

Brunner, Bernd. 2008. *Bears: A Brief History*. New Haven, CT: Yale University Press.

Butler, Judith. 2010. *Frames of War: When Is Life Grievable?* London: Verso.

Canada Post Corporation. 1996. "Winnie the Pooh at Walt Disney World, 1996." Postage Stamp Guide. www.canadianpostagestamps.ca/stamps/16968/winnie-the-pooh-at-walt -disney-world-1996-1996-canada-postage-stamp-winnie-the-poohw. Accessed December 2, 2018.

Canada's Historic Places. n.d. "Assiniboine Park Pavilion." www.historicplaces.ca/en/rep-reg/place-lieu.aspx?id=8233. Accessed January 13, 2019.

Canadian Broadcasting Corporation (CBC). n.d. "Winnie Takes a Trip," *The Real-Life Canadian Story of Winnie-the-Pooh*. CBC Kids. https://www.cbc.ca/kidscbc2/the-feed /the-real-life-canadian-story-of-winnie-the-pooh. Accessed November 13, 2018.

Canadian Broadcasting Corporation (CBC). 1987. "Winnie-the-Pooh Makes His Literary Debut." June 3. www.cbc.ca/player/play/1435067886.

Canadian Broadcasting Corporation (CBC). 1989. "Winnie-the-Pooh's Canadian Connection." April 24. www.cbc.ca/player/play/1290974275868.

Canadian Broadcasting Corporation (CBC). 2014. "The Winnipeg Connection to Winnie the Pooh." CBC News. YouTube, October 29. www.youtube.com/watch?v=enVonjSGlas.

Canadian Broadcasting Corporation (CBC). 2015. "22 Minutes: Heritage Minute, Winnie the Pooh." CBC Comedy. YouTube, March 31. https://youtu.be/Gp3FBQ1B23A.

Day, Lisa. 2015. "Book Time Interviews Beach Resident Lindsay Mattick about *Finding Winnie*, the True Story of Winnie-the-Pooh." Toronto.com, October 28. www.toronto .com/blogs/post/6036027-book-time-interviews-beach-resident-lindsay-mattick-about -finding-winnie-the-true-story-of-winnie-t/. Accessed December 10, 2018.

Disneyland Paris. 2018. "Disneyland Paris: The Little Duck." YouTube, December 25. www .youtube.com/watch?time_continue=2&v=G4qMqbL9ACo. Accessed March 11, 2019.

Dominion Street. 2020a. "*Winnie the Bear*, Awards." www.winniethebear.com/pages/awards. Accessed October 19, 2020.

Dominion Street. 2020b. "*Winnie the Bear* and the Royal Visit." www.winniethebear.com /blogs/news. Accessed October 19, 2020.

Fort Garry Horse Kit Shop. 2020. "Winnie the Bear, 20" Black Bear Wearing Cadpat Uniform." www.fortgarryhorse.ca/FGHKitShop/product/winnie-the-bear/. Accessed October 20, 2020.

Frost, Warwick. 2011. "From Winnie-the-Pooh to Madagascar: Fictional Media Images of the Zoo Experience." In *Zoos and Tourism: Conservation, Education, Entertainment?*, edited by Warwick Frost, 217–26. Bristol: Channel View Publications.

Ganea, Patricia A., Caitlin F. Canfield, Kadria Simons-Ghafari, and Tommy Chou. 2014. "Do Cavies Talk? The Effect of Anthropomorphic Picture Books on Children's Knowledge about Animals." *Frontiers in Psychology* 5, no. 283 (April 10). doi:10.3389/fpsyg.2014.00283.

Graham, Heidi. 1987. "Pooh Bear's Name Is Winnie as in Winnipeg." *Winnipeg Free Press*, May 2, 1, 4.

HappyTravels. 2018. "The Pooh Gallery." YouTube, January 1. www.youtube.com/watch?v=3LbDL89PQ6A. Accessed December 2, 2018.

Harfeld, Jes Lynning. 2013. "Telos and the Ethics of Animal Farming." *Journal of Agricultural Environmental Ethics* 26, no. 3 (June): 691–709. doi.org/10.1007/s10806-012-9422-y.

Harrison, John Kent, dir. 2004. *A Bear Named Winnie*. Canadian Broadcasting Corporation.

Historica Canada. n.d.(a). "About." http://www.historicacanada.ca/about. Accessed November 15, 2018.

Historica Canada. n.d.(b). *Winnie*. Heritage Minutes. www.historicacanada.ca/content/heritage-minutes/winnie. Accessed November 15, 2018.

Historica Canada. 2017. "The Real Winnie-the-Pooh." *The Canadian Encyclopedia*, January 18. www.thecanadianencyclopedia.ca/en/article/the-real-winnie-the-pooh. Accessed December 2, 2018.

Hodgins, Peter. 2003. "The Canadian Dream-Work: History, Myth and Nostalgia in the Heritage Minutes." PhD diss., Carleton University. www.curve.carleton.ca/e5715913-7778-4eab-82d3-3f9c831bd408. Accessed November 15, 2018.

Hodgins, Peter. 2012. "Why Must Halifax Keep Exploding? English-Canadian Nationalism and the Search for a Usable Disaster." In *Settling and Unsettling Memories: Essays in Canadian Public History*, edited by Nicole Neatby and Peter Hodgins, 725–59. Toronto: University of Toronto Press.

Hogan, Walter. 2009. *Animals in Young Adult Fiction*. Lanham, MD: Scarecrow Press.

Hurt, Lindsay Schafer. 2014. "Fuzzy Toys and Fuzzy Feelings: How the 'Disney' Culture Provides the Necessary Psychological Link to Improving Animal Welfare." *Journal of Animal and Natural Resource Law* 10: 253–72.

König, Gudrun M. 2016. "Displaying Things: Perspectives from Cultural Anthropology." In *On Display: Visual Politics, Material Culture, and Education*, edited by Karin Priem and Kerstin te Heesen, 35–46. Münster, Germany: Waxmann Verlag.

Mainland, Leslie G. 1925. *Secrets of the Zoo*. London: Partridge Publishers.

Malamud, Randy. 2012. *An Introduction to Animals and Visual Culture*. Basingstoke, Hants., England: Palgrave Macmillan.

Mattick, Lindsay. 2015. *Finding Winnie: The True Story of the World's Most Famous Bear*. Boston: Little, Brown.

Mattick, Lindsay, and Josh Greenhut. 2018. *Winnie's Great War*. New York: HarperCollins.

Meanwhile in Canada. n.d. "About." Facebook. www.facebook.com/pg/MeanwhileinCanada1/about/?ref=page_internal. Accessed June 4, 2019.

Meanwhile in Canada. 2019. "102 years ago, a Canadian soldier . . ." Facebook, January 18, 12:27 p.m. www.facebook.com/MeanwhileinCanada1/posts/2047739008606453. Accessed January 18, 2019.

Milne, A. A. 1948. *When We Were Very Young*. New York: E. P. Dutton.

Monteiro, Rute, and Giuliano Reis. 2018. "Animals 'Я' Us: Egomorphism in/for Science and Environmental Education." *Society and Animals*, Advance Articles, August 28. doi:10.1163/15685306–12341526.

Paul Seven Lewis. 2012. "Steiff Winnipeg Teddy and the Winnie the Pooh Connection." YouTube, February 15. www.youtube.com/watch?v=WF9-X9cQRFg. Accessed February 18, 2019.

Ross, Bob. 2016. "Honey Lover." *Naturalist News*. Texas Master Naturalist, Elm Fork Chapter. April, 8–9. www.txmn.org/elmfork/chapter-newsletter/2016-newsletters/. Accessed December 2, 2018.

Ryerson University. n.d. "Remembering the Real Winnie." https://therealwinnie.ryerson.ca /collection/. Accessed December 2, 2018.

Sears, Roebuck and Company. 1966. *Sears 1966 Christmas Book*. http://www.wishbookweb .com/FB/1966_Sears_Christmas_Book/#173/z. Accessed April 26, 2020.

Serpell, James. 2003. "Anthropomorphism and Anthropomorphic Selection: Beyond the Cute Response." *Society and Animals* 11, no. 1: 83–100.

Sharp, Margaret. 1987. "Princess Patricias Bare Winnie the Pooh Facts." *Calgary Herald*, April 19, A1, A2.

Shushkewich, Val. 2005. *The Real Winnie: A One-of-a-Kind Bear*. Toronto: Natural Heritage.

Sibley, Brian. 1991. *Three Cheers for Pooh: A Celebration of the Best Bear in All the World*. London: Methuen.

Sidebotham, Helen. 1925. *Behind the Scenes at the Zoo*. London: Cassel and Company.

Steiff. n.d.(a). "Steiff Baby Grizzly Bear Winnipeg." https://www.curiosity-corner.com/prod detail.asp?prod=steiffbabygrizzleybearwinnipeg. Accessed February 18, 2019.

Steiff. n.d.(b). "Steiff Winnipeg Mohair Teddy Bear." https://www.curiosity-corner.com /proddetail.asp?prod=steiffwinnipegbear. Accessed February 18, 2019.

Thwaite, Ann. 1990. *A. A. Milne: The Man behind Winnie-the-Pooh*. New York: Random House.

Thwaite, Ann. 1992. *The Brilliant Career of Winnie-the-Pooh: The Story of A. A. Milne and His Writing for Children*. London: Methuen.

Varga, Donna. 2009a. "Babes in the Woods: Wilderness Aesthetics in Children's Stories and Toys, 1830–1915." *Society and Animals* 17, no. 3: 187–205. doi:10.1163/156853009 X445370.

Varga, Donna. 2009b. "Gifting the Bear and a Nostalgic Desire for Childhood Innocence." *Cultural Analysis* 8, 71–96. www.ocf.berkeley.edu/~culturalanalysis/volume8/vol8 _article4.html.

Varga, Donna. 2009c. "Teddy's Bear and the Sociocultural Transfiguration of Savage Beasts into Innocent Children, 1890–1920." *Journal of American Culture* 32, no. 2 (June): 98–112. doi:10.1111/j.1542–734X.2009.00701.x.

Varga, Donna, and Victoria Dempsey. 2016. "Happy Captives and Monstrous Hybrids: The Flamingo in Children's Stories." In *Flamingos: Behavior, Biology, and Relationship with Humans*, edited by Matthew J. Anderson, 309–26. Hauppauge, NY: Nova Science Publishers.

Vaughan, Vicki. 1989. "Pooh's Hometown Can Put Up His Statue." *Orlando Sentinel*, September 8. www.orlandosentinel.com/news/os-xpm-1989-09-08-8909086366-story .html. Accessed June 4, 2019.

Walker, Sally M. 2015. *Winnie: The True Story of the Bear Who Inspired Winnie-the-Pooh*. New York: Henry Holt.

Waxman, Sandra R., Patricia Herrmann, Jennie Woodring, and Douglas L. Medin. 2014. "Humans (Really) Are Animals: Picture-Book Reading Influences 5-Year-Old Urban Children's Construal of the Relation between Humans and Non-Human Animals." *Frontiers in Psychology* 5, no. 172 (March 17). doi:10.3389/fpsyg.2014.00172.

Weatherhead, Ted. 1989. "In Which Pooh Joins the Army and Lands in the Zoo." *The Beaver*, October–November, 35–36, 38.

White River, Ontario. n.d. www.whiteriver.ca/article/welcome-to-white-river-1.asp. Accessed November 15, 2018.

Yarhi, Eli. 2013. "Winnie-the-Pooh." *The Canadian Encyclopedia*. Historica Canada, April 22, updated November 14, 2016. www.thecanadianencyclopedia.ca/en/article/winnie-the-pooh. Accessed June 2, 2019.

Yarhi, Eli. 2015. "In Conversation with Lindsay Mattick." *The Canadian Encyclopedia*. Historica Canada, October 15. www.thecanadianencyclopedia.ca/en/article/in-conversation-with-lindsay-mattick. Accessed December 2, 2018.

Yorkshire Evening Post. 1934. "'Winnie the Pooh' Dead." May 14, 6.

Zavatsky, Lisa. 2019. Comment, Meanwhile in Canada, "102 years ago, a Canadian soldier . . ." Facebook, January 18, 2019, 2:06 p.m. www.facebook.com/MeanwhileinCanada1/posts/2047739008606453. Accessed January 18, 2019.

Zoological Society of London (ZSL). 2014. *The Bear Who Inspired Winnie-the-Pooh*. YouTube, January 18. https://youtu.be/AdOymRprTqM. Accessed December 2, 2018.

CHAPTER 3

Always Playing
The Spectral Nostalgia of Cinematic *Pooh*

Zoe Jaques

There is something distinctly unsettling about these two quotations, one from the father and one from the son, which emerges especially when they are considered side by side:

> "Pooh, promise you won't forget about me, ever. Not even when I'm a hundred."
>
> Pooh thought for a little.
>
> "How old shall *I* be then?"
>
> "Ninety-nine."
>
> Pooh nodded.
>
> "I promise," he said.
>
> Still with his eyes on the world Christopher Robin put out a hand and felt for Pooh's paw.
>
> "Pooh," said Christopher Robin earnestly, "if I—if I'm not quite—" he stopped and tried again—"Pooh, *whatever* happens, you *will* understand, won't you?"
>
> "Understand what?"
>
> "Oh, nothing." He laughed and jumped to his feet. "Come on!"
>
> "Where?" said Pooh.

"Anywhere," said Christopher Robin.

So they went off together. But wherever they go, and whatever happens to them on the way, in that enchanted place on the top of the Forest a little boy and his bear will always be playing.

—A. A. Milne, *The House at Pooh Corner*

If you saw them today, your immediate reaction would be: "How old and battered and lifeless they look." But of course they are old *and* battered *and* lifeless. They are only toys and you are mistaking them for the real animals who lived in the forest . . . So, if I am asked "Aren't you sad that the animals are not in their glass case with you today?" I must answer "Not really," and hope that this doesn't seem too unkind. I like to have around me the things I like today, not the things I once liked many years ago. I don't want a house to be a museum . . . But my Pooh is different, you say: he is *the* Pooh. No, this only makes him different to you, not different to me.

—C. R. Milne, *The Enchanted Places*

The ending of the Winnie-the-Pooh stories—if we can call the lost-in-time, perpetual play with which *The House at Pooh Corner* closes "an ending"—is a voyeuristic, syrupy, mawkish affair, which many critics have noted is out of step and out of time with the main body of the narratives. It is a stiff, romanticized close, but an appealing one, at least for adult sensibilities—its sentimentalism a beguiling pool where the reflecting reader can wallow in the fantasy of childhood stood still, or what Henry Jenkins calls in a nod to A. A. Milne's friend J. M. Barrie, "the never-never-land" of nostalgic desire (1998, 4). Christopher Milne's own comment on the status of the toys, however, feels blunt and cold in its refusal to maintain possession of this childhood play through treasuring the objects that facilitated it (as his plea not to be viewed as "too unkind" alludes). Its lack of nostalgia—or at least the form of nostalgia that envelops and consumes the past through "a yearning for a different time—the time of our childhood, the slower rhythms of our dreams" (Boym 2001, xv)—sits awkwardly against the authorial promise that a boy and his bear will always be playing. It is challenging reconciling the *particularity* of the real individuals—the boy, Billy Moon, who lived, grew up, put away his childish things, and became Christopher Milne—and the *universality* of the idea of the boy and the bear, forever at play, which was meant by design to enchant. The word "enchant," of course, is suggestive of magic and delight, but also means "[t]o influence irresistibly or powerfully, as if by a charm; to hold spellbound; in bad sense, to delude, befool" (OED 2019). Held under such an enchantment of delight and delusion, pondering too long the fate of "*the* Pooh"—stuck in time as a museum exhibit while thousands of nonparticular visitors trudge by year-on-year—is a situation that might well lead contemporary readers to fear that this Bear of Very Little Brain would ultimately not come to understand his lengthy afterlife at all.

The problem is not merely authorial trickery but is ontological in nature: it is hard to separate being and nonbeing in the case of Pooh and his friends. On the one hand, toys are "transitional objects" (Winnicott 1971, 2) that are meant to be outgrown. Marjorie Taylor makes the case in her psychological study of imaginary companions that the passing of such fantastic play is rarely mourned by children as they grow up; such beings "tend to be abandoned when they have outlived their usefulness" in a manner that "underlines the utilitarian nature of these friends" (1999, 120). Children's literature, however, is usually authored by the reflecting adult, not the experiencing child—as such, it struggles to give up on its companions quite so easily. Lois Kuznets makes the case that the toy—when animated through narrative into a living being—becomes "an independent subject or self rather than an object" (1994, 2). Through that process, the toy can become "real" in a way that troubles the easy rejection of a disposable plaything. This point is made explicit in Margery Williams's *The Velveteen Rabbit* (1922): "You become. It takes a long time. . . . Generally, by the time you are Real, most of your hair has been loved off, and your eyes drop out and you get loose in the joints and very shabby" (10–11). The Skin Horse's description here resonates strongly with Christopher Milne's recollections of his "old and battered toys," although they differ on the matter of being "real" versus "lifeless." While Roland Barthes claims that "toys *always mean something*" ([1957] 1993, 53), Christopher Milne makes clear in *The Enchanted Places* that what they mean and to whom vary enormously. The sense that Winnie-the-Pooh is a "being"—that he possesses an ontology—can haunt the reader, just as we know that his fame came to haunt the boy upon which the stories were based. There is an uncanny ethereality to a being made alive yet forever left to "live" within a glass case; Christopher Milne's "writing back" against such an interpretation can itself be read as an attempt to see this toy-ghost finally laid to rest. The enchantment at work here is therefore as spectral as it is magical.

I will start with the famous dualism of father and son, adult and child, which also happens to tap into one of the central conceits of children's literature studies. The unequal power dynamic between children and adults in the literature of childhood—what Maria Nikolajeva termed "aetonormativity" in 2010 but which circulated by other names even before then—has long been the bedrock of critical discussion within the discipline, at least until more recent work by scholars such as Marah Gubar, Victoria Ford Smith, Justyna Deszcz-Tryhubczak, and Alison Waller began to question the purely coercive power of the adult and emphasize instead the actual agency of children. *Pooh* provides a curious and contradictory commentary on this issue, haunted as it is by its origin story. For Dennis Butts and Peter Hunt, the "driving force" behind *Pooh* is "the tension between the adult and the child" (2013, 83), an assertion that perhaps seems odd at first glance, given that the stories themselves are largely devoid of conflict and that adult characters appear almost entirely absent throughout. The child also makes only intermittent entrances into the Hundred Acre Wood, bringing with him the authority of a governing adult to his childlike toys in a manner that is never hostile and is "more like a kindly uncle than a child" (Boyce 2017). Age-based identities in the stories are thus unstable and interlinked—a point made more persuasive when the books themselves are considered as "intergenerational collaborations" (Smith 2017, 36) that A. A. Milne produced *with*, rather than simply created *about*, his young son—but they rarely seem particularly fractious. Yet the biographical narrative surrounding the *Pooh* stories cannot help but cast such collaboration in shadow. The story of the creation and commercialization of *Pooh* becomes one of an author-father forever eclipsed by what he later described as "[t]hose four trifles for the young" (Thwaite 1980, 480) and of a child-muse equally, but rather differently, enveloped by the play he was perpetually expected to enact—a play that loses its *particularity* to the *universality* of its nostalgic appeal. The static image of the *Pooh* toys in their museum case, cooed over by bemused onlookers, thus provides something of a simulacrum for Christopher Milne's own childhood, forever trapped under the glass, never allowed to fade. Placed under this critical spotlight, the sense that the *Pooh* stories are indeed haunted by the disruptive specter of adult-child friction, Milne's "love-hate relationship with [his] fictional namesake" (C. Milne 1974, 97), seems entirely appropriate.

The purpose of this chapter, then, is to consider these tensions—nearly one hundred years on—through the lens of two recent cinematic narratives that creatively respond to the relationship of A. A. Milne and his son. Winnie-the-Pooh has of course been no stranger to the big screen since Disney acquired the rights in 1961, but two recent filmic treatments of the narratives—*Goodbye Christopher Robin* (2017) from Fox Searchlight Pictures (itself a subsidiary film studio of the Disney Company) and Walt Disney Pictures' own *Christopher Robin* (2018)—have departed from a focus on the original stories. Instead, both films attend to some of the issues I have highlighted thus far, namely the specific place of the adult in the landscape of Winnie-the-Pooh; the curious, spectral haunting of these stories by their own biographies; and the nostalgic, voyeuristic, both comforting and uncomfortable state of perpetual play in which they appear suspended. *Goodbye Christopher Robin* provides a playful dramatization of *Pooh*'s construction, inflected and itself somewhat haunted by the recollections of father and son in their respective autobiographical writings, explicating the events that will lead to the separation of boy and bear. *Christopher Robin*, conversely, conjures a vision of an alternative ending, refashioning the inevitability of Pooh bear's necessary abandonment and giving physical form to the story's phantom of perpetual play. Both films enact a form of rereading, or returning, to this text from a new position—a reorientation of the stories and their foundations. They provide imaginative responses to both the origin story of *Pooh* and his autobiographical afterlives, while being true to neither; in doing so, they hint at Alison Waller's claim, in her recent research titled *Rereading Childhood Books*, that "[r]emembering and rereading are imaginative process for reclaiming the private relationships that child selves once had" with our texts (2019, 2). It is perhaps telling that Waller found A. A. Milne's *Pooh* stories and poetry to be some of the most frequently mentioned by interviewees as "successful shared childhood books" with the "potential for shared pleasures across different aged readers," which has "prompted their regular use as family texts across generations" (137). What emerges in these filmic rereadings and reappropriations, however, is attention to both the readerly, universal pleasures (the escapism) and the biographical, particular traumas (the deceptions) of these "enchanted" narratives.

In her edited collection *Reinventing Childhood Nostalgia*, Elizabeth Wesseling pointedly highlights that "hardly anybody ever questions the unholy trinity of nostalgia, deception and escapism," locating Svetlana Boym's work on differentiating between "restorative" and "reflective" nostalgia as "a rare exception to this rule" (Wesseling 2018, 2). I would venture that while each film shows elements of both Boym's more conservative "reflective nostalgia" and the more critical modes of its "restorative" counterpoint, what these films proffer for the most part is a third mode of remembrance that might usefully be thought of as spectral nostalgia. Spectral nostalgia can be defined as a wistful looking back to the past, certainly, but via a backward glance that is specifically attentive to its hauntings and echoes, the way specters not only emerge from the past but can shape and inflect the present and future. Reading A. A. Milne's narratives as affected by nostalgia is almost axiomatic—Christopher Milne himself reflected that nostalgia "was the only emotion that [his father] seemed to delight in both feeling and showing" (C. Milne 1974, 146). Yet in reading that nostalgia through the lens of spectrality and via the fantastical, quasi-biographical filmic reimaginings of recent years, we find a working through of the uncanny sense of mourning, discomfort, loss, and absence that haunts the seemingly idealized imagery of *Pooh*'s everlasting play. Lisa Kröger and Melanie Anderson argue that "[f]ilm, as a medium, lends itself well to spectrality" (2013, xiv), and the combination of the haunting foundational narratives of *Pooh*, along with its affecting afterlives and the possibilities inherent in the filmic form, make for a compelling spectral route by which to return to these narratives at the one hundredth anniversary of Christopher Milne's birth. The *Pooh* stories and their history combine the inherent contradictions of nostalgia—its combination of "bitterness and sweetness, the lost and the found, the far and the near, the new and the familiar, absence and presence" (Harper 1966, 128)—with the "liminal position between visibility and invisibility, life and death, materiality and immateriality" that marks the specter (Pilar Blanco and Peeren 2013, 2). The ghost, as Jacques Derrida has argued, is "neither living nor dead, present nor absent" (Derrida [1993] 2006, 63)—much like the simultaneously real and lifeless Pooh, forever stuck behind glass, or the memory of a universal boy perpetually playing above the Hundred Acre Wood long after the real boy's death. Considered in this light, the ontology of *Pooh* becomes more of a "*hauntology*" (Derrida [1993] 2006, 10), one that emerges potently in these recent revisionings.

When Butts and Hunt reflect upon the presence of adulthood in *Winnie-the-Pooh*, they conclude that there are five adults to be found lurking in the forest: "[I]n ascending order of disruptiveness they are Kanga, Eeyore, Owl, Rabbit, and A. A. Milne" (2013, 83). If the *Pooh* books are marked by the "intrusive adult voice of the adult narrator" (Hunt 1992, 114), then *Goodbye Christopher Robin* gives full rein to such interloping; the titular character may be the boy-inspiration, but the focus remains predominately on the author-father—a redress, perhaps, to the near eclipsing of the author by the child, which Milne himself satirically and prophetically described as early as 1929: "[T]he hero of *When We Were Very Young* was not, as I had modestly expected, the author, but a curiously-named child" (Milne [1929] 1931, 204). While the film therefore echoes what some critics find to be the focalizing narrative voice of Milne in the original stories, it also differs remarkably on other matters; in particular, as a form of biographical homage, it expands the stories' timeline to consider what came before and what came after Winnie-the-Pooh's rise to fame. Critics have variously argued that the *Pooh* stories are "only a set of incidents which could be put in almost any order" (Carpenter 1985, 202) and Milne's verse "a nostalgic retreat into a fantasy of an extra or atemporal childhood space" (Wake 2009, 28). If *Pooh* here functions like a phantom—"[a]s an entity out of place in time, as something from the past that emerges into the present [. . . and] calls into question the linearity of history" (Weinstock 2004, 62) through the creation of a nostalgic longing for perpetual childhood—then *Goodbye Christopher Robin* provides an exorcism that puts both the bear and the childhood firmly back into their temporal sphere.

That is not to say that *Goodbye* abides by linear rules in its exposition of the narrative nor indeed that it attempts to be a truthful account of history; the film, in fact, begins at its eventual close, recalling *The House at Pooh Corner*'s opening "Contradiction" of having an introduction serve "to say Good-bye" (Milne 1928, ix). The initial scenes are characterized by this curious doubleness, optimizing what Boym locates as the "cinematic image" of nostalgia: "a double exposure, or superimposition of two images—of home and abroad, of past and present, of dream and everyday life" (2001, xiii–xiv). The camera flits between the narrative's present and its past; recollections of Christopher Milne shift in an eye-blink from his childhood to adolescence in a manner that serves to highlight and amplify his absence. The film locates and time-stamps its opening as "Ashdown Forest, Sussex 1941," depicting the arrival of a telegram reporting the fate of Christopher in World War II (here dramatized as a notice that "2nd Lt C. R. Milne is missing presumed dead"; in reality, the telegram would not be delivered until some years later in October 1944, reporting that he had suffered "a penetrating shell wound in the right upper occipital region and was seriously ill" [Cohen 2017, 172]). As light shines through the bucolic canopy of trees, we see the postwoman slowly wind her way through the pathways and over the bridges of *Pooh*'s creation to bear her traumatic news, thrusting the viewer into a space haunted by images of the young boy and his playthings in a mode that is liminally neither entirely true nor completely false, drawing attention to the "storiedness" of its history. The fact that the film alters and embellishes is somewhat in keeping with that history; as it turned out, Christopher Milne was not seriously injured by the shell (he needed treatment only under local anesthetic), just as the film finally concludes by seeing Christopher Milne, not dead, returning home—depicted emerging hazily through the darkness in a disembodied and decidedly spectral fashion, flickering out of death and into being, bringing light to the shadow that war casts over the story.

The opening scene of the film concludes by showing Milne, upon receipt of the telegram, striding through the broken pastoral idyll of the forest to hurl away a cricket ball (a token that throughout the film will serve as a recurrent simulacrum for childhood play). The ball here immediately "breaks the frame" and "burns the surface" (Boym 2001, xiv) as it blasts backward through time, transforming into an explosion that shifts the story and transports Milne in period and geography to "the Western Front, France 1916." Within the first two minutes, then, we see both world wars intervene in the bucolic bubble of the Hundred Acre Wood, as haunting wartime atrocity and spectral play crash together. Perhaps the most striking element of *Goodbye*'s reorientation is in fact this careful situation of the creation, reproduction, and lived experience of Winnie-the-Pooh firmly in the context of these dual world wars. It is well established that the rustic arcadia of the *Pooh* stories offered an "escape from a modern industrial world . . . reeling from the lingering consequences of the First World War" (Hemmings 2007, 72–73) and reflect "a greater cultural nostalgia for a prewar era" (Nance-Carroll 2015, 69). Yet at the time of their authoring, the 1914–1918 conflict was not known as "the First" World War; it was thought to be, in H. G. Wells's words, "the War that will end War" (a refrain that *Goodbye* has A. A. Milne parrot on more than one occasion). By immediately highlighting its interwar context, the film draws attention from its opening to the period of Winnie-the-Pooh's creation not merely as an anti-dote to what came before but as indicative of "the way in which the future is always already populated with certain possibilities derived from the past; the way in which it is constrained, circumscribed, inscribed by the past; the way in which it is haunted before we make and enter it" (Brown 2000, 168). The film thus establishes the construction of *Pooh* as haunted not only by its history but by its future; as Boym writes, "[n]ostalgia is not always about the past; it can be retrospective but also prospective" (2001, xvi). The specters of A. A. Milne's wartime experiences are also here characterized as leaving a ghostly impression upon the shaping of the *Pooh* books. Flashbacks to the Somme penetrate Milne's play with his son and thus the creation of the stories that follow—the sound of bees recalls the relentless buzzing of flies in the trenches, the bursting of balloons is haunted by the memory of close-range explosions. While clearly a fantastical overlapping, recasting infamous episodes of the *Pooh* stories in this context has a particularly spectral effect; it "signals the unbidden imposition of parts of the past on the present" (Brown 2000, 36), exposing "those singular, yet repetitive instances when home becomes unfamiliar, when your bearings on the world lose direction, when the over-and-done-with comes alive" (Gordon [1997] 2008, xvi). But such haunting also, and importantly, serves a purpose—it is "distinctive for producing a something-to-be-done" (xvi). In life, it would be the pacifist tract *Peace with Honour: An Enquiry into the War Convention* (1934) that Milne would view as his greatest literary contribution in this regard. In *Goodbye*, the *Pooh* books themselves operate as that "something"—not just as a form of nostalgic escapism, a retreating back in time, but as an intervention in their author's own haunting that "forc[es] a confrontation, forking the future and the past" (Gordon [1997] 2008, xvii). The film will later conclude with a grown-up Christopher Robin, returned from war, recalling a moment when "in the desert, we were under fire, and one of the men started singing one of the hums of Pooh." Nostalgic haunted echoes operate in dual directions.

In their introduction to *The Spectralities Reader*, María del Pilar Blanco and Esther Peeren suggest that "the ghost is a figure of surprise that does not necessarily reappear in exactly the same manner or guise" (2013, 13). *Goodbye's* navigation of the spectral effects of wartime atrocity functions in this mode, resurfacing intermittently and in decidedly different forms. Yet if ghosts, as Wendy Brown argues, "come and go as they please," then they "can also be conjured and exorcised—solicited, beckoned, invoked, dismissed" (2000, 35). The overall narrative of the film operates within just this domain of both conjuring and exorcizing, drawing upon various talismanic specters from the *Pooh* stories and scraps from their biographical history to frame its dramatizing of the tension between adult and child that emerged as a consequence of the commodification and perpetuation of play that was meant, so the story suggests, to be only cathartic and temporary. One method deployed here is to create uncanny moments in which Christopher Milne and his bear appear conjoined or doubled, recalling the role of the doppelgänger that "takes the form of a lookalike and has paranormal connotations as a harbinger of bad luck or doom" (Shaw 2018, 95). Paula T. Connolly has argued that A. A. Milne "tried to differentiate between the two Christopher Robins" (1999, 189), referring to the author's own claim that "I have not exploited the legal Christopher Robin. All I have got from Christopher Robin is a name which he never uses, an introduction to his friends . . . and a gleam which I have tried to follow" (Milne [1929] 1931, 205). The filmic version of the history, however, blending and dramatizing from the autobiographical recollections of the son as well as the father, is less inclined to respect such implied separation. From Christopher's mother's articulation that the toy bear will "stay little forever, like my boy" through to the intrusion of the capturing hand of E. H. Shepard into the otherwise unfixed woodland play ("Just get everything you can," says A. A. Milne to the illustrator; "We'll pick and choose later"), the film revels in highlighting moments of uncanny doubling that predict the eventual haunting of the child by his own ghost, which will indeed, if not doom, then severely hamper adult-child relations. As viewers witness the fixing in time of the living boy by the artist's pencil—the film overlaying the frenetic movements of the child at play with the static lines that will forever memorialize him—the story appears haunted by Milne's own admission that "the distinction, if clear to me, is not so clear to others" and "the dividing line between the imaginary and the legal Christopher Robin becomes fainter with each book" (Milne [1929] 1931, 205).

The dissolution of easy divisions between the child as subject and object is central to *Goodbye Christopher Robin*'s troubled reflections on *Pooh*'s history, a history it exorcises through attention to canonical moments of its representation. Julian Wolfreys makes the case that the specter resists nomenclature: "Names conventionally applied, fix the limits of an identity. . . . [T]his 'strange name'—*spectre*—names nothing as such" (2002, xi). *Goodbye* takes pains to emphasize that there is nothing conventional about naming or being named in *Pooh*, the inadequate distinctions between names sufficiently potent so as to lead Christopher Milne in *The Enchanted Places* to provide a glossary of them, to accompany his observation that "I have suffered—if not all my life, then at least for the first thirty years of it—from an embarrassment of names" (1974, 17). Both the boy and his bear have an unsettled relationship with their representational names, in keeping with their unfixed and unstable identities.

"I don't like that name," declares the young child in *Goodbye* when gifted a teddy called Edward, but the rejection refers as much to his own identity as to his toy's. When asking his father what his own name will be in book form, he is told "not Billy Moon because that is what we call you" but "Christopher Robin, then, because it's your real name but it's not who you really are." His bear's identity is similarly unsettled. *Goodbye* has A. A. Milne observe his unearthly nature: "Winnie-the-Pooh is a creature of bedtime. He's either just got up or just going off. He's reverie in bear form." The toy is thus not easily fixed in time or title: on occasions he is Edward, at others he is Winnie, and eventually Winnie-the-Pooh, yoking together a London Zoo bear and a Sussex swan. The confusion, collision, and metamorphosis at work is as deliberately unclear in the film as it is in the stories: "Here is Edward Bear, coming downstairs now, bump, bump, bump . . . here he is at the bottom, and ready to be introduced to you. Winnie-the-Pooh" (Milne 1926, 1). The film's rendering of Shepard and Milne in dialogue has the creative pair pointedly summarize: "Winnie-the-Pooh. That's rather . . . Inexplicable." There is a significant ontological gap here that makes both boy and bear particularly ethereal.

If "the name is always related to death, to the structural possibility that the one who gives, receives, or bears the name will be absent from it" (Brault and Naas 2003, 13), then the conscription to, resistance of, and confusion over the names Edward Bear/Winnie-the-Pooh and Christopher Robin/Billy Moon is uncannily destabilizing, rendering both subjects spectral in a manner that hauntingly predicts their long afterlives. The same can be said of *Goodbye*'s repeated inclusion of an imitation of the famous sepia-toned photograph by Howard Coster in which A. A. Milne holds his son on his lap—the adult's eyes turned to the viewer, the boy's not returning the gaze, the toy bear clutched to the child's side, one paw extended as if seeking to break the frame. Roland Barthes drew attention to the voyeuristic, spectral nature of photography, in which "the person or thing photographed is the target, the referent, a kind of little simulacrum" not dissimilar to the toys in their museum case, capturing and making a "spectacle" of "that rather terrible thing that is in every photograph: the return of the dead" (1980, 9). Such a return is made all the more uncanny in the case of the film's re-creation of a re-creation, the already-lost-to-history-at-the-moment-of-creation scene reformed through the bodies of actors, a filmic restoration of a photographic impression that fixes bodies in place as doubles of doubles. As Ann Thwaite observes, "Christopher Milne would say of the photograph that his father never held him like that" (2017, 183).

Both photography and naming here are locations of absence; the film attends to the modes by which the *Pooh* narratives are always already haunted in their attempt to fix in place that which can never stay and never truly was, what Boym calls "a longing for a home that no longer exists or has never existed" (2001, xiii). As the title of the film suggests, the whole of *Goodbye Christopher Robin* can be read as a story of departure; the narrative is full of spectral shadows, of absent forces, of something missing or gone. The role of both the central female figures in the narrative—the mother, Daphne, and the nanny, Nou—are examples of such haunting absence. It is Daphne who provides both the physical toys and their voices, while Nou provides safe spaces in which the boy might play and grow, but both frequently slither into the background of the film (as indeed they did in the books), creating in their absence a void into which father and son are forced to build their own adventures in a decidedly nonperpetual manner. (As an older Christopher Milne puts it in the film, "When I was Billy Moon . . . we played in the woods . . . and then you wrote that book and it all stopped. As if it has all been a piece of research. You never came back.") Even the toys are remarkably noncentral to the story as told here—they elide the focus, largely because the narrative is not primarily invested in soliciting sentimental longing for simulacra in its audience but in opening up the gaps between the particularity and universality of *Pooh*'s appeal. Absences aren't merely wistful and are not meant to seduce or enchant; the film undoubtedly partakes of the nostalgic mode, but it does so in a manner actively attentive to its fractures, absences, and ghosts. The light from the sun that so frequently filters through the trees is for the most part cooler than it is warming, the atemporal idyll of *Pooh* placed in the context of its production, framed and haunted by what is to follow on both a collective and individual level (the Second World War for a nation and the devolving of a parent-child bond for the Milnes). The film is not interested in creating an alternative vision; it allows these tensions to be present, playing with the frayed edges of biography, snatching up a thread here and there, mending or exacerbating a rent in its tapestry.

Goodbye Christopher Robin thus generally resists the nostalgic lure to create "a phantom homeland" (Boym 2001, xvi), focusing instead on exposing and to some extent exorcising the phantoms that haunt *Pooh*'s textual history. Released a year later, Disney's own take in *Christopher Robin* appears to work entirely in the opposite direction; it returns to the titular character's childhood only to posit an alternative ending to his life post-Pooh, focusing almost completely on a fantasy adulthood that bears little semblance to biography. Yet while this tongue-in-cheek, playful fantasy seems on the surface to be mere whimsy, its phantasmagoria is nonetheless attentive to many of the same frictions and specters of the more overtly biographical treatment in *Goodbye*, providing an alternative working through of some of the discomforts and tensions that haunt the story in a manner that is both nostalgic and resistant to that mode. Its fantastic approach to the place of the adult in *Pooh*'s history can therefore be read as a study "of ghosts and haunting [. . . that does] more than obsessively recall a fixed past"; in an "active, dynamic engagement," it reveals "the insufficiency of the present moment, as well as the disconsolations and erasures of the past, and a tentative hopefulness for future resolutions" (Pilar Blanco and Peeren 2013, 16).

Christopher Robin is comfortable both playing with and drawing attention to time, beginning with a young Christopher Robin saying "fairwel" to his toys (more evidence of strong association of *Pooh* with absence and departures) but then moving through the remainder of his childhood and adolescence at some speed. Like *Goodbye*, the film fixes childhood moments in place by sketching over the action, literally, in the representation of a moving pencil, highlighting connections to the textual history but here also utilizing the aesthetic device of metaphorically depicting the passing of a life as the flipping through of pages of a book (rather akin to Milne's own sense that his life was pinned down by the printing of *Pooh*). The film thus skims through yellowing leaves to depart "Chapter I—In Which Christopher Robin leaves his childhood behind," cutting to the boy setting "out into a new world" of boarding school and settling on "Chapter III—In Which Christopher Robin hears very sad news." The collapsing of Christopher Robin's growth into so few moments is here set in the specific context of the death of his father: "You're the man of the house now, dear," the child is told in a device that rather ironically deploys death to overcome the haunting effect A. A. Milne had in life on his son. The narrative then grows the boy into his role as paternal adult; the next few "chapters" see Christopher Robin meet his future wife (here named Evelyn, not Lesley), depart for war, and return to meet his three-year-old daughter (here Madeline, not Clare). The adult Christopher is then shown retreating from contact with his family, repeatedly resisting attempts to engage him in any form of play and encouraging his child as she grows to "do something useful" by focusing on schoolwork over frivolity and adventure. As in *Goodbye*, the first few minutes of the narrative are a speedy assemblage of a warped history, creating an effect of uncomfortable atemporal generational looping in which past, present, and future appear to collide as the boy embodies the tropes of his spectral father, a cold distancing between parent and child fictionally revisiting the adult imitation Christopher just as it did the real child.

Particularly potent in this opening montage is the offsetting of the meta-morphosing movement of Christopher Robin with the stasis of his childhood toys. Episodes depicting the child's growth are intersected with cuts to Winnie-the-Pooh, sometimes accompanied by Piglet, still living in the Hundred Acre Wood and staring wistfully at the enchanted door, moving through the seasons of spring to winter in a mode that is hauntingly melancholic in its emphasis on the long-felt absence of his child friend. Danielle O'Connor has made the case that "[t]ime does not matter for Pooh" (2018, 31); in this version of the narrative, there is a strong sense that time matters a great deal to the bear, with the toys stuck in a perpetual woodland purgatory that is as distinctly lacking in play as the depiction of city life for adult Christopher Robin. Of course, Disney animation is adept at using neotenizing anthropomorphism for distorting effect; Jean Baudrillard famously argued that "whole Walt Disney philosophy eats out of your hand with these pretty little sentimental creatures in grey fur coats," behind whose "smiling eyes there lurks a cold, ferocious beast fearfully stalking us" ([1986] 1989, 48). Such criticism of Disneyfication is notoriously cynical although indicative of what David Whitley more neutrally labels Disney's "deliberate attempts to court and cultivate sentiment" (2008, 2). Disney's characterization of the lonely Pooh—wandering the foggy and abandoned woods, "all gloomy and sad," listening to the atemporal spectral echoes of Christopher Robin's childhood voice—cannot fail to be viewed as sentimental and nostalgic. But it also creates an atmosphere that is highly attuned to the same discomforts that haunt the image of the real-life toys in their museum case, so many years on from their last playtime. If Pooh has an ontology, then being left behind in time is particularly troubling, be that in museum or woods. Niall Nance-Carroll makes the case that "the fictional world (and Pooh himself) . . . will loyally wait for Christopher Robin even when he is one hundred" (2015, 77); Disney's animation of that fantasy gives viewers an unpleasant window into what such incessant waiting might look like. Where *Goodbye* avoids placing too much emotional investment on the bodies of the toys themselves, *Christopher Robin* relies upon it.

The actual bodily design of the toys in Disney's version further extends this uncanny spectrality. Physically, the toys are rendered disheveled—they appear "old and battered," to recall Christopher Milne's description of his playthings. The distinct incarnations of Milne and Shepard's Pooh compared with that of Walt Disney tend to be read as addressing "different cultures, different times, and even different views of childhood" (Connolly 1999, 188), but here we have a collapsing of those differences, a yoking together of the unblemished aesthetic of Disney's sanitized version with the real, tangible look of toys that bear the traces of actual, spectral play. They are *distinctly toys* in a manner that differs from Disney's traditional animations of the characters. Pooh is permitted minimal expression—his eyes unblinking, his body stiff and movements awkward—creating the impression that he is a vessel "filled with 'mana,' possessed by physic energy or even a 'soul'" (Michanczyk 1973, 161). What Nance-Carroll calls their "flatness of character" (2015, 68) feels troubling in such three-dimensional, living bodies. The alignment, then, of these hollow toys with an inherent "liveliness" takes on a peculiar quality; as a taxi driver in the film puts it, "there's something strange going on with them— something spooky." Such a comment provides a wry nod to the double uncanniness of these characters in both animated form and narrative function—the hyperrealism of the CGI, which makes the animations appear unnaturally "alive," blends with the story's stance that Pooh and his friends are not merely imagined into being via childhood play but *really are* living beings roaming the streets of London. Just as the story permits Pooh to break the enchanted frame of the Hundred Acre Wood by passing through Christopher Robin's normally one-way arboreal door, so too does it allow the toys to violate this nearly universal rule of toy-come-to-life narratives. Winnie-the-Pooh and his friends are often shown to animate before the eyes of human onlookers in *Christopher Robin*—that the reactions to such animation range from shock to screaming (with Christopher's Robin's own daughter initially decidedly unsettled by the toys' emergence from the hedgerows) offers a playful allusion to the fact that in any other genre such eerie enlivenment would be a locus of horror, with only the toys' Disneyfied cuteness preventing them from being decidedly too creepy.

Yet the most overwhelmingly spectral quality of the story is the echo of absent play, for which these strangely, spookily enlivened toys provide a perpetual synecdoche. Peppered with references to lost playtimes—from abandoned tennis courts to phantom games of gin rummy—the film strongly works to emphasize the value of diversion. Its overall narrative thrust is to reshape the adult Christopher Robin's obsessive attitude to work (itself imagined as a kind of woozle that recalls Milne's ethereal version of the monster rather than Disney's corporeal one), by filling the void imposed by his repeated refrain that "nothing can come of nothing" with the resolution that "doing nothing can lead to the very best something." It is a lesson, of course, that a child Christopher Robin teaches his bear: "'How do you Nothing?' asked Pooh, after he had wondered for a long time. 'Well, it's when people call out at you just as you're going off to do it "What are you going to do, Christopher Robin?" and you say "Oh, nothing," and then you go and do it'" (Milne 1928, 171). Here it is Pooh who returns the favor, and in doing so provides both an antidote to the tensions between adult and child that haunt the origin story and a respite to the perpetual waiting of the toys made manifest either in the hauntedness of the empty woods or the stasis of life in a museum. The film's resolution echoes the similarly nostalgic ending to Disney-Pixar's *Toy Story 3* (2010), with Christopher Robin's toys finding fresh playfulness in Madeline just as Andy's do in Bonnie, the recyclability of the relationship between toy and child papering over the unsettling fact that such beings can eternally outlive their human companions, even as they become tattered and frayed. At the same time, however, Pooh remains attentive to and questioning of the conditions of linear history, resisting both his past and futurity but aware of the spectral effects of each: "[T]oday," he explains, is "my favorite day. . . . Yesterday, when it was tomorrow, it was too much day for me." Pooh here explores "ways of inhabiting many places at once and imagining different time zones" (Boym 2001, xviii), but in doing so he remains troubled by the perpetual "too much" tomorrow that has haunted his yesteryears, and that might well be said to have been the locus of tension for Christopher Milne's actual childhood experience through his father's authorial assurance that a boy and his bear would always be playing. Through a spectral form of nostalgia, then, Pooh retrieves what Connolly sees as "thoroughly expunged" (1999, 200) in previous Disney animations of the silly old bear, namely his sense of insight into both himself and the world around him.

Both recent filmic interpretations of the making of *Pooh* and the life of Christopher Milne play differently with the nostalgic mode, taking the energies that haunt the story of the production of the books in different directions. Michael Kammen writes: "Nostalgia, with its wistful memories, is essentially history without guilt" ([1991] 1993, 688); the films examined here each partake in some of this contemplative exorcism, indulging in escapist fantasies of frictions fantastically overcome and wrongs magically righted. Yet, as this chapter has shown, neither film is entirely invested in a pure or linear over-writing of the narrative's history with such deceptive enchantments. These stories are each endowed with the momentums of the ghost, "that which inter-rupts the presentness of the present," indicating that "beneath the surface of received history, there lurks another narrative, an untold story that calls into question the veracity of the authorized version of events" (Weinstock 2004, 5). While both of these filmic dramatizations of the life of Christopher Robin are fantastic in their interpretative forms, they each find ways to highlight the tensions surrounding an illusion of perpetual play with which the books are forever associated and to creatively respond to the spectral forces that haunt the chronicle of their creation.

At the same time, however, neither film can resist the draw of the *Pooh* stories' ultimate site of nostalgic longing. Each of the films concludes at "that enchanted place on the top of the Forest" with which this chapter began and with which the *Pooh* books themselves end. For *Christopher Robin*, the loca-tion is very much one of return and revivification—it is here that Madeline and the toys will restart the fantasy of perpetual playtime made forever pos-sible while there is sufficient stuffing in the bear and a new child with whom to frolic. *Goodbye* is more pointed in its reflections, bringing together the desire to rewrite history with an awareness that that past will always haunt the present and future. The depiction of A. A. Milne with his adult son, in that enchanted place but without the troublesome toys for company, offers a surface resolution not possible in the real biographies of the individuals; the father apologizes for giving away his son's childhood, the son reflects that his childhood "was wonderful" in a denial of his rather sharper, real-world reflec-tions that his father "got where he was by climbing on my infant shoulders" (C. Milne 1974, 165). Yet even as this moment appears to rely on syrup to overcome salt, the film reverts to its opening unsettling and liminal flicker-ing between past and present, adult and child, embodied and ghostly. "Who would have guessed that bear would swallow us up," states A. A. Milne, as the adult Christopher metamorphoses backward into his child form via the same double exposure that begins the film. But it is not simply a case of the narrative slipping back to the comforts of a nostalgically conceived history here, as the adult and child get an opportunity to go back and magically rewrite their past, but a recognition of the way in which the past reverberates through history. "There is an echo, listen," says young Christopher Milne (itself an echo of an earlier point in the narrative), crying out into the reverberating hillside; "I'm Billy Moon, and I'll be back soon." Where the Disney film finds comfort in this prospect of timely return—Christopher Robin will be back, after all, in the form of his daughter's re-creation of his play with the toys—*Goodbye* is less secure in its convictions. The film's final two images bring together the actual photograph that was earlier imitated, in which the real A. A. Milne holds his son and bear, alongside a picture of the real toys, trapped in their static afterlife: "The toys are on display at the New York Public Library where they attract 750,000 visitors a year." In drawing attention in its final moments to these spectral absent forms that have troubled the story throughout, the film thus concludes where this chapter began—reminding us that while nostalgia might well mean a longing to return home, in the case of Pooh and his friends, that home is a haunted as well as an enchanted place.

Bibliography

Barthes, Roland. 1980. *Camera Lucida: Reflections on Photography*. Translated by Richard Howard. New York: Hill and Wang.

Barthes, Roland. (1957) 1993. *Mythologies*. Translated by Annette Lavers. London: Vintage.

Baudrillard, Jean. (1986) 1989. *America*. London: Verso.

Boyce, Frank Cottrell. 2017. "A. A. Milne, Christopher Robin and the Curse of Winnie-the-Pooh." *Guardian*, September 27. https://www.theguardian.com/books/2017/sep/23/how-aa-milne-and-christopher-robin-fell-under-the-curse-of-pooh-bear. Accessed June 4, 2019.

Boym, Svetlana. 2001. *The Future of Nostalgia*. New York: Basic Books.

Brault, Pascale-Anne, and Michael Naas. 2003. "To Reckon with the Dead: Jacques Derrida's Politics of Mourning." In *The Work of Mourning*, by Jacques Derrida, edited by Pascale-Anne Brault and Michael Naas, 1–30. Chicago: University of Chicago Press.

Brown, Wendy. 2000. "Specters and Angels at the End of History." In *Vocations of Political Theory*, edited by Jason A. Frank and John Tambornino, 25–58. Minneapolis: University of Minnesota Press.

Butts, Dennis, and Peter Hunt. 2013. *How Did Long John Silver Lose His Legs? And Twenty-Six Other Mysteries of Children's Literature*. Cambridge: Lutterworth Press.

Carpenter, Humphrey. 1985. *Secret Gardens: A Study of the Golden Age of Children's Literature*. Ithaca, NY: Cornell University Press.

Cohen, Nadia. 2017. *The Extraordinary Life of A. A. Milne*. Barnsley, Yorks., England: Pen and Sword History.

Connolly, Paula T. 1999. "The Marketing of Romantic Childhood: Milne, Disney, and a Very Popular Stuffed Bear." In *Literature and the Child: Romantic Continuations, Postmodern Contestations*, edited by James Holt McGavran, 188–207. Iowa City: University of Iowa Press.

Curtis, Simon, dir. 2017. *Goodbye Christopher Robin*. Fox Searchlight Pictures.

Derrida, Jacques. (1993) 2006. *Specters of Marx*. Translated by Peggy Kamuf. London: Routledge.

Forster, Marc, dir. 2018. *Christopher Robin*. Walt Disney Pictures.

Gordon, Avery F. (1997) 2008. *Ghostly Matters: Haunting and the Sociological Imagination*. Minneapolis: University of Minnesota Press.

Harper, Ralph. 1966. *Nostalgia: An Existential Exploration of Longing and Fulfilment in the Modern Age*. Cleveland: Press of Western Reserve University.

Hemmings, Robert. 2007. "A Taste of Nostalgia: Children's Books from the Golden Ages— Carroll, Grahame, and Milne." *Children's Literature* 35, no. 1 (January): 54–79.

Hunt, Peter. 1992. "*Winnie-the-Pooh* and Domestic Fantasy." In *Stories and Society: Children's Literature in Its Social Context*, edited by Dennis Butts, 112–24. London: Palgrave Macmillan.

Jenkins, Henry. 1998. "Introduction: Childhood Innocence and Other Modern Myths." In *The Children's Culture Reader*, edited by Henry Jenkins, 1–37. New York: New York University Press.

Kammen, Michael. (1991) 1993. *Mystic Chords of Memory: The Transformation of Tradition in American Culture*. London: Vintage.

Kröger, Lisa, and Melanie R. Anderson, eds. 2013. *The Ghostly and the Ghosted in Literature and Film: Spectral Identities*. Newark: University of Delaware Press.

Kuznets, Lois. 1994. *When Toys Come Alive: Narratives of Animation, Metamorphosis, and Development*. New Haven, CT: Yale University Press.

Michanczyk, Michael. 1973. "The Puppet Immortals of Children's Literature." *Children's Literature* 2: 159–65.

Milne, A. A. 1926. *Winnie-the-Pooh*. London: Methuen.

Milne, A. A. 1928. *The House at Pooh Corner*. London: Methuen.

Milne, A. A. (1929) 1931. *By Way of Introduction*. London: Methuen.

Milne, A. A. 1934. *Peace with Honour: An Enquiry into the War Convention*. London: Methuen.

Milne, Christopher Robin. 1974. *The Enchanted Places*. London: Eyre Methuen.

Nance-Carroll, Niall. 2015. "Not Only, But Also: Entwined Modes and the Fantastic in A. A. Milne's Pooh Stories." *Lion and the Unicorn* 39, no. 1 (January): 63–81.

Nikolajeva, Maria. 2010. *Power, Voice and Subjectivity in Literature for Young Readers*. New York: Routledge.

O'Connor, Danielle A. 2018. "Frozen Rivers, Moving Homes, and Crossing Bridges: Liminal Space and Time in Neil Gaiman's *Odd and the Frost Giants* and A. A. Milne's *The House at Pooh Corner*." *Children's Literature Association Quarterly* 43, no. 1 (Spring): 28–46.

Oxford English Dictionary (OED). 2019. S.v. "enchant, v., n. 2." OED Online, May. www.oed.com/viewdictionaryentry/Entry/61656. Accessed May 18, 2019.

Pilar Blanco, María del, and Esther Peeren, eds. 2013. *The Spectralities Reader: Ghosts and Haunting in Contemporary Cultural Theory*. London: Bloomsbury.

Shaw, Katy. 2018. *Hauntology: The Presence of the Past in Twenty-First Century English Literature*. London: Palgrave Macmillan.

Smith, Victoria Ford. 2017. *Between Generations: Collaborative Authorship in the Golden Age of Children's Literature*. Jackson: University Press of Mississippi.

Taylor, Marjorie. 1999. *Imaginary Creatures and the Children Who Create Them*. Oxford: Oxford University Press.

Thwaite, Ann. 1980. *A. A. Milne: His Life*. London: Faber and Faber.

Thwaite, Ann. 2017. *Goodbye Christopher Robin: A. A. Milne and the Making of Winnie-the-Pooh*. London: Pan Books.

Wake, Paul. 2009. "Waiting in the Hundred Acre Wood: Childhood, Narrative and Time in A. A. Milne's Works for Children." *Lion and the Unicorn* 33, no. 1 (January): 26–43.

Waller, Alison. 2019. *Rereading Childhood Books: A Poetics*. London: Bloomsbury.

Weinstock, Jeffrey Andrew, ed. 2004. *Spectral America: Phantoms and the National Imagination*. Madison: University of Wisconsin Press.

Wesseling, Elizabeth, ed. 2018. *Reinventing Childhood Nostalgia: Books, Toys, and Contemporary Media Culture*. London: Routledge.

Whitley, David. 2008. *The Idea of Nature in Disney Animation*. Farnham, Surrey, England: Ashgate.

Williams, Margery. (1922) 1989. *The Velveteen Rabbit; or, How Toys Become Real*. N.p.: Little Mammoth.

Winnicott, Donald Woods. 1971. *Playing and Reality*. London: Routledge.

Wolfreys, Julian. 2002. *Victorian Hauntings: Spectrality, Gothic, the Uncanny and Literature*. Basingstoke, Hants., England: Palgrave.

CHAPTER 4

Latecomers to the Hundred Acre Wood

The Tension between Nostalgia and Updating in *Return to the Hundred Acre Wood* and *The Best Bear in All the World*

Niall Nance-Carroll

For eighty-one years, A. A. Milne's *Winnie-the-Pooh* and *The House at Pooh Corner* were the only canonical Pooh stories. While other versions of Pooh swirled about—from pop psychology and business management to Disney movies to fan art that reimagined them as Star Wars characters—there were no official sequels. This changed with the publication of *Return to the Hundred Acre Wood* in 2009, followed by *The Best Bear in All the World* in 2016. Neither received the widespread acclaim of the original books, but both offered readers the opportunity to nostalgically walk the Hundred Acre Wood again among childhood friends.

Svetlana Boym, drawing on Michael Kammen's description of nostalgia as "history without guilt," describes one understanding of nostalgia as "an abdication of personal responsibility, a guilt-free homecoming, an ethical and aesthetic failure" (2001, xiv). The official returns to the Hundred Acre Wood certainly risk this. Milne's ethical vision is often an agreeable one, and if one were picking a childhood text as the site of nostalgic return, there is much to recommend the Pooh books: they offer texts that are kind, gentle, and largely free of the negative cultural baggage that sometimes surrounds *Peter Pan* or *Alice in Wonderland*. A nostalgic return to childhood is always fraught with ethical concerns, however, for to wish to return to that age is also to free oneself of the responsibilities of the present and of adulthood.

The nostalgic draw of the Pooh stories is not limited to returning to the same two texts that Milne wrote; there is an ever-expanding universe of Pooh materials. While most people currently become familiar with the characters through their continuing appearance in Disney properties (not only the animated films but also the video games, theme parks, and merchandise), Disney makes little effort to canonically continue the world of the older Pooh stories; indeed, the Disney Pooh stories swiftly abandoned the practice of animating the original Milne texts and took Pooh on other adventures. *Return to the Hundred Acre Wood* and *The Best Bear in All the World*, however, attempt to return quite precisely to Milne's Hundred Acre Wood, not the Disney version inspired by it and not a reboot that modernizes the location or the characters. In this chapter, I will discuss the ways in which these texts engage with the original stories, through both nostalgia and revisionism.

A Wider World of Winnie-the-Pooh

The fan-created metatext of Pooh is complex, encompassing not only the Milne texts and these new sequels but also the Disney versions, the real A. A. and Christopher Milne, and the many other Pooh texts that have emerged. Kenneth Kidd describes "Poohology, or Pooh-centric discourse," which is rooted in pop cultural Pooh works, but he begins with the Latin translation of Pooh and then moves to Frederick Crews's satires: "Poohology mobilizes *Pooh* toward various ends, which might be generally called pedagogical" (Kidd 2011, 36). In the vein of Poohology, *Return to the Hundred Acre Wood* functions as a progressive revision of the Pooh metatext, whereas *The Best Bear in All the World* is a more purely nostalgic text.

To begin with, these are authorized sequels produced for the eightieth and ninetieth anniversaries of the publications of the initial book, *Winnie-the-Pooh*. *Return to the Hundred Acre Wood* was actually substantially late on that front, as it was released in 2009. *The Best Bear in All the World* was more precisely an anniversary text, being released in 2016. Both of these recent sequels have illustrator Mark Burgess approximating the illustrations of E. H. Shepard, although they have different authors who try (with questionable success) to approximate both Milne's world and his style.

Milne's Hundred Acre Wood is an attractive site for pastoral nostalgia. As Boym explains: "The rapid pace of industrialization and modernization increased the intensity of people's longing for the slower rhythms of the past, for continuity, social cohesion and tradition" (2001, 16). While Boym describes the rise of nostalgia toward the end of the nineteenth century in these terms, the twentieth and twenty-first centuries have not seen a rejection of nostalgia but an ever-evolving embrace of it. The two modern Pooh books represent two differing traditions of nostalgia, even though both are additions to the official and canonical world of Pooh.

Boym contrasts *restorative* and *reflective* varieties of nostalgia; the former "proposes to rebuild the lost home and patch up memory gaps" whereas the latter "dwells . . . in longing and loss" (41). Restorative nostalgia aims for "total reconstructions of monuments of the past, while reflective nostalgia lingers on ruins, the patina of time and history" (41). While neither *Return to the Hundred Acre Wood* nor *The Best Bear in All the World* feature ruins, the latter seeks a timelessness that is clearly restorative—it seeks to be *Winnie-the-Pooh* exactly as it was—whereas *The Return to the Hundred Acre Wood* presents more of a patina: Christopher Robin is still aging, and the world of the Hundred Acre Wood changes.

The analysis of nostalgia in Milne's writing has been explored by Robert Hemmings, who saw Milne's Hundred Acre Wood as an "impossibly sanitized and Edenic time and Space" (2007, 55), and Roger Sale, who saw nostalgia as a key component of the "man reading" of the text, contrasting with the "child reading" (1972, 169). In "Not Only, But Also: Entwined Modes and the Fantastic in A. A. Milne's Pooh Stories" (2015), I engaged with their arguments and asserted that the text "entwined" the nostalgic reading with credulous and comic readings (borrowing the notion of entwined modes from Mike Cadden [2005]). The lens of entwined modes may enrich the analysis of these newer Pooh stories, but they are a more expressly nostalgic product, and I think the analysis must begin there. Hemmings asserts that Milne's writing should be seen as a product of "the Victorian and Edwardian cultural movement" in which he was raised (rather than the post–World War I era in which *Winnie-the-Pooh* was published); the Hundred Acre Wood evokes "the myth of an Arcadian rural England," which functions as "a pastoral counterpoint to industrialization and modernization" (54). From this perspective, the sequels are nostalgic reconstructions of what was already for Milne a nostalgic reconstruction. This is not a unique position; many texts and eras become sites of nostalgic return for people whose connection to those eras is primarily imagination; they keenly miss places and times they never experienced.

The difference in titles also hints at the sequels' differing relationships to Milne's Pooh books—David Benedictus, author of the first sequel, is explicitly returning to the Wood; we have left them and neither they nor we are precisely the same by the time we return (akin to Boym's reflective nostalgia, which acknowledges the inaccessibility of the past exactly as it was). *The Best Bear in All the World* does not have a sense of linear time; it is not *after* the earlier Pooh books except that Kanga and Tigger are already present. The four chapters are divided by seasons, hinting at a more cyclical relationship with time. Such yearning for return to an unchanging place fits with Boym's definition of restorative nostalgia, which tries to rebuild exactly what there used to be.

Which *Pooh*? And Why Does It Matter?

Lynn Neary's review of *Return to the Hundred Acre Wood* (2009) begins: "It used to be that all good things would come to an end, but these days, at least in the world of books and movies, there is always 'the sequel.'" Matt Berman's review (n.d.) is even harsher: "For reasons that pass understanding, someone decided a sequel was needed to Milne's original books, and Milne's estate gave its permission—a big mistake." Neary and Berman view *Return to the Hundred Acre Wood* more as a symptom of the general tendency toward sequels, no matter how unnecessary, than a uniquely guilty party. *Return to the Hundred Acre Wood* is much more unambiguously a sequel than *The Best Bear in All the World*—it advances the plot and recognizes the passage of time. *The Best Bear in All the World* is much closer to fan fiction despite its authorized status. This assessment, though, is not intended to malign the text but rather to explore the differing function that fan fiction serves from sequels.

Fan fiction, Kimberley Reynolds asserts, "denies" the literary pleasure that Roland Barthes observes "is bound up with knowing from the first page that a book will end" (Reynolds 2007, 183). Instead, fan fiction "exists to extend indefinitely the textual experience," assuring readers that "fictions featuring favourite characters will be available indefinitely" (183). The cyclical time of *Best Bear in All the World* and the reassurance of a Christopher Robin who will always be able to return emphasize this reaccessibility. Such reassurance contrasts with the endings of *The House at Pooh Corner* and *Return to the Hundred Acre Wood*, which emphasize that growth is inevitably taking Christopher Robin away from the Hundred Acre Wood.

The pleasure of a fictional world that is indefinitely available, one of fan fiction's strongest draws, is not limited to fan fiction. Gary Saul Morson writes of Tolstoy's work: "[A]t any point in the novel, some plot lines are just beginning, others developing strongly, still others disappearing; which is why the work has so many loose ends and is incapable of achieving closure. Instead, it achieves the quite different effect of what I call *aperture*: principled openness" (2013, 117). While *The Best Bear in All the World* is not necessarily quite as open-ended as *War and Peace*, "which is literally interminable in the sense that, no matter how many parts Tolstoy added, he could have added more," it does function more as what Morson calls "a process work," which offers only a "partial closure that might round off a chapter or a part, and ties up some of the loose ends of the work" (116). In *Return to the Hundred Acre Wood*, Christopher Robin's return is supposed by a hum that Pooh composes: "He left us all wondering: Gone for good? / No! He'll be back to our lovely wood," but the hum only says that "[o]ne day perhaps . . . [he'll be] back again to spend time with" them (Benedictus 2009, 200). Pooh and Piglet end the text together remembering that Christopher Robin "wouldn't be there tomorrow, or the next day" and walking "until they are swallowed up by the mist" (201). *The Best Bear in All the World* instead ends with Christopher Robin still happily in the Hundred Acre Wood saying "Dear old bear!" to Pooh, who, after deciding "there isn't anything nicer" than "a summer tea party," has decided to "stop thinking" (Bright et al. 2016, 102). While *The Best Bear in All the World* has finished its cycle of seasons, it has not drawn the story of Pooh any closer to an ending or pushed Christopher Robin any closer to adulthood. The decision by Pooh to "stop thinking" may be merely a temporary signal that he's going to take a nap, but it points to the worrying potential of restorative nostalgia: it rejects thinking, whereas reflective nostalgia is much more about provoking thoughts than escaping them.

Return to the Hundred Acre Wood and *The Best Bear in All the World* are fan works—the authors identify themselves as fans—but they are not *fan fiction* in the typical sense because they are authorized sequels. The Winnie-the-Pooh of the animated Disney films is not the Winnie-the-Pooh of the Milne books—this claim is not about quality nor about the faithfulness of the Disney films but rather about the diverging continuities. I use "continuity" here in the sense that it is used to discuss the multiple simultaneous canonical versions of comic book characters, as in the Marvel Cinematic Universe maintaining continuity across the films but not with the comic books. While the distinction between continuities might initially seem trivial, and it is not necessary to trace a complete Many Poohs Theory to describe the separation between Disney's Pooh, Milne's, and those of ancillary texts such as *The Tao of Pooh*, it is nonetheless important to distinguish which Pooh is being extended in the authorized sequels to better describe the relationship between these texts and the originals. *Return to the Hundred Acre Wood* and *The Best Bear in All the World* do not mention Disney, and they emulate the style of Shepard's illustrations, not the Disney version of Pooh. In contrast to these books, one can consider books such as Benjamin Hoff's *The Tao of Pooh*, which are fully fan works and under no circumstances will have repercussions for the "real" Winnie-the-Pooh of the Milne books. The expanded universe of Pooh, comprising texts such as this, has been well examined as "Poohology" by Kenneth Kidd in *Freud in Oz*, but those texts are fan works rather than official sequels. As the canonical continuation of A. A. Milne's Pooh stories, *Return to the Hundred Acre Wood* and *The Best Bear in All the World* must balance the competing demands of faithfulness to the original and a desire to address elements that were lacking.

The distinction between official sequels and fan works is necessarily malleable—fan-created content or fan theories of content can become so prevalent as to function almost as canon, whereas the author is not necessarily infallible in their own creation of canon (the fan reaction to some of J. K. Rowling's *The Cursed Child* and her own continual tweaks of her creations demonstrate such struggle). To establish their claims to legitimacy, both *Return to the Hundred Acre Wood* and *The Best Bear in All the World* are marketed based on the establishment of a connection to the original texts. More than simply a claim that these are stories set in the same world, these connections assert an authority to write supported by marketing claims. For example, before *Return to the Hundred Acre Wood* was released, David Benedictus was presented as "familiar with the world of Winnie the Pooh after adapting and producing audio versions of the books starring Judi Dench, Stephen Fry and Jane Horrocks" (Flood 2009). By establishing his credibility in relation to Milne's texts, Benedictus does not challenge the authority of those texts by the addition of his sequel.

Unlike in most sequels (and quite like the "indefinitely [extended] . . . textual experience" Reynolds describes as common in fan fiction), the status quo is expected to be maintained; the characters, their relationships, and the world they live in are not supposed to be subject to drastic permanent change (Reynolds 2007, 183). In this way, these sequels reflect the sensibilities of fan fiction that produce an infinitely prolonged extension of the middle for canonical texts, in which the major events of the stories are fixed, but more can always be added between those events, fleshing out the time that the canonical texts skip over. *The Best Bear in All the World* fits this idea almost perfectly—ending in the middle of a tea party without signaling any trajectory out of the Wood for Christopher Robin—but *Return to the Hundred Acre Wood* fits this paradigm more subtly. While it is set after the first novels and when Christopher Robin is older, Alison Flood notes that Benedictus has "promised that the book would both 'complement and maintain Milne's idea that whatever happens, a little boy and his bear will always be playing.'" Such a promise signals that the book will not significantly depart from the rest of the Pooh books, but also that it does not disrupt the ending of *The House at Pooh Corner*—that story remains true.

If there is an implied child reader of *The Best Bear in All the World*, it is a nostalgic reconstruction of oneself as a child wholly separate from oneself as an adult—the prelapsarian child whose time is measured only cyclically while ignoring the trajectory toward adulthood. In this sense, the Christopher Robin of *The Best Bear in All the World* is *not* the Christopher Robin of the rest of the canon, unless *The Best Bear in All the World* is not to be understood as a sequel but rather an "inter-quel." None of these stories challenge the continuity of the world established in the series, and none of them expand it. Each disappears without a trace. This fits with the nostalgic reconstruction of an unending innocent childhood, but the Christopher Robin of *Winnie-the-Pooh*, *The House at Pooh Corner*, and *Return to the Hundred Acre Wood* is not a "child who never grows up" à la Peter Pan: he is growing constantly, gaining competence, knowledge, and even (depending on the illustration) height. Taken together, the two authorized sequels reflect differing approaches to nostalgically returning to older childhood texts: *Return to the Hundred Acre Wood* seeks to remedy the issue of representation and (at least subtly) acknowledge the passage of time, while *The Best Bear in All the World* insists on avoiding any disruption of the textual world.

The Response to the Sequels

Philip Nel describes *Return to the Hundred Acre Wood* as "almost like reading someone else's memory of A. A. Milne and E. H. Shepard. . . . It's a pleasant memory, but why wouldn't you read the original? It's not like they've disappeared" (qtd. in Neary 2009). Furthermore, Nel sees it as an imitation—one that gets the broad strokes of the characters right ("Pooh is ruled by [his] tummy. Piglet is timid. Eeyore tends to be sarcastic and depressed") but expands little on them (qtd. in Neary 2009). This is perhaps a bit too harsh: Piglet may be timid, but his development into a very brave small animal from *The House at Pooh Corner* is not wholly forgotten. However, it is tough not to see the scene of Piglet being lowered into a well (Benedictus 2009, 69) as a retread of Piglet being raised to the roof so that he can escape Owl's fallen house in *The House at Pooh Corner* (Milne 1928, 282).

Philip Womack's review in the *Telegraph* (2009) admits that "[t]he introduction of a new character is sure to ruffle some feathers" but assures potential readers that Lottie, a female otter invented by Benedictus, "doesn't feel as if she was made up by a committee to compensate for the lack of female characters." I disagree with Womack in the sense that Lottie clearly is intended to revise the Hundred Acre Wood and fix that fairly glaring issue. However, I assert that the other premise of Womack's statement is also in error—that if Lottie is there to fix what is wrong, then the enjoyment of the Pooh stories would be tainted. Such a statement suggests that the admission that the originals were flawed and in need of revising might destroy the enjoyment; the pleasant nostalgia of childhood would be replaced with the more clear-eyed assessment that a children's book written by an upper-middle-class male author in the 1920s was sexist. Furthermore, the "made up by a committee" comment seems to suggest that there is something wrong with making changes for ideologically progressive reasons—which points to a rather naïve vision of writing in which ideology is, or should be, absent from children's texts.

I would assert that one can maintain—and indeed, these texts require that one does maintain—a nostalgic view of the Hundred Acre Wood as a site of perpetual childhood return *and* celebrate the addition of a character who makes the Wood more inclusive. This is not to say that there are no issues with Lottie. There are the perennial issues of adding new characters to the sequel—they take away page space from the beloved characters and are often disliked as a result. Their tone or characterization may appear unreasonable in comparison to the established characters, even when those characters are already un-alike; because they are not already embedded in the group dynamics, they risk disrupting those dynamics by taking over an established role—for example, Rabbit's insistence on rules makes him unlike the other animals in Milne's books, but Lottie shares or even exceeds Rabbit's penchant for social norms. Perhaps to combat those issues, Lottie is used sparingly, although she is more fully integrated into daily life in the Hundred Acre Wood than Penguin, who visits in *The Best Bear in All the World*. *Return to the Hundred Acre Wood* presents a world still open to the potential for long-term changes, such as the addition of a gramophone and a new character, whereas *The Best Bear in All the World* presents a world that is fixed in time, reaccessible but unchanging.

Animals of the Hundred Acre Wood

The original animals of the Hundred Acre Wood are at once "real" animals (who eat, experience pain from bee stings, and move about on their own) and stuffed animals (who can be lifted by a balloon and fall from it with no injury and have a tail nailed onto them as a repair without causing an injury). They slip easily from one state to another without a transitional period; however, broadly speaking, they could be assigned a coherent set of physical characteristics: their bodies are generally recognized to be stuffed (rather than flesh), but their minds are those of anthropomorphic animals, not anthropomorphic *stuffed* animals. They are not like the stuffed creatures in *The Velveteen Rabbit* or the *Toy Story* series, who are explicitly not "alive" and never "living" in a standard sense.

Lottie differs from the earlier Hundred Acre Wood companions in that she maintains more of the physical characteristics of real otters, such as sleekness and sharp teeth, whereas such attributes are not in evidence for most of the other creatures. While this physical difference might seem minor, it points to the ways that Lottie is not a standard stuffed friend—she has no stuffed antecedent in the real world, having been added many decades after the real Christopher Robin was a child. While Owl and Rabbit did not exist as stuffed toys, they are written as native inhabitants of the Hundred Acre Wood and not newcomers. Lottie is disruptive to the gentle play of the Hundred Acre Wood. This disruption is not necessarily a bad thing: Kanga, Roo, and Tigger were all disruptive previously, and Lottie is indeed treated more kindly than they were as newcomers. What is particularly unusual from a social standpoint in the Hundred Acre Wood is that Lottie wins at games and even outscores Christopher Robin in cricket (Benedictus 2009, 154). Both cricket and "Doing the Ditch," which is a race down a muddy track, almost like luge or skeleton[1] but without the sled (72), are games of skill and athleticism in comparison to the game of Poohsticks of the original texts, which, while Roo contended one could drop one's stick in a "twitchy" sort of way to win (Milne 1928, 249), is evident even within the text to be a game of chance. This differentiation between games of chance and games of skill suggests a clear recognition of Christopher Robin's advancement between *The House at Pooh Corner* and *Return to the Hundred Acre Wood*. Rather than being obviously and quite permanently above the animals, here Christopher Robin can be in real competition and even lose. By presenting the more mature Christopher Robin, *Return to the Hundred Acre Wood* acknowledges growth and thus admits that he is impelled toward adulthood (neither he nor the Hundred Acre Wood can be the same forever).

Penguin is less disruptive, leaving the Hundred Acre Wood at the end of his chapter in *The Best Bear in All the World*, but nonetheless he is more firmly rooted in the characteristics of a real penguin than a stuffed one—in particular in his ability to slide down a snowy hill without the aid of a toboggan (Bright et al. 2016, 50). He does not, however, have the appetite of a real animal, consuming only hot chocolate and an ice lollipop during the characters' Special Winter Picnic (53). While Piglet does seem to be focused overmuch on Penguin's beak when they meet, the apparent issue is about the politeness of staring rather than anxiety of being attacked. Lottie, on the other hand, is the only carnivore of the Hundred Acre Wood, consuming sardines and explaining that Otters typically eat eels and frogs (Benedictus 2009, 61). Lottie's teeth, "which are sharp enough, I can promise you, when they need to be" (59), and her insistence on colder water in the bath (61) also emphasize her as a "real" otter rather than a stuffed one. The ambiguous stuffed/real/anthropomorphic nature of Milne's animals is maintained slightly more faithfully in *The Best Bear in All the World*, but ultimately both of the texts seem more interested in real animals than in stuffed ones. The characters' existence as "real" animals undermines some of the gentleness of Milne's forest, in which no creatures, even beetles such as Very Small Beetle (commonly called "Small"), are considered food. While the nostalgia in these texts may emphasize the welcoming nature of the (stuffed) animal society in the Hundred Acre

Wood, the slightly more realistic depiction of animals works subtly against the open-ended imaginative play of the initial texts, which ignored concerns about the animals rooted in realism.

What Does the Nostalgia Mean?

Milne's Pooh stories are exceedingly gentle; the new texts do little to change that, but there is one aspect in which they actually become gentler than Milne's initial texts (presenting the lesson of mutual care and acceptance of difference that is learned in the original books as already known in these sequels). In each of the original Pooh books, a new character is introduced, and the other characters react to their presence. In *Winnie-the-Pooh*, it is Kanga and Roo; in *The House at Pooh Corner* it is Tigger. In the sequels, this trend continues. In *Return to the Hundred Acre Wood*, it is Lottie the Otter; in *The Best Bear in All the World* it is Penguin. Superficially, this is the same; one newcomer per book (assuming that Kanga and Roo count as one, as their split name and role as mother/child rather than fully realized independent characters indicates); however, the responses in Milne's books were negative, in particular by Rabbit, who used a kidnapping plot to attempt to rid himself of Kanga and Roo and who planned to "lose" Tigger in the woods to make him less bouncy. In contrast, their treatment of Lottie and Penguin is more positive: both are welcomed to the Hundred Acre Wood without such hostility. In the case of Lottie, her sharp teeth might present a deterrent, but a more compelling explanation would be that Benedictus did not want the almost exclusively male inhabitants of the Hundred Acre Wood seeking to oust or mistreat the arriving girl otter. They model better behavior than they did back in the Milne books. In *The Best Bear in All the World*, Penguin's arrival is mostly focused on getting a proper introduction made, and he is only a visitor, soon to be leaving. Penguin's presence is perhaps less of a threat because he is merely a visitor, but also the gentle acceptance that needed to be learned in Milne's books is presented as the new status quo.

Each of these books is steeped in nostalgia, and one would expect no different from anniversary returns to a childhood text, but their relationship to Milne's stories differs and nowhere is that more evident than in the use of the new characters. Lottie the Otter adds something that was missing from the early Pooh stories. The initial Pooh stories are deeply sexist—only one woman appears, and her role is exclusively confined to that of the mother obsessed with her child. Lottie the Otter is feisty, dangerous, and sporty. The inclusion of Lottie is akin to what Boym describes as reflective nostalgia—which acknowledges the radical inaccessibility of the past and does not seek to reenter it but rather to look upon the remaining ruins. *Return to the Hundred Acre Wood* does not wholly fit this paradigm, though, because the Hundred Acre Wood is not in ruins, but perhaps (to the savvier adult reader) we see instead that the past was always already corrupted, not by impending adulthood but by subtle prejudices that permeated even the supposedly idyllic enchanted places. With the help of this otter, however, a new past, a fundamentally better and more thoroughly egalitarian past, can be created. In her introductory chapter, a new game is added to the Hundred Acre Wood called "Doing the Ditch," in which "the nimbler animals would run up to Galleon's Lap and throw themselves into the ditch and be washed all the way down the hill to Eeyore's place. Lottie was the quickest at it because her skin was the sleekest, and she would add little twists and turns along the way" (Benedictus 2009, 72). Later, she proves herself the ablest cricketer of the Hundred Acre Wood, outscoring even Christopher Robin. Benedictus is not trying to make it seem as if she is a likely fit for the Wood: rather, she is an unlikely one. She is unlike any character that Milne wrote: the Pooh stories present a world inhabited almost exclusively by boys.

In *The Best Bear in All the World*, Penguin's relationship to the Hundred Acre Wood is different from Lottie's. While the in-text relationship is also different, I want to begin with the out-of-text justification for this inclusion. Brian Sibley, a coauthor of the sequel, explains that he saw a photograph of Christopher Robin with a stuffed penguin, and thus the penguin is already among the animals who inhabit the Hundred Acre Wood. The initial news stories about the collection focus on this fact—indeed, Clarisse Loughrey, in the *Independent* (2016), determines that it is likely a stuffed version of Squeak from the comic strip *Pip, Squeak, and Wilfred* and was among the stuffed animals available in the 1922 Harrods catalog. There is something touching about the desire for fidelity here, although admittedly strange. Whether or not the real Christopher Robin Milne played with a stuffed penguin, A. A. Milne did not write such a character, so Christopher Robin, the creature of ink and paper, has never met Penguin—and so Penguin is no more a part of the original cast than Lottie (who claims no stuffed antecedent). The emphasis on justifying the addition of Penguin is particularly significant given his relatively modest presence in the text and his position as a visitor rather than a long-term addition. Both the temporary nature of Penguin's stay and the use of photographic justification featuring the real Christopher Robin make it clear that Sibley is avoiding disrupting the Hundred Acre Wood. This Forest is forever the same, and Penguin's presence in only a single chapter marks him as a visitor more than an interloper. He does not change the Wood.

The oft-studied ending of *The House at Pooh Corner* presents a Christopher Robin acutely aware of his trajectory out of the Hundred Acre Wood; the new texts are less certain about this growth. Christopher Robin is taller by the end of *Return to the Hundred Acre Wood*, but he tells Pooh that he will be "away for awhile again" (Benedictus 2009, 198), which is a far cry from the ending to *The House at Pooh Corner*, when he struggles to speak: "'Pooh,' said Christopher Robin earnestly, 'If I—if I'm not quite—' he stopped and tried again—'Pooh, *whatever* happens, you *will* understand, won't you?'" (Milne 1928, 313). Well, Pooh quite clearly won't understand in this book; he responds "understand what?," and Christopher Robin abandons the question to go off "anywhere" with Pooh (313). *Return to the Hundred Acre Wood* ends after Christopher Robin has left, with Pooh and Piglet talking and reflecting on how Christopher Robin is gone and shall be away for a while. In *The Best Bear in All the World*, Christopher Robin is not only still there, but there is no particular mention of his leaving—Kate Saunders's story is the last of the collection and ends with Pooh and Christopher Robin reflecting that they cannot think of anything nicer than a summer tea party (which they have just had). This emphasizes again that these stories take place in an infinitely reaccessible time, rather than a specific and lost time.

Escapism or Revisionism? How the Sequels Change Pooh

Gary Saul Morson and Caryl Emerson describe two of the most important aspects of Mikhail Bakhtin's notion of prosaics as form-shaping ideologies concerning "the novel's special sense of language" and "its sense of social space, historical time, character, and human action" (1990, 308). Morson and Emerson contrast Bakhtin's view, that "[t]he prosaic is truly interesting and the ordinary is what is truly noteworthy," with that of the "Formalists and Futurists" who "were attracted to bohemian romanticism—to slaps in the face of public taste, dramatic beginnings and endings, crises, the storming of barricades, to unrequited love and 'braked' emotion, to apocalyptic time and historical leaps" (22–23). While Lottie is not a revolutionary character at the 2009 publication of *Return to the Hundred Acre Wood*, she would also not have been revolutionary as an addition in the 1920s to Milne's books—the literary world already had Jo March and Alice, and women's suffrage was making significant strides. Lottie is, however, a significant expansion of the roles modeled by female characters in the Hundred Acre Wood. She is confident, athletic, cultured, and talented—in many ways a rounder character than most of her compatriots (perhaps because, as one of only two female characters in the book, she must represent a wide variety of characteristics lest the text present a limited view of women). David Lodge responds to Lennard J. Davis's polemic that views novel reading as preventing social change. Lodge admits that "[i]f you oppose life to art, acting to reading, rather than including the second term of these pairs in the first, if you think that the important thing is not to interpret the world but to change it, then the novel will seem at best an irrelevance, at worst an obstacle" (1990, 21). However, Lodge argues, the novel has never been as conservative as Davis constructs it; novelists "from Cervantes to Martin Amis" have built "resistance to fictional stereotypes and conventions into the novel itself" (21). *Return to the Hundred Acre Wood* attempts to remediate the conventional division between the male characters who act throughout the original Pooh stories and the one female character who worries about her son.

Morson contends that "novels are best able to capture the messiness of the world" because "[p]rosaic facts have been best represented in prosaic art" (2013, 15). While "prosaic facts" are often overlooked, they are the core of many texts for children. "Hidden by our familiarity, the prosaic events that truly shape our lives—that truly *are* our lives—escape our notice," argues Morson (19); "Tolstoy explained that the shape of traditional novels misrepresents history, which is shaped by events that might very well not have happened" (109). Even when not looking at major historical moments, the traditional novel gives the impression of life moving toward specific goals. *Return to the Hundred Acre Wood* more fully embraces the project of the traditional novel than *The Best Bear in All the World*—Benedictus continues Christopher Robin's progress toward adulthood and away from the open-ended imaginative play of his nursery days that typifies *Winnie-the-Pooh* and begins to fade as he spends more time at school.

The Best Bear in All the World offers an ever-available return to the familiar fictional space of childhood. Jennifer Barnes observes that while previous studies established that "[m]any adults develop strong emotional attachments to fictional characters [. . .], and becoming absorbed in a fictional world can serve as a means of escape," these studies have focused on people "interacting with the fictional characters [. . .] by watching, reading, re-watching, or re-reading these narratives" (2015, 70). Barnes asserts that "daydreaming about these characters—imagining further adventures or playing out our hypothetical interactions with them—seems to be a reasonable alternative" (70). In her view, fan fiction is a form of imaginary play, a written form of daydreams. While daydreams about fictional characters are "correlated with self-reported loneliness and negatively correlated with social support" (Barnes 2015, 71), this does not suggest that such daydreams cause such loneliness but rather that they may be a response to it. This is consistent with Barnes's assertion that "the writing of fanfiction [is] a social activity, as well as a creative one" and furthermore "tends to be based not only on the primary text, but also on the 'metatext' developed as part of the collective fandom imagination" (73). As a multiauthor collection, *The Best Bear in All the World* reminds readers that their fan experience is a shared one and that the nostalgia is not an isolating force but a profoundly communal one.

In conclusion, these new Pooh books occupy a strange space. Are they truly children's texts? Are these books primarily sold to be read by children, perhaps after they have devoured Milne's Pooh books and are eager for more? In this sense, they capture some of the infinite reaccessibility that puts the pleasures of fan fiction into the realm of nostalgia, where a reader can continue to dwell in a world indefinitely as new stories are constantly spun within it. They assume a preexisting knowledge of the characters, even approximating Shepard's original illustrations (differing, then, from the Disney characters with whom many children are now familiar). On the other hand, perhaps these sequels are more oriented toward an adult audience, who would be reading the stories to children. This is not unusual in the realm of children's books; it is a truth universally understood that one must appeal to the adult purchasing the book, sometimes even more than the child to whom it will be read. So a double audience is perhaps established.[2] If this double address is occurring, we might assume that the adult pleasure of these texts is to nostalgically return to one's own childhood connection to the Hundred Acre Wood, whereas the child (who presumably ignores or is not read the section labeled "exposition" in these books in which the authors are clearly trading in such nostalgic stock and who likely cares little that the authorship and illustration have been passed on) is excited to hear of more adventures. If we assume such a credulous child reader, then the re-creation of a more inclusive Hundred Acre Wood that Benedictus aims for is successful. These stories become a larger canon of Pooh stories, and this generation of readers need not experience the Hundred Acre Wood as a boys' club with only a nagging mother figure. Perhaps in this way, the text veers away from nostalgia, self-consciously creating a false past that satisfies present needs—in this case, the innocence of the upper middle-class rural childhood combined with a more progressive world view of the present. The Hundred Acre Wood of 2009 and 2016 is different from that of 1926 and 1928, but so is the world beyond the Wood. Both authorized sequels are nostalgic, but *Return to the Hundred Acre Wood* moves time forward (albeit slightly), both in representation and also in the growth of the characters and the changing of the Hundred Acre Wood society, while *The Best Bear in All the World* attempts to remain timeless, the stories having no impact beyond their chapter and the Hundred Acre Wood remaining precisely as it was. If *The Best Bear in All the World* achieves timelessness, it is by making itself ephemeral. *Return to the Hundred Acre Wood* updates Milne's world while remaining nostalgic and suggests that the Hundred Acre Wood was always already large enough to hold a cricket pitch, a gramophone, and a sporty otter girl.

Notes

1. These are sports that consist of racing down an icy track on a small sled; internationally, they are most familiar as Winter Olympics events.

2. Here, the term "double audience" is used in the sense that Barbara Wall uses it, differentiating between the different forms of address—single for texts addressing only children, double for texts that address adults and children differently, and dual for texts that simultaneously address adults and children in the same ways (1992, 9).

Bibliography

Barnes, Jennifer L. 2015. "Fanfiction as Imaginary Play: What Fan-Written Stories Can Tell Us about the Cognitive Science of Fiction." *Poetics* 48 (February): 69–82.

Benedictus, David. 2009. *The Return to the Hundred Acre Wood*. New York: E. P. Dutton.

Berman, Matt. n.d. "Review of *The Return to the Hundred Acre Wood*." Common Sense Media. https://www.commonsensemedia.org/book-reviews/return-to-the-hundred -acre-wood.

Boym, Svetlana. 2001. *The Future of Nostalgia*. New York: Basic Books.

Bright, Paul, Brian Sibley, Jeanne Willis, and Kate Saunders. 2016. *The Best Bear in All the World*. New York: E. P. Dutton.

Cadden, Mike. 2005. "Simultaneous Emotions: Entwining Modes in Children's Books."
    Children's Literature in Education 36, no. 3: 285–98.
Flood, Alison. 2009. "After 90 Years, Pooh Returns to Hundred Acre Wood in Sequel."
    Guardian, January 9. https://www.theguardian.com/books/2009/jan/10/pooh-bear
    -sequel-david-benedictus.
Hemmings, Robert. 2007. "A Taste of Nostalgia: Children's Books from the Golden Age—
    Carroll, Grahame, and Milne." *Children's Literature* 35, no. 1 (January): 54–79.
Kidd, Kenneth. 2011. *Freud in Oz: At the Intersections of Psychoanalysis and Children's
    Literature.* Minneapolis: University of Minnesota Press.
Lodge, David. 1990. *After Bakhtin: Essays on Fiction and Criticism.* New York: Routledge.
Loughrey, Clarisse. 2016. "New Winnie-the-Pooh Character Added to Celebrate 90th
    Anniversary." *Independent*, September 18. https://www.independent.co.uk/arts-enter
    tainment/books/news/new-winnie-the-pooh-character-added-to-celebrate-90th-anni
    versary-a7314561.html.
Milne, A. A. 1926. *Winnie-the-Pooh.* In *The World of Pooh*, 1–149. New York: E. P. Dutton,
    1957.
Milne, A. A. 1928. *The House at Pooh Corner.* In *The World of Pooh*, 151–314. New York: E. P.
    Dutton, 1957.
Morson, Gary Saul. 2013. *Prosaics and Other Provocations: Empathy, Open Time, and the
    Novel.* Brighton, MA: Academic Studies Press.
Morson, Gary Saul, and Caryl Emerson. 1990. *Mikhail Bakhtin: Creation of a Prosaics.*
    Stanford, CA: Stanford University Press.
Nance-Carroll, Niall. 2015. "Not Only, But Also: Entwined Modes and the Fantastic in
    A. A. Milne's Pooh Stories." *Lion and the Unicorn* 39, no. 1 (January): 63–81.
Neary, Lynn. 2009. "Pooh Faithful Return to the Hundred Acre Wood." National Public
    Radio, October 2. https://www.npr.org/2009/10/02/113406207/pooh-faithful-return
    -to-the-hundred-acre-wood.
Reynolds, Kimberley. 2007. *Radical Children's Literature: Future Visions and Aesthetic
    Transformations in Juvenile Fiction.* Basingstoke, Hants., England: Palgrave Macmillan.
Sale, Roger. 1972. "Child Reading and Man Reading: Oz, Babar, and Pooh." *Children's
    Literature* 1: 162–72.
Wall, Barbara. 1992. *The Narrator's Voice: The Dilemma of Children's Fiction.* New York:
    Palgrave Macmillan.
Womack, Philip. 2009. "Winnie the Pooh *Return to the Hundred Acre Wood* Review."
    Telegraph, October 5. https://www.telegraph.co.uk/culture/books/children_sbook
    reviews/6262332/Winnie-the-Pooh-Return-to-the-Hundred-Acre-Wood-review.html.

CHAPTER 5

The Curious Disappearance of Christopher Robin

A New Understanding of Narratives in *The Many Adventures of Winnie-the-Pooh* in Hong Kong Disneyland

Tsang Chun Ngai, Jonathan

Christopher Robin has long occupied a central role in the Winnie-the-Pooh world. A. A. Milne's original books start with him being told a story and end with his departure from the Hundred Acre Wood. His figure is present in later adaptations, notably the Disney animated feature (Reitherman and Lounsbery 1977), cementing the popularity of the story, in which he continues to be a young boy who solves problems for his anthropomorphic friends. Furthermore, in the movie *Christopher Robin* (Forster 2018), a grown-up version features as the titular character, catering to the nostalgic sentiments of long-time readers.

This chapter will focus on an attraction in Hong Kong Disneyland, *The Many Adventures of Winnie-the-Pooh*. Present since the theme park opened in 2005, it is an indoor amusement with honeypot-shaped guided vehicles traveling through different scenes, which themselves include animation, sounds, music, and special effects. For three minutes and fifteen seconds, guests get to experience five acts—A Blustery Day in Hundred Acre Wood, Bounce with

Tigger, Heffalumps and Woozles, A Rainy Place, and A Party for Pooh—with animatronic versions of the characters reenacting parts of the story. These acts draw content from chapters 5, 9, and 10 of *Winnie-the-Pooh* (Milne [1926] 2016) and chapters 2, 3, 4, 7, 8, and 9 of *The House at Pooh Corner* (Milne [1928] 2016). A key feature of the amusement is the giant storybook pages, which extend from ground to ceiling with Disney illustrations accompanying the texts from Milne. These appear at the queuing and unloading areas as well as during significant junctures of the narrative within the ride. In the words of Disneyland's promotional materials, this ride takes you "through a color-ful, song-filled storybook wonderland [to] experience a menagerie of kooky adventures" (Hong Kong Disneyland n.d.).

In this chapter, I will examine how the employment of narratological tools to analyze a thematic park ride may offer new insights into the way attractions engage with their audiences and how they offer a range of subject positions. I will first posit that the marginalized role that this specific adaptation assigns to Christopher Robin is fostered through a specific focalization and creates the unique effect of positioning the riders in his place. Guests of this attraction experience the narrative world and make choices of their own, with a narrating voice and different genre-specific means guiding this experience of the nar-rative. I will explore how analyzing this ride through narratology reveals the potential of the medium to create a different engagement with the audience in comparison to others that can be understood through the study of focaliza-tion and the interplay between diegesis and mimesis. Finally, I will proceed to examine how the range of subject positionings offered must be understood within the specific cultural context of Hong Kong Disneyland, and how park rides themselves can be understood as spaces for negotiating glocalization.

When considering the prominence of Disneyland parks within the Disney corporation and the global success of the format, in tandem with Hong Kong Disneyland's popularity just in terms of visitor numbers, it can be argued that they constitute a key experience of children's culture. Both the study of Disneyland rides as a format and their adaptation into a specific cultural context are, however, limited and not systematic. In light of this, and given the nontextual nature of the subject text, I will provide some definitions with regard to terminology. The term "ride" refers to the experience from the moment the riders settle into the carts until they disembark; whereas "attrac-tion" comprises the ride along with the entire structure related to the expe-rience, encompassing the signage, queuing area, and shop area encountered after the ride. The term "riders" refers to the people who go on the ride, while "guests" is used when discussing, more broadly, Disneyland visitors. With this text being an attraction that is physically experienced, the word "audience" is used in a sense analogous to "readers" of a word-based text.

Constructing the Story World with an Intruding Narrator

A narrative, as defined by Gérard Genette, is "[an] event that consists of someone recounting something, the act of narrating taken in itself" (1980, 25). *The Many Adventures of Winnie-the-Pooh* ride appears to be fertile ground for a discussion of this practice. It foregrounds the diegetic storytelling act but has its generic foundations in a mimetic (akin to theatrical) story world. In contrast to the less active modes of the text or the animation, in this attraction, full mimesis is possible, as it employs semiotic signifiers that go beyond language, presenting a narrative in the physical, embodied realm. This analysis would hence strive to unravel how diegesis and mimesis interact.

A commonality found between the original text and the adaptations is the oral tradition being sustained through the narrator-narratee relationship. This is key to how Milne's texts are experienced, as Roger Sale sees that their charm depends on them "being read aloud in the spirit of a cosy relation between reader and read to" (1972, 167). This relationship can be exemplified in Milne's description of the first meeting between Pooh and Christopher Robin:

> "Good morning, Christopher Robin," he said.
> "Good morning, Winnie-ther-Pooh," said you. (Milne [1926] 2016, 8)

In the example above, we observe how the second-person "you" seems to intrude. Milne utilizes the oral tradition of an adult reading the text aloud to a child, making the adult a "teller-surrogate" (Wall 1991, 19). This feature accommodates the implied double reader characteristic of the children's literature genre, in which the assumption of this role allows involvement by adult readers while entertaining a child audience. Breaking down the two lines, the first is presumably spoken by the (adult) narrator, while the second continues with an invitation to participate extended to the person being narrated to, quite likely a child. This kind of direct address is sustained through the rest of the opening chapter after this quotation. It positions the implied narratee in a participatory role with the continued use of "you said" and in phrases like "you both went out" (Milne [1926] 2016, 11), "you laughed to yourself" (13), and "you aimed . . . and fired" (16). The listening child is encouraged to identify with the character-narratee, Christopher Robin, and imagine taking similar actions by the use of the inclusive second person. The verbs (went out, laughed, aimed, fired) in the quoted phrases are "attributive signs"—verbs that communicate perception and indicate shifts from one focalization level to another (Bal 2009, 162)—which also coax readers of the text to mimic Christopher Robin's actions. Therefore, the consistent use of a direct address acts as a means of focalization, leading the listener-child to experience the story from Christopher Robin's (the metadiegetic character's) perspective, vicariously interacting with the different toy/animal characters in his place.

Such foregrounded use of the narrator is intensified as a narrative strategy in the animated feature (Reitherman and Lounsbery 1977). The extradiegetic narrator intrudes more frequently at points to change settings and comment on the characters' actions. He even breaks down the layers of diegesis to address the diegetic characters directly. Conversely, Christopher Robin's role in this adaptation is reduced when compared to Milne's novels, as in the latter he is relatively highlighted as the intended narratee and comments on the action. There are sections of the animation in which he becomes absent from the narrative, only to reappear at critical junctures when a solution is required. He is portrayed as the savior to many of their problems, like when Pooh gets stuck in the entrance to Rabbit's burrow or when Roo and Tigger bounce too high and cannot get down from a tree.

When it comes to Disneyland's ride adaptation, this key feature is maintained, in which riders encounter a narrator who is similarly intrusive and bears the voice of authority. There are altogether four interventions by the narrator:

1. The ride starts off Act 1 with a mature, genial male narrator's voice just as the visuals appear, opening with "One day in the Hundred Acre Wood."

2. A voice right before Act 3 can arguably be attributed to the narrator, announcing the demons that Pooh faces in the subsequent scene: "Heffalumps and Woozles . . . Beware! Beware!" The vocal quality of this line is distorted with a "spooky" timbre.

3. In Act 4, shifting the setting from the dream of Heffalumps and Woozles back to the Wood, where the characters struggle with a

heavy flood, a voice cautions, "There was a bit of a cloudburst. It got rainier and rainier!"

4. In Act 5, to bring the ride to a conclusion, the voice concludes: "And at last, everyone gathered together to say," with the characters answering in refrain, "Hooray!" as they are depicted in a party scene celebrating Pooh's heroism.

Drawing together these intrusions, the narrator in the ride signals to riders the shifting environment and navigates them across worlds that blur fantasy and reality. These shifts are akin to how Milne jumps between layers of diegesis to signal different story worlds, or how the narrator "turns the page" in the animated feature. In the beginning, the narrating voice brings the riders from the outside world into the realm where Pooh and friends reside. The opening declaration of "one day" recalls the tradition of the opening lines of fairy tales, which transport readers to an "ageless, therapeutic, miraculous, undetermined" world (Zipes 1991, 2). The second and third interventions frame the shifts between the story world (the Hundred Acre Wood) and the dream world, immersing riders into, then waking them up from, the dream of Heffalumps. The third intervention also anchors the story in the dire predicaments the characters are in and explains the bad dream (the encroaching flood). Then, in its final intervention, the narrator skips ahead, quickly resolving the danger the characters confronted and increasing the pace of the narrative toward a jubilant finish.

Examining these four appearances of the narrator, it seems that the ride accentuates a collaboration of both diegetic and mimetic presentations; in other words, the story is both told and shown to the audience, complementing the embodied experience of the ride while sustaining the sensation of "being read to." The narrative is presented by a "heterodiegetic" narrator, one who is "absent from the story he tells" (Genette 1980, 245). Similar to Milne's text, this narrator continues the use of an intruding adult voice—a feature commonly seen in children's fiction to "'correct' whatever erroneous conclusions that readers can draw about characters" (Nikolajeva 2014, 93). This form of narrative address emphasizes the "authorial persona" of the narrator; although it is now considered dated, it was commonly employed by Milne and his contemporaries in their works written for children (Wall 1991, 5). In the ride, the narrator is deployed in such an unnatural way, mostly reduced to a force that signals to riders the arrival of the next scene, causing some unexplained jumps in the narrative. The narrator's final appearance can be quite confusing for riders, as those who are closely following will question how the crisis is resolved and why Pooh happens to be the hero. Both in Milne's text and in the animation, the narrator performs the function of an adult voice that colludes with the adult audience, speaking "over the heads" of the child audience in a bid for humor; yet with the ride, this narrative strategy is not deployed.

While such insistence on the diegetic elements is peculiar when considering the nature of the attraction, I would suggest that the mimetic and the diegetic work in tandem to create the narrative world. The rider encounters mimetic elements overlapped with the narrator's incursions, and the experience arising from the physical nature of the attraction adaptation, distinct from the novel or the animation, cannot be overlooked. To explore their interaction, I will first take a broader view to look at how the story world is built when placed in the context of Hong Kong Disneyland, then proceed to study how specifically the attraction mimetically aids the rider's immersion into the Hundred Acre Wood.

First, taking a macroscopic view, an understanding of the narrative and the rider's entire experience cannot be dissociated from the context within which this narrative is staged—a theme park. The creation of an alternate world that engages visitors' immersion and willing suspension of disbelief is the main premise of Disneyland. The park is subdivided into various themed areas, demarcated by music (as discussed in Charles Carson's analysis of Disneyland thematic lands [2004]) and other elements such as architecture, park layout, and the presence of iconic characters. Milne creates a "Secondary World" in his text (Hunt 1992, 114), just as Disney constructs this alternate reality through a theme park. To get to the park, guests first go on a Disney-themed train that takes them to the Disneyland stop. After entering the park, they head to the Winnie-the-Pooh attraction, which is located in Fantasyland, a themed area that hosts other fantasy worlds such as *Sleeping Beauty's Castle* and *Alice's Mad Hatter Tea Cups*. The Hundred Acre Wood of *The Many Adventures of Winnie-the-Pooh* is delineated from the rest of Fantasyland with signs, music, and character sculptures. These elements are varied, nontextual semiotic resources that guide park guests to the fantasy world of their choice. The Disney theme park experience aims to create "a whole new world," and to experience this, guests must take an active role in engaging with "the complex and circular network of images, sounds, and commodities" (Carson 2004, 233). The act of moving through the different worlds, from the moment guests step on the train to get to the theme park, to getting into the honeypots, helps prime them for accepting and embodying the world of Winnie-the-Pooh. In text-based narratives or movies, "readers can never be actually transported to a fictional world," with their presence in the fictional world remaining "virtual" (Caracciolo 2014, 161). The experience of an attraction, by contrast, becomes one that works in the flesh, with the deliberate trip to this attraction standing as a physical metaphor of transportation theory, which is the "process of becoming fully engaged in the story" (Green, Brock, and Kaufman 2004, 312). Guests of the attraction gradually leave the normative world to arrive at a fantasy one. This trip extends the virtual embodied experience of the narrative to beyond the narrated world itself, where the staging of worlds becomes a crucial process in leading the immersion of riders into the story.

In his discussion of world-making strategies, David Herman (2009) points out that the procedures for creating a narrative and a nonnarrative world are distinct. The overall stance taken in the previous paragraph could, in this light, be refuted by arguing that the elements mentioned are simply strategies to create themed worlds, but unrelated to a narrative world. However, the Winnie-the-Pooh ride draws from both diegetic and mimetic features to construct the Hundred Acre Wood, namely by making sustained use of a narrator's voice combined with mimetic devices and the "establishing shot" of the story world, its opening section.

The relationship between the diegesis and the mimesis in this ride is inherently collaborative. First, the authorial, intruding narrative voice is aligned with mimetic shifts in the environment. As previously discussed, the narrator's voice signals a change in story world diegetically, but this is not exclusive to his role, for shifts in time and locale are also effected mimetically to create the story worlds through "the semiotic cues available in a given medium" (Herman 2009, 75). In this case, shifts between acts are indicated through the visuals (comprising animatronics, projections, and storybook pages), music, and the movement of the honeypot cart. This combination of mimesis and diegesis directs the rider's understanding of the story world. An example of this feature is the third appearance of the narrator before act 4, A Rainy Place. While the narrator declares the new setting, the riders see a giant storybook page depicting a water bucket that is overlaid with a projection of it overflowing and "washing away" the text beneath it. The collaboration is intensified when the honeypots transition to a rocking motion that mimics a floating boat in a flood. In the background, a tune is heard, with the alliterative lyrics "the rain rain rain came down down down" and a melody that goes down stepwise in a repetitive rhythm, musically evoking the pitter-patter of rainfall. The ambient lighting is dark, but strobe lights imitate falling rain. In this context, the narrator's line "There was a bit of a cloudburst. It got floodier and floodier!" is therefore not merely declared diegetically but also demonstrated mimetically.

Following the trajectory of Herman's argument, the narrative practices of world making are better revealed when looking at "narrative beginnings" (2009, 79). The second aspect I will focus on is the opening section, which comprises the pre-ride area to its first storybook page, including elements such as the signage, the storybook pages presented in the queuing area, and the first appearance of the narrator accompanying the first page. Considering once again the affordances of this medium, the narrative—and, by extension, the construction of the story world—does not begin at the ride but upon entering the attraction. The overhead sign displaying the attraction name, *The Many Adventures of Winnie-the-Pooh*, is flanked by sculpted versions of the titular character and his companions in the Wood (with Christopher Robin conspicuously absent). Outside the queuing area is a map of the Hundred Acre Wood, and at its entrance is a giant storybook page with an illustration of Winnie-the-Pooh eating honey, continued with other pages featuring one of the other characters in turn throughout the queuing area. These "paratextual" elements frame the introduction to the "textual." The ride starts with a page showing Winnie-the-Pooh, along with the narrator's voice, who intrudes to open with "One day," evoking a fairy-tale opening as aforementioned.

The Winnie-the-Pooh ride experience is rendered unique mainly due to the way the audience is exposed to both diegetic and mimetic elements and is thus enabled to combine all the macroscopic and microscopic semiotic cues that frame a particular sentiment toward its story world. Such a foray into Winnie-the-Pooh's world suggests an experience, evidenced by transportation theory, of "temporarily leaving one's reality behind and emerging from the narrative somehow different from the person one was before entering the milieu of the narrative" (Green, Brock, and Kaufman 2004, 315), in which the realistically rendered mimetic features in the ride help the audience immerse into the narrative as they are transported away from the normative world. This fantastic experience echoes the central sentiment of Milne's work, as suggested by Alison Lurie—a nostalgia for simpler times, or the childhood memory of creating and inhabiting one's own story world. By visiting this Disneyland attraction, the audience's yearning for a "lost paradise" (Lurie 1973, 16) can perhaps be similarly satiated.

Narrative Focalization and Embodiment
in a Theme Park Attraction

To confirm the potential of the sentiment of nostalgia, particularly that directed toward the audience of the attraction, requires an analysis that goes beyond the narrative beginnings. While the narrator and various semiotic cues, as argued, put riders in the story worlds, I have yet to explicate how the attraction frames them explicitly as the now-absent Christopher Robin, for thus far the experiencer could very well be a generic participant or an external focalizer, with no connection to the narrative. In this section, I will explain how a deliberate focalization accompanies the story, accomplished through two steps: first, framing the rider as focalizer, and second, having the rider embody the role of Christopher Robin.

Focalization, in its simplest definition, refers to how a narrative is "seen": in Mieke Bal's definition, it is "the relationship between the 'vision,' the agent that sees, and that which is seen" (2009, 149). This encompasses two entities, the active agent being the focalizer and the passive object being the focalized. Gérard Genette (1980) was the first to systematically present the notion of focalization, proposing the following three types: "zero focalization," which does not fix the perspective to any character; "internal focalization," which limits the vision to just one character and reveals that character's internal thoughts and feelings; and "external focalization," which follows a character in an "over-the-shoulder" manner, following their vision but not delving into their internal world. In text-based narratives, both the focalizer and the narrator can only be realized through language. Therefore, the narrator's voice (the speaker) and the focalizer (the seer) are intertwined, with the narrator's involvement differing in the three types: the narrator says more than what the focalizer sees in a zero-focalized narrative; says exactly what the focalizer sees in an internally focalized one; and says much less for external focalization (Grünbaum 2013, 113).

This categorization has been questioned among narratologists regarding whether there is subjective input from the audience, whether vision predominates over other senses, and whether a narrative can be unfocalized. Bal believes that there can only be either "character-focalization" (akin to internal focalization) and "external focalization," thereby refuting the presence of zero focalization (2009, 152). In later work, Genette equivocates with a vague qualification of his original definition that zero focalization implies "variable, and sometimes zero, focalization" (1988, 74). Thor Grünbaum proposes some interesting refinements to focalization relevant to our discussion here. He first finds the restriction on vision "arbitrary" and criticizes the neglect of the reader's presence in Genette's model (2013, 114–15). Subsequently, he proposes, building upon a "visual"-oriented conceptualization of focalization, a refinement that arrives at "perceptual" focalization. This reformation includes the audience in the process of focalization, with the text assisting readers' immersion into the narrative world, and their memory and understanding of the narrative (127).

Grünbaum's suggestion that focalization is perceptual coincides with the generic affordances of a theme park ride. Contrasting the narrative strategies with those deployed in Milne's text and Disney's animated feature, I would argue that the multimodal possibilities of the ride allow a higher degree of immersion, which may challenge traditional categories of focalization. In her analysis of picture books, Maria Nikolajeva points out the potential for transmedial texts to both build engagement with the character and relate "directly to the imagery," with the immersion arising from a "synergetic effect" seen through the interplay of the verbal (the narrator) and the visual (2014, 106). With the ride being a physical experience, it is an embodied narrative in the literal sense, with sensory input on top of the visual component. Refocusing Grünbaum's narratological tools to examine this experiential narrative, I would propose another qualification to focalization that can be seen in this ride and, more broadly, rides of a participatory nature. As the attraction here is an embodied text, with various sensual input provided to the riders directly, it concretizes the core of focalization as "perceptual" yet no longer in the imaginary realm nor elicited through text. When we ask "who experiences" the narrative as a tool to identify the focalizer, it is clear that the riders are put in this role. This type of focalization requires further characterization extended from the debates outlined above. Under the conditions that (1) *the focalization is not linked to any character in the narrative* (in a way affirming Genette's assertion that there can indeed be zero focalization); and (2) *the narrative is experienced through an extradiegetic* (real-life rider) *narratee's perspective*, I would like to coin a new type of focalization revealed by this ride and other texts in this medium: *intrinsic* focalization. The word "intrinsic" points to something that comes from within, but when applied in this case, it also implies a contradictory position. The first implication lies with the focalizer. An intrinsic focalizer is distinct from one internally focalized, as this extradiegetic audience is not one of the characters within the diegesis, and a view into the inner thoughts of these characters is not offered. However, at the same time, the riders embody the focalizing perspective, with an internalized perception of an actualized fictional world. This intrinsic focalizer lies both within and without the metadiegetic world, as it would be psychologically external to the characters in the narrative yet physically internal to it. Another implication of such focalization concerns the narrator. Under such focalization, the narrator and focalizer are now discrete entities, as the narrative voice is dissociated from the perceptual perspective. In the case of this ride, the narrator is a disembodied voice not identified with any character, and one that intrudes in the embodied experience from time to time to signal world shifts, among other elements. In summary, an intrinsic focalizer is characterized by being positioned with the experiencer-narratee instead of the narrating voice, thus differing from traditional (text-based) narrative practices.

With the medium no longer restricted to the textual, the attraction utilizes new resources to engender focalization. The means of focalizing intrinsically can be separated into active focalization, referring to the rider's act of perceiving, and passive focalization, referring to the semiotic resources provided by the attraction to direct their perception. In *The Many Adventures of Winnie-the-Pooh*, the rider is free to make active choices as to which elements to focus on along the ride. There are sweeping scenes that extend beyond a rider's field of vision, depicting settings of a field and a falling house (act 1), a dream world (act 3), and a flood (act 4). The rider's choice of what to focalize on is, therefore, significant in these scenes, with it being physically impossible to look at everything at once.[1] This act of volition points to the uniqueness of intrinsic focalization of these embodied adaptations, a feature extending from an internally focalized or first-person narrative. In first-person narratives, there is limited access to the mind of only one character, a "visual as well as psychological constraint," leading to authenticity in such narratives as this perspective mimics the limitation we experience in real life (Martin 1986, 133). Intrinsic focalization comes with this quality and further imposes physical limitations, as one cannot freely enter the minds of the characters. In this attraction, the experience of the narrative is only allowed from the physical location of the rider, as determined by the position of the cart. Other than engaging in the active act of perceiving, the rider is also passively guided by ride elements to notice some aspects above others. An immediate element is the mimetic performance of animatronic characters. As the diegetic narrator sets the scene, the characters' dialogue and movements direct the gaze of riders, suggesting to them whose actions to focus on. Familiarity with the characters' voices from previous exposure to the animated movie may be required, but then the mimetic can be understood together with the movement along the track. The characters always speak in turn, and only as the cart passes them by. The sequential manner of the presentation, therefore, guides riders to focalize primarily on the one element they are in front of. Another passive element that guides focalization is lighting. In the sequence with Tigger (act 2), his apparitions are indicated not merely with his mimetic performance but also by spotlights. This invites further analysis at a possible intersection between narratology and theater semiotics, where the use of lights as semiotic resources is explored (Gostand 1980). Finally, the tracks are an essential guide to the rider's vision. The orientation and length of a track section, as well as the speed at which the carts move along it, determine how long a rider will "naturally" look at a scene. Summing up the various means effecting focalization, they correspond to Bal's definition of the term. The "active" means pertain to the focalizer, the seer (or the experiencer, in a broader definition following Grünbaum); and the passive elements, to the focalized, the seen (the experienced). Intrinsic focalization is achieved by directing the focalizer's perception through a combination of the rider's physical constraints (active) and the ride elements (passive).

As mentioned at the beginning of this chapter, Christopher Robin is marginalized in the attraction as he does not appear in the ride. The discussion on intrinsic focalization leads to my second point regarding the focalization practices in *The Many Adventures of Winnie-the-Pooh*, that, in his absence, riders are placed in the role of the original focalizer, Christopher Robin. This modifies how intrinsic focalization functions and exemplifies how it can be placed in a contradictory position. The internal mind of Christopher Robin is still not offered, following how the experience of the narrative is externalized, but the attraction offers indications that position riders in his role. In other words, by intrinsically focalizing a character, the text invites the audience to embody the focalizer's perspective; yet, a genuinely internal view is not (as a narrative choice) and cannot be (as a physical limitation for the focalizer) offered.

The framing is achieved through his appearances in two "paratextual" locations. First, in the aforementioned illustrated pages of characters around the queuing area, Christopher Robin meets the riders on the last pre-ride page before they clamber onto the honeypots. He is presented as a boy extending his arm, holding a balloon to the direction of a nearby page that features Winnie-the-Pooh. At the conclusion of the ride, before the riders leave the honey-pots, the penultimate storybook page illustrates a scene in which Christopher Robin takes Winnie-the-Pooh's hand and leads him off along a path that points toward the ride's exit. The text accompanying this illustration says:

> "Wasn't that fun Christopher Robin?" asked Pooh.
> "Oh, yes Pooh," said Christopher Robin as he happily walked along with his friend. "It was grand!"

These two pages are significant to the understanding of the attraction in terms of its world-building practices and focalization. First, their presence provides yet another means to create the story world. In the illustrations, the directions of the giving hand and the winding path suggest an invitation to take the balloon and enter the story world, and to exit, respectively. More significantly, the world-building capacities of these two pages can be extended to focalization practices, especially when considering the positioning of the narrator. Milne's work is characterized by the layers of diegesis, with the *extradiegetic* level involving Milne, the author, the *diegetic* level having the narrator in the story speaking to the character-narratee, and the *metadiegetic* being the fantasy world of the Hundred Acre Wood. Narrative levels can also be deployed analogously when considering the attraction. Assuming that the narrator in the ride is the same entity as the implied narrator (A. A. Milne) in the pre-ride areas (for the illustrated pages), this entity would sustain the diegetic-metadiegetic difference in the text as well as the attraction-ride boundary in this attraction. Taking the attraction as a whole, the area outside the ride (i.e., the queuing area) would be the diegetic, and the ride itself would be the metadiegetic. If it can be assumed that the books' practice of having the real Christopher Robin as the narratee is continued on these two pages, the rider experiences the ride embodying Christopher Robin from the point when they cross the boundary from the diegetic into the metadiegetic. The narrator of the ride can be seen as the diegetic narrator taking the narratee, Christopher Robin, into the metadiegetic, then becoming the intruding narrator narrating the ride for the focalizer. The narrator in the illustrated pages, through opposition, constructs the narratee in the diegetic and the focalizer in the metadiegetic. The opening pages, therefore, transport the riders between worlds and transform them from an extradiegetic observer of the narrative to an intrinsic focalizer.

Being transported, the rider is now an experiencer physically and psychologically in the metadiegetic, playing the role of Christopher Robin. In Marco Caracciolo's discussion of how immersion is achieved in fictional texts, the process of embodiment is triggered when the text invites readers "to enact the experiences of fictional characters, causing an overlap between their own story-driven experience and the experience that they attribute to characters" (2014, 158). This process is coined the "fictionalization of the reader's body"—there would be a "fictionally actual body" (a concretized focalizer that exists in the fictional world), which "can help the reader position his or her virtual body within the fictional world" (163). While in text-based fiction this can only be done through the narrating voice, I would argue that the ride is narratively distinct by offering other means to achieve embodiment.

There are passive means along the ride that fictionalize riders as Christopher Robin. Each cart goes into a bouncing motion as it enters the scenes with Tigger (act 2) and rocks gently from side to side to mimic floating in a flood (act 4), echoing what the characters fictionally experience in the book and animation. These kinesthetic simulations assist the riders' embodiment as Christopher Robin, as they, in the vein of a narratee's participation in storytelling, take part in the story with their movements. They allow for a state of narratee-narrator relationship that Barbara Wall terms "playing together," "a felt partnership, almost a collusion" (1991, 258). All these elements combine to form an effective practice of riders' transportation into the Hundred Acre Wood, with them encompassing the tripartite of persuasive communication—attention, imagery, and feelings (Green, Brock, and Kaufman 2004, 312). Riders can be fully engaged in this imagery-laden narrative because they are intrinsically focalized to experience it directly in an embodied manner. Without Christopher Robin's absence, there would not be the possibility for riders to project themselves as him. I would further posit that intrinsic focalization is the ideal practice for narrative-based theme park rides like our example here, as this allows both more immersive audience engagement and better use of the generic affordances of the medium.

Positioning the Audience

In the last two sections, I have built a case of how this attraction creates a narrative world, how it focalizes the rider intrinsically, and eventually how it positions the rider as Christopher Robin. In this section, I will discuss how audience engagement can vary depending on the extent to which the rider embodies the absent Christopher Robin and the sociocultural implications of this narrative strategy, with consideration to the ride's site of production, Hong Kong Disneyland.

A significant effect of intrinsic focalization is that it allows for an "ageless" appeal. Generally speaking, the layers of diegesis and narration can be framed and considered different literary modes, which further leads to the multiple positioning of riders. In Niall Nance-Carroll's survey on critical readings of *Winnie-the-Pooh*, three modes of the Pooh story are found: first, the romantic comic mode meant for young readers, as discussed by Ellen Tremper; second, Roger Sale's view of the narrative as ironic comedy meant for adults or a sophisticated audience; and third, Robert Hemmings's observation of the ultimate tragic exit of Christopher Robin from the story world, and thus the story serving as a nostalgic re-creation of the past (Nance-Carroll 2015, 66). These three modes are not distinct; the audience may be "hailed by the differing modes at different times according to mood and circumstances . . . [or] multiple modes simultaneously" (67) (although it may be argued that children, the primary target reader, might access some modes more readily than others). This merging of modes is similarly displayed in this adaptation, which is achieved by intrinsically focalizing riders as Christopher Robin. While the ironic mode seems faint if not absent, the two other modes are relevant to the target audience of the attraction. Young children may indeed be amazed by the technical display and multimodal experience of a narrative, and appreciate this ride with childlike wonder, just like Christopher Robin, being ushered into an actualized story world. Adult riders, in turn, when focalized as Christopher Robin, are put into the perspective of a child, experiencing make-believe through a nostalgic lens. The adult experience coheres with the modus operandi of Disneyland, which seeks to create "immense nostalgia machines whose staging and specific attractions are generationally coded to strike a chord with the various age categories of its guests" (Project on Disney 1995, 10). With the malleable perspectives that the focalizer Christopher Robin allows, the mode of experience depends on the rider. Furthermore, the attraction here adds to the practice of focalization, echoing Bal's statement that for a reader, the focalizer determines the range of completeness of the image of a character (2009, 164). With intrinsic focalization, the audience itself is now positioned as the focalizer. In this situation, the understanding, or the completeness, of the character is determined by how familiar the focalizer-rider is with it—the character being Christopher Robin in this case. This is aptly described by Caracciolo's characterization of a spectrum of readers' engagement that fluctuates between "consciousness-attribution" and "consciousness-enactment" (2014, 110). These two strategies "overlap" in varying degrees, meaning that the narrative is experienced more in the first-person perspective (consciousness-enactment) when there is a high degree of overlapping between the rider's story-experience and the focalizing character, or more as the third-person (consciousness-attribution) if the overlapping of these two is low (Caracciolo 2014, 110). In an extreme case in which the rider completely dissociates the focalizer of the ride from the protagonist, this would be a case of consciousness-attribution. Characterization becomes limited, but then it allows for the indeterminacy that this figure, Christopher Robin, requires. On the other end, the ride can also be experienced through channeling the rider's prior understanding of Christopher Robin, leading to consciousness-enactment. The attraction, therefore, enables the multiple positions that Christopher Robin first inhabits in Milne's texts. Depending on whether he is understood as a character, a narratee, or the writer's son in the flesh, riders would subsequently be entering a world where his subject positioning would range from a place where he resides, that he creates, or that is created for him, to one where he simply encounters a fantasy world wholly dissociated from him. This experience would depend on how much guests' knowledge of Christopher Robin and their experience with the ride itself overlap.

On a contextual level, intrinsic focalization can have further implications when considering the site of reception. Opened in 2005 to attract more mainland Chinese tourists to the city, Hong Kong Disneyland (HKDL) was the first Disney theme park to be built in the Greater China area and remained the only one until Shanghai Disneyland opened in 2016. The theme park is a site for meaning-contention; Wing Yee Kimburley Choi asserts that it gives the Hong Kong government, in this joint venture with the Walt Disney Company, an opportunity to "re-narrativize the East-meets-West clichés" in the search for a "Hong Kong identity" (2007, 138). Choi's coincidental selection of the word suggests a useful frame of reference when considering how HKDL "narrates" a story of postcolonial Hong Kong. The territory differs from other postcolonial communities in the sense that it does not have a precolonial past; its identity comes from its colonial days. Hong Kong has long acted as "a translational space where Chinese-ness was interpreted for 'Westerners' and Western-ness was translated for Chinese," without an identity of its own (Louie 2010, 2). The postcolonial narrative that the Hong Kong government chose to build with HKDL, with it representing the "West," may be distilled down to a consumerist culture, enhancing Hong Kong's reputation as a shopper's paradise. Tourists enter the park to consume an "authentic" experience of Disney/Western culture, celebrating the magic of an alternative world. Reframing the discussion to *The Many Adventures of Winnie-the-Pooh*, it is understandable that Anthony Fung and Micky Lee argue that guests of the attraction in its HKDL incarnation may only "enjoy the form over the content" and summarize the experience as one for riders to be bedazzled by the display of technology (2009, 204). When this attraction, primarily American in origin and mediated through Disney's lens, is presented to park-goers of a mostly Chinese/East Asian demographic, a group understandably less familiar with Milne's text or the Disney animated movie, it can potentially have a foreignizing effect on them. Their reading of the attraction would tend more toward one of consciousness-attribution, as they fail to embody Christopher Robin. With the insistence on an "authentic" experience, the characters are already set in the context of a foreign culture, and the liberal use of narrative intrusion does not help with following a plot that riders might not be familiar with. This, however, does play to the advantage of HKDL, with such foreign but authentically Western experiences of the attraction serving its consumeristic intentions. By being immersed into the attraction world and impressed with this decidedly different experience, guests might more likely spend their money on merchandise at the shop after exiting the ride, achieving Disney's corporate aims.

A further consideration is how HKDL incorporates local elements into the otherwise westernized park. Glocalization—the synergy of both foreign and local elements in cultural contact—in HKDL is a topic of investigation for local scholars. Jonathan Matusitz believes that the park "illustrates that glocalization works" from a business perspective (2011, 677), and Kimburley Choi observes that "Disney's power is not absolute" in its management practices and allows room for a "reshaping of local culture and identity" in local actors' resistance to Disney's corporate politics (2012, 395). However, their work focuses mostly on the business practices of HKDL, neglecting the guests' core experience of the park—attractions. These embodied narratives have the potential to "bridge the ontological gap between reality and fiction"

(Caracciolo 2014, 161). With a focalizer (no matter whether embodied through consciousness-attribution or consciousness-enactment) that riders can project on as a stand-in as they experience this actual but fictional world, this virtual body allows them to be "detached from the here and now, and projected into another here and now" (Caracciolo 2014, 162). It gives room for the imagination of and immersion into an alternative world that riders may not have previously fathomed.

Returning to *The Many Adventures of Winnie-the-Pooh*, it can be argued that there are not many "local" elements present at all, and the attraction may serve more as a vessel to bring local urbanites into the Arcadian world of Disneyland. Nevertheless, this cultural exchange is present with far greater richness in newer attractions, interestingly in those featuring an intrinsically focalized narrative, displaying in more depth how HKDL can become a place where "Chinese-ness" is incorporated in the process of glocalization. Examples of this process are two Marvel-themed attractions, namely *Iron Man Experience*, completed in 2017, and *Ant-Man and the Wasp: Nano Battles*, opened in 2019. Both attractions intrinsically focalize riders as actors within their narratives, with the latter even giving participants active volition in picking which targets to hit with their laser guns. Local elements are called upon by the use of local actors speaking in Cantonese to interact with the Marvel superheroes, in backdrops of eminent local architecture. Both attractions provide immersive sites where elements of contrasting origins can come together. Along with this, when examined through narratological tools, they reveal the potential that intrinsically focalized narratives have in reshaping cultural contact by allowing the audience to embody a new perspective in an imaginary world where East meets West.

Thematic park rides and fantasy lands as emblematic as Disneyland are a prominent feature of current children's culture and thus a concern not to be dismissed by children's studies. While park rides are usually the object of research when exploring Disneyland's corporate strategies or consumerism, I posit that analyzing them through narratology has rife potential to offer insight into their relationship to audiences. Through an analysis of a specific case in HKDL, *The Many Adventures of Winnie-the-Pooh*, many interesting issues are raised regarding the subject positioning of its riders. I have posed how Christopher Robin's absence in this ride offers a deliberate void to be filled by participants. The affordance of the embodied narrative in play with the diegetic levels of the original work extends the diegetic means to the mimetic and aids in the immersion of the audience in an alternative world. This creates a range of subject positionings, which is further nuanced by the cultural context of this park ride, revealing thematic park rides as interesting sites of cultural negotiation.

Notes

1. The intricate details of the ride may also be a deliberate strategy of Disneyland to encourage return visits. As it is impossible to grasp the ride elements all at once, the audience (especially children) would want to revisit the ride for a more complete understanding.

Bibliography

Bal, Mieke. 2009. *Narratology: Introduction to the Theory of Narrative*. 3rd ed. Toronto: University of Toronto Press.

Caracciolo, Marco. 2014. *The Experientiality of Narrative: An Enactivist Approach*. Berlin: De Gruyter.

Carson, Charles. 2004. "'Whole New Worlds': Music and the Disney Theme Park Experience." *Ethnomusicology Forum* 13, no. 2 (November): 228–35.

Choi, Kimburley. 2012. "Disneyfication and Localization: The Cultural Globalisation Process of Hong Kong Disneyland." *Urban Studies* 49, no. 2 (February): 383–97.

Choi, Wing Yee Kimburley. 2007. "Remade in Hong Kong: How Hong Kong People Use Hong Kong Disneyland." Doctor's thesis, Lingnan University, Hong Kong.

Forster, Marc, dir. 2018. *Christopher Robin*. Walt Disney Pictures.

Fung, Anthony, and Micky Lee. 2009. "Localizing a Global Amusement Park: Hong Kong Disneyland." *Continuum* 23, no. 2 (April): 197–208.

Genette, Gérard. 1980. *Narrative Discourse: An Essay in Method*. Ithaca, NY: Cornell University Press.

Genette, Gérard. 1988. *Narrative Discourse Revisited*. Ithaca, NY: Cornell University Press.

Gostand, Reba. 1980. "Verbal and Non-Verbal Communication: Drama as Translation." In *The Languages of Theatre: Problems in the Translation and Transposition of Drama*, edited by Ortrun Zuber-Skerritt, 1–9. Oxford: Pergamon.

Green, Melanie C., Timothy C. Brock, and Geoff F. Kaufman. 2004. "Understanding Media Enjoyment: The Role of Transportation into Narrative Worlds." *Communication Theory* 14, no. 4 (November): 311–27.

Grünbaum, Thor. 2013. "Sensory Imagination and Narrative Perspective: Explaining Perceptual Focalization." *Semiotica* 2013, no. 194 (January): 111–36.

Hemmings, Robert. 2007. "A Taste of Nostalgia: Children's Books from the Golden Age— Carroll, Grahame, and Milne." *Children's Literature* 35, no. 1 (January): 54–79.

Herman, David. 2009. "Narrative Ways of Worldmaking." In *Narratology in the Age of Cross-Disciplinary Narrative Research*, edited by Sandra Heinen and Roy Sommer, 71–87. Berlin: De Gruyter.

Hong Kong Disneyland. n.d. "The Many Adventures of Winnie the Pooh." https://www
.hongkongdisneyland.com/attractions/many-adventures-of-winnie-the-pooh/. Accessed
June 10, 2019.

Hunt, Peter. 1992. "Winnie-the-Pooh and Domestic Fantasy." In *Stories and Society:
Children's Literature in Its Social Context*, edited by Dennis Butts, 112–24. London:
Palgrave Macmillan.

Louie, Kam. 2010. *Hong Kong Culture: Word and Image*. Hong Kong: Hong Kong
University Press.

Lurie, Alison. 1973. "Back to Pooh Corner." *Children's Literature* 2: 11–17.

Martin, Wallace. 1986. *Recent Theories of Narrative*. Ithaca, NY: Cornell University Press.

Matusitz, Jonathan. 2011. "Disney's Successful Adaptation in Hong Kong: A Glocalization
Perspective." *Asia Pacific Journal of Management* 28, no. 4 (December): 667–81.

Milne, A. A. (1926) 2016. *Winnie-the-Pooh*. London: Egmont UK.

Milne, A. A. (1928) 2016. *The House at Pooh Corner*. London: Egmont UK.

Nance-Carroll, Niall. 2015. "Not Only, But Also: Entwined Modes and the Fantastic in
A. A. Milne's Pooh Stories." *Lion and the Unicorn* 39, no. 1 (January): 63–81.

Nikolajeva, Maria. 2014. *Reading for Learning: Cognitive Approaches to Children's
Literature*. Amsterdam: John Benjamins.

Project on Disney. 1995. *Inside the Mouse: Work and Play at Disney World*. Durham, NC:
Duke University Press.

Reitherman, Wolfgang, and John Lounsbery, dirs. 1977. *The Many Adventures of Winnie the
Pooh*. Walt Disney Productions.

Sale, Roger. 1972. "Child Reading and Man Reading: Oz, Babar, and Pooh." *Children's
Literature* 1, no. 1: 162–72.

Tremper, Ellen. 1977. "Instigating Winnie the Pooh." *Lion and the Unicorn* 1, no. 1: 33–46.

Wall, Barbara. 1991. *The Narrator's Voice: The Dilemma of Children's Fiction*. London:
Palgrave Macmillan.

Zipes, Jack. 1991. *Fairy Tales and the Art of Subversion: The Classical Genre for Children and
the Process of Civilization*. London: Routledge.

CHAPTER 6

Bringing Winnie Home
The World of Pooh in a Canadian Context

Megan De Roover

When you think of Winnie-the-Pooh, you may very well imagine the iconic
scruffy beige bear as illustrated by E. H. Shepard. Or perhaps your mind
conjures the additional red shirt, as depicted by Disney. Certainly the yellow bear with his hand perpetually in a pot marked "hunny" has a global
following, but maybe, just maybe, when you think of Winnie you might
think of something rather different: a sweet, gentle black bear with her
paws in a brown paper bag hunting for oranges, hugging the leg of a dash-
ing Canadian soldier.

At the outbreak of the First World War, Lieutenant Harry Colebourn was
en route to Quebec with the Canadian Army Veterinary Corps, the last staging
area before being sent to England. When the train stopped at White River,
a small town in northwestern Ontario between Thunder Bay and Sault Ste.
Marie, a small orphaned bear tied to the armrest of a bench caught his eye.
Val Shushkewich, author of *The Real Winnie: A One-of-a-Kind Bear*, explains
that Colebourn's journal entry for that fateful day read: "August 24, 1914.
Left Port Arthur 7A. In train all day. Bought bear. $20" (2003, 8). Colebourn
named the female cub Winnipeg-Bear, after the Canadian city he had settled
in. Winnipeg-Bear, or Winnie for short, became the official mascot of the

Second Canadian Infantry Brigade, sleeping under Colebourn's cot, following around soldiers, and playing games. As she grew,

> her playful, accepting nature and willingness to please were apparent to the men, and her constantly gentle nature was especially endearing. Her presence helped take their minds off their ongoing soggy circumstances and off the prospect of the conflict to come. Group photographs frequently included Winnie, front and centre, a position of honour. (Shushkewich 2003, 21–22)

When dispatched to Salisbury Plain on the SS *Manitou*, Winnie traveled with the brigade across the Atlantic to England. The brigade's departure to the front lines was imminent, but there was no place for a bear. Records show that Colebourn managed to get the use of a car to sneak Winnie into London and arrange for her keeping at London Zoo (Shushkewich 2003, 26). This way, the bear who had lifted the spirits of soldiers bound for war would remain safe and cared for while her caretakers faced uncertain odds in Europe. According to Shushkewich: "Winnie was the first of six black bear cubs presented to the London Zoo by various contingents of the Canadian forces during the beginning of the First World War. However, only Harry Colebourn's Winnie seems to stand out" (30–31). Despite the fact that he was stationed close to the front lines in mainland Europe, Colebourn was able to visit Winnie throughout the war, and he expressed on several occasions his intention to eventually return the bear to Canada. However, by 1919 Winnie had become so beloved by zoogoers that Colebourn was convinced to officially donate her. A permanent attraction at the zoo, she would continue to enjoy the affection, treats, and "Winnie's cocktails" (condensed milk and syrup) she had become accustomed to, until her death in 1934.

While Winnie had many adult and child visitors at London Zoo, Alan Milne contributed most directly to the bear's fame, as he and his four-year-old son Christopher were frequent visitors. Milne describes their visits in the introduction to *The World of Pooh*:

> So when Christopher Robin goes to the Zoo, he goes to where the Polar Bears are, and he whispers something to the third keeper from the left, and doors are unlocked, and we wander through dark passages and up steep stairs, until at last we come to the special cage, and the cage is opened, and out trots something brown and furry, and with a happy cry of "Oh, Bear!" Christopher

Robin rushes into its arms. Now this bear's name is Winnie, which shows what
a good name for bears it is. (Milne 1958, 13–14)

Winnie's gentle and playful nature set her apart from the many other charismatic bears at the zoo. The polar bear enclosure near Winnie, for example,
included the well-known Sam, who had a habit of stealing umbrellas by
placing a fish on an upper ledge of his enclosure and "whining piteously . . .
pretending the fish was beyond his reach" (Shushkewich 2003, 50). Well-
meaning visitors who tried to help knock the fish from the ledge would
soon contribute to the "collection of mutilated umbrellas at the bottom
of his pond" (Shushkewich 2003, 50). But as impressive, charismatic, and
exotic as Sam may have been, Winnie stood out because of her unparal-
leled gentleness. A major feature of her appeal for visitors was the fact that
children (including Christopher Milne) could enter the bear enclosure to
play with her, ride on her back, and feed her cocktails. Given the surrounding context of more dangerous bears, this thrilling but safe way of engaging
with bears was highly sought out and made Winnie famous in London even
prior to Milne's stories.

From their Canadian origins, stories of Christopher Robin and Winnie-
the-Pooh have left an indelible mark on the global landscape of children's
literature. To reclaim Winnie's historical roots, several Canadian books and
films have told her story. Shushkewich offers historical insights about the
legacies of the bear as well as practical information and primary materials (as
cited earlier), whereas Mia Sokoloski's children's book *The Romance of the
Captain and Winnie the Bear* (1992) tells the story of the little black bear's
adventures from northern Ontario to England in verse. A 2004 television
drama by John Kent Harrison, *A Bear Named Winnie*, likewise tells the
story of Winnie's adventures, starring Michael Fassbender, David Suchet,
and Stephen Fry, although the film avoids any mention of Winnie-the-
Pooh to avoid copyright infringement. The award-winning *Finding Winnie*
by Lindsay Mattick in 2015 is perhaps the best-known story of Winnie's
origins published outside of Canada, in part due to the author being the
great-granddaughter of Harry Colebourn. Elsewhere in this collection,
Donna Varga analyzes Mattick's depiction of Winnie (in *Finding Winnie*
and its 2018 sequel, coauthored with Josh Greenhut, *Winnie's Great War*)
as being teddy-bear- or toy-like, more akin to Winnie-the-Pooh than to the

historical animal. Even the most popular depictions of the "real" Winnie, then, enter the realm of fantasy.

Milne's books have strongly contributed to a tradition that transforms bears into toys, producing a sociocultural understanding of bears as safe/fun/cuddly (in effect, not bear-like at all). Because of this positioning, real bears are by proxy either themselves transformed into toys or vilified for being "too dangerous." Real bears are forced to occupy a liminal space where their animal nature and their cultural use oppose one another unless, like Winnie, they happen to have an ideal demeanor. The juxtaposition between bears as toys/friends and bears as military symbols is one such example that richly illustrates the complexity of Winnie-the-Pooh's origins. Transforming an animal as dangerous as a bear into a cuddly toy occurs figuratively in Milne's encounters with Winnie the bear at London Zoo, and literally in his rendition of Winnie as Pooh in the books. Similarly, themes of exploration and hunting are transformed into fun and imaginative childhood pastimes in the world of story, while such outside the Hundred Acre Wood are dangerous activities with serious consequences.

An emphasis on the live bear to reclaim a part of the story—now internationally famous—presents its own problems in interpretation. While the iconic bear of biography and fiction shares a name with the black bear at London Zoo, the stories themselves in *The World of Pooh* are more in keeping with child's play than the historical events. And yet, in claiming the origins of Winnie in Canada, there is a subsequent claiming of the stories as well. In a Canadian context, the stories take on new layers that contribute to the national imaginary while simultaneously complicating the relationship between Canada and the natural world. *The World of Pooh* in a Canadian context of the "real" Winnie introduces contradictory themes of peace and safety in a time of war, protection and control over imaginary and real animals, and relationships with the natural world based on either conquest or stewardship. Reconciling these contradictions is the task of understanding Winnie in Canada—particularly in those cities that have laid claim to the origins of Winnie, Winnipeg and White River—and unpacking the different paths forward presented by Winnie the bear versus Winnie-the-Pooh in Canadian-bear interactions. Understanding the real bear and the circumstances that led to Milne's text exposes a longer, richer history of attitudes and engagements with bears in Canada—one that has helped shape the popularity of Pooh even if it is a history that is largely unknown.

Bears and Canadian Nationalism

Of all Milne's stories in *The World of Pooh*, the most obviously connected to a Canadian imaginary is "In Which Christopher Robin Leads an Expotition to the North Pole." It is no surprise that imaginaries of "the North" are deeply entwined with Canadian identity, given that one of the most common self-descriptors of the country, arising from its national anthem, is the "True North." The North, and even to some degree the North Pole, is just specific and ambiguous enough to always be displaced. The imaginary/imagery of "the North" hints at locations anywhere from boreal forest to tundra to ice floe, just so long as those places offer an illusion of being sparsely populated and ruggedly challenging. The most important part of a story set in such a landscape is the perseverance of the individuals exploring it.

> At the turn of the twentieth century, expeditions to the North and South Poles were big news and people had fantastical ideas about the kinds of worlds at the poles.... These expeditions took unbelievable fortitude. A certain type of person was primed for the hardships and courage required for them. (Aalto 2015, 140)

Nationalism based on the idea of surviving an inhospitable northern terrain developed in North America out of a long march of colonial narratives. It became a very popular theme in international narrativization during the modern age of Arctic exploration, which largely transpired from the early 1800s to the mid-1900s (Kolbert 2007). In many famously publicized accounts by John F. Franklin and others, the Arctic offered the imminent threats of freezing, starvation, and entrapment while simultaneously being noted for its beauty, wonder, and potentially valuable resources. As Geneviève King Ruel argues in her article "The (Arctic) Show Must Go On" (2011), the general representation of the Arctic in media "stress[es] the sense of northernness as a central aspect of Canadian identity"; it "leav[es] Canadian citizens with the idea that the Arctic is entirely theirs, that it contains unimaginable riches, and that its territory is under threat" (829–30, 826). Within these narratives lies a contradictory sentimentalization that both idealizes and demonizes the region and its inhabitants, constructing hierarchies of ownership and control and justifying acts of conquest as well as stewardship. This rhetoric of the expedition is indicative of most colonial ideologies, but in the context of Arctic exploration, narrative functioned as a tactical strategy for convincing readers back home to send much-needed funds to support continuing expeditions. When the narrator or protagonist conquers these amazing odds, as disseminated to the public through narrative accounts, themes of pride and sovereignty become abundant in the writing and in the audience response.

A gun, provisions, an ambush, a rescue, a hero, and proof of discovery—the "expotition" to the North Pole in *The World of Pooh* has every glamorous element of polar expeditions to rival those of Richard Byrd or Robert Peary, with none of the gruesome details that often accompanied such adventures such as scurvy, starvation, and hypothermia. Instead, the fantasy of exploration occurs in a friendly and safe world: the gun is never used, the provisions are eaten in one sitting, the ambush is transformed into a gorse-bush, Roo swims happily in the river, and Pooh's heroism and discovery of a large pole are amusingly delightful. Johan Huizinga's theory of play exemplifies the mechanics of this tamed version of an expedition, as for him, "all play is a voluntary activity" (1970, 7), "distinct from 'ordinary' life both as to locality and duration" (9). Moreover, play "is 'played out' within certain limits of time and place," which "are temporary worlds within the ordinary world" (9, 10). In this manner, the Hundred Acre Wood is the realm of play for Christopher Robin, who exists in the real world, while the games, such as the "expotition," conjure imaginary play worlds for the characters who exist within the Hundred Acre Wood. The elements of reality may be essential to the play narrative, but the distinction is that those elements are contained and voluntary, and pose no real threat.

The narrative of Arctic conquest is strikingly at odds with that of the fun and friendly "expotition" by Christopher Robin and company, even though the latter emerges from the historical narrative. Similarly, the idea of conquering the North and its wild inhabitants is at odds with the relationship between humans and nature as constructed by the Colebourn and Winnie story. I argue that in many ways, the historical Winnie story in Canada conjures that same "temporary world" away from the horrors of war that is ever present in Milne's Hundred Acre Wood. In the historical story, man and bear can coexist in a manner that reflects a stewardship model of interacting with nature rather than the conquest model implied by a colonizing attitude toward the North. Jennifer Welchman, a Canadian philosopher, offers a historical examination of attitudes toward stewardship and puts forward a new definition that provides a "promising way of construing morally decent conduct towards the environment" (2012, 297), which reflects more readily the attitudes being supported in the Canadian adoption of the Winnie narrative. Her definition, which challenges existing ideas of stewardship in environmental studies, is as follows:

> Environmental stewardship is the responsible management of human activity affecting the natural environment to ensure the conservation and preservation of natural resources and values for the sake of future generations of human and other life on the planet, with the acceptance of significant answerability for one's conduct to society. (303)

Welchman presents stewardship as an environmentally friendly model rooted in guardianship, emerging from similar historical origins as those of the conquest of the natural world.

At the time of Milne's publication of *The World of Pooh*, the golden era of Arctic exploration had been overshadowed by the First World War. In creating the settings and stories in *The World of Pooh*, "Milne created a fantasy world around his son and his toy bear, named for Colebourn's beloved pet. In a traumatized post-war era, this imagined, safe world commanded legions of fans" (Gammel and Addleman-Frankel 2018). Not only a safe world, but safe inhabitants of that world, where bears and tigers are friendly rather than fearsome animals. To transplant that safe world into a Canadian context that holds this imaginary as a very real part of the national identity conflates the real with the fictional. The safety of the Hundred Acre Wood offers Christopher Robin and the other characters the possibility of playing at games of northern discovery and adventure without ever entering the realm of dangerous consequences. Similarly, the narrative relationship between Colebourn and Winnie presents the traumatized postwar readership with a safe relationship between us and them, the human and the other, which emphasizes values of responsibility (Colebourn), gentleness (Winnie), and kindness to each other.

In a Canadian context, it is nearly impossible to discuss northern expeditions (or "expotitions") and bears without evoking that enduring symbol of the North, the polar bear—a "fierce animal" by all accounts. Churchill, Manitoba, situated on the western shore of Hudson Bay and dubbed the "polar bear capital of the world," has developed a vibrant tourism industry built precisely around its access to polar bears and other "northern" elements such as the aurora borealis and beluga whales. While the North Pole itself is nowhere close to Churchill, the town does offer many of the same elements of northern exploration and capitalizes on them: "Located on the edge of the

Arctic, Churchill offers the feel of a frontier town with the amenities of an international tourist destination" (Travel Manitoba 2014). Modern tourists can, like Christopher Robin and his friends, play at northern exploration in a relatively safe context. The bear connection is absolute and ubiquitous: "Polar bears are everywhere—on murals, signs, souvenirs, and sculptures—and the live version occasionally wanders into town as well!" (Travel Manitoba 2014). Una Chaudhuri, an animal studies and ecocritical studies scholar, explains that "by ceaselessly troping [the animal] and rendering it a metaphor for humanity, modernity erases the animal even as it makes it discursively ubiquitous" (2003, 648). The overwhelming symbolic presence of the polar bear in Churchill in many ways diminished its otherness, its animalness, into a kind of game for the "expotition" experience. One of Churchill's unique facilities is known as the Polar Bear Jail, where nuisance bears are "incarcerated" before being released far away from the town. When orphaned bear cubs are found, however, they are transferred to the Leatherdale International Polar Bear Conservation Center, located at Assiniboine Park Zoo in Winnipeg, a stone's throw away from the Winnie the Bear statue, which celebrates the famous orphaned black bear. It may have been a century since Lieutenant Colebourn rescued the orphaned Winnie from a railway station in northwestern Ontario, but the city of Winnipeg is maintaining Colebourn's legacy by rescuing orphaned cubs from certain death and transforming them into ambassadors of the Canadian North (Assiniboine Park Conservancy 2018). As it transforms these bear cubs into a metaphor of Canada, the impact of Milne's legacy is fundamentally about caring for the other and creating a safe space in the face of traumatic experience, whether that is war or climate change.

Rescuing or adopting bear cubs has been a long-standing practice in Canada; as noted by several sources, including Val Shushkewich, Canadians have had something of a habit of adopting wild animals as mascots, from coyotes to beavers to bears. According to Mike Commito and Ben Bradley in an article for the website Canada's History Society, Winnie's exceptional story is, in many ways, a familiar one. Across the country bears were kept as pets, mascots, and attractions into the twentieth century, albeit few gained as much popularity as Winnie. In the Canadian military, photographic evidence of at least two fully grown black bears living with various Canadian regiments during World War I is archived at the Prince Albert Historical Museum in Prince Albert, Saskatchewan (Nault 2011). Outside of the military, eager to attract customers or tourists, some entrepreneurs featured bears at roadside stops in a practice that was wildly successful even as it was dangerous, only beginning "a gradual decline in the 1950s, as Canadians recognized the dangers and liabilities of displaying these animals" (Commito and Bradley 2017). Even with the changes in attitude that Commito and Bradley identify, the desire to see and interact with bears as "roadside attractions" lingers, with enthusiastic campers trespassing into provincial and national park garbage dumps in hopes of glimpsing the bears that frequent them: "[A]lthough the practice of ordinary Canadians keeping bears as pets and mascots has fallen by the wayside, what lives on is the public's desire to observe bears—in the wild, beside a highway, in zoos and wildlife parks, on the printed page, and online" (Commito and Bradley 2017). Continuing today, the official Canadian army mascot is a cartoon polar bear named Juno, departing from the originally popular black bears who were "recruited" into the army due to their availability in the region and more manageable size. The polar bear, in this context, is transformed into a safe, engaging character in much the same way that Winnie the bear was transformed into Winnie the Pooh. Some power and strength remain, but the more dangerous aspects of a polar bear's animal nature are diminished in the service of the story the Canadian army seeks to tell. As Chaudhuri identifies: "Not only do we exploit animals as beasts of burden and subjects of scientific experimentation . . . we have also made them creatures of somatization, forcing them to carry our symbolic and psychological baggage. As pets, as performers, and as literary symbols, animals are forced to perform us—our fantasies and fears, our questions and quarrels, our hopes and horrors" (2003, 648). And whether it is through polar bears or Winnie, nowhere is this performance clearer than in their use to promote nationhood.

In the context of the Canadian military, polar bears evoke an iconic imaginary of Canadian northernness more readily than black bears like Winnie. In a media release, Brigadier General David Patterson explains:

> Why choose a polar bear as a mascot for the Canadian army? Polar bears are brave, strong, resilient, tenacious, agile, and more than capable of defending themselves, just like our Canadian soldiers. The polar bear is also an enduring symbol of our North, strong and free, as is our Canadian army. (Patterson 2016)

After the popularity of the cartoon mascot took off, the character of Juno was intentionally attached to a live polar bear by the Canadian army, in much the same way that the famous American Smokey Bear (or Smokey the Bear) cartoon mascot, created for fire safety programming, was later associated with a living bear. Smokey Bear began featuring in posters and advertisements for fire prevention in 1944, after the forest service lost the rights to use characters from Walt Disney's animated film *Bambi*. In 1950, after a wildfire burned seventeen thousand acres of Lincoln National Forest in New Mexico, a game warden rescued an injured black bear cub and later renamed him after the mascot. Smokey Bear was moved to the National Zoo in Washington, DC, where he became a public icon, receiving his own ZIP code from the US postal service due to the sheer volume of letters and pots of honey mailed to him (US Forest Service 2018). Similarly, Juno—a costumed cartoon bear created in 2003—was attached to a young polar bear at Toronto Zoo in a ceremony in 2016. Juno, fortuitously born at Toronto Zoo on Remembrance Day (November 11) in 2015, was named after "the hundreds of Canadian soldiers who were killed or wounded during the 1944 allied storming of Juno Beach on D-Day" (Lockie 2016). At five months old, Juno was adopted into the Canadian army and immediately promoted to the rank of private. In 2017, the Canadian army "deployed" Juno to Assiniboine Park Zoo in Winnipeg for "Operation SOCIALIZATION" to allow her to interact with other polar bears and transition to adulthood (Canadian Army 2017). The recurring theme of the (often) orphaned bear standing in as a symbol for safety, friendship, bravery, or nationhood in a context of war is evidently popular, as Juno is not the first bear to hold an official army rank, although perhaps she is the first polar bear. Another bear, Wojtek, led a very similar life to Winnie the bear, albeit during the Second rather than the First World War. Like Winnie, Wojtek was adopted as an orphaned bear cub at a railway station (by the Polish II Corps); he was raised in the Poles' camps as they traveled to Italy for combat, nursed with "condensed milk in a vodka bottle," and "treated . . . like a baby, perhaps because [the soldiers'] own families had been torn apart" (Waxman 2017). Unlike Winnie, who spent World War I safe and comfortable at London Zoo, Wojtek served during World War II as an enlisted solider and saw active duty in Italy, contributing by moving heavy ammunition. After the war, he lived out the rest of his life on a farm in Scotland, as his caretakers "didn't want him to go back to Poland because they were afraid that the fledgling Soviet-controlled government would adopt the bear as a symbol for communism" (Waxman 2017). Winnie and Wojtek both served as morale boosters in their respective wars, and later as important symbols for their countries of origin—a legacy that continues today with Juno's participation in the Canadian army. Where Winnie was beloved by children and fed sweets by eager visitors, Wojtek was beloved by soldiers and veterans, who would visit and feed him cigarettes and beer—habits he picked up from his army days. For Canadian audiences, bears and the military are linked. Juno will very likely never see battle like Wojtek did, but a bear standing in for the military evokes an imaginary that goes back a century to when Canadians were experimenting with wild mascots and bears in captivity—the same experimentation that led directly to Winnie being tamed and brought to London Zoo. Featuring bears as mascots contributes to an overall performance of Canadian identity as one that can literally "tame" the symbols of the North.

However, the act of reclaiming Winnie in Canada presents a central problem: the conflation between the historical bear and the fictional one. The two bears, literal and fictional, are usually held apart from one another (consider Harrison's *A Bear Named Winnie*, which strictly avoids any crossover references), but in places like Winnipeg and White River, the conflation of the two presents curious possibilities. The Pooh connection, which these Canadian towns have worked hard to cement, introduces a complicated synthesis of the real and the imaginary. If Winnie has indeed "come home" to Canada through the celebration of Winnie's origins, how do the stories of a friendly toy bear set in an idyllic English wood resonate in a hundred acres (or more) of boreal forest where black bears are often deemed dangerous and hunting them is a popular pastime?

Winnie: A Black Bear in Manitoba and a Yellow Bear in Ontario

Winnipeg, Manitoba, has made strides to explicitly celebrate its connection both to Harry Colebourn and the bear he named after his adopted hometown. In 1992, a larger-than-life "Winnie-the-Bear" was sculpted by William Epp and dedicated to the "children of the world" on the accompanying plaque. Located in Assiniboine Park on the west side of Winnipeg, the sculpture features the lieutenant standing hand in paw with a small black bear cub. To further commemorate the connection between Winnipeg and Winnie-the-Pooh, an exhibition presenting the story of "Colebourn's adoption, transportation, and donation to the London Zoo of a Canadian female black bear that would later inspire a literary icon" (Gammel and Addleman-Frankel 2018) is featured at Assiniboine Park to mark the centenary of the adoption. The curated story is told through Colebourn's personal photographs, journals, and more. Curators Irene Gammel and Kate Addleman-Frankel explain: "Torn and stained from age and use, inscribed with names and dates, these image-objects embody a story that belongs equally to Canadian culture and to global literature at the centenary of the Great War" (2018). Photos and descriptions of a female Canadian black bear celebrate a Canadian narrative of taking responsibility and caring for others while presenting the real Winnie as a counterpart to the "Silly old Bear" (Milne 1958, 43) who has enchanted the world over. The fact that Winnie is a Canadian bear icon and *not* a polar bear demonstrates a commitment to the historical accuracy of the story and to a stewardship of nature that values both charismatic polar bears and common black bears.

While Winnipeg's claims to the Winnie-the-Pooh origins and legacy are obvious given Winnie's name, another Canadian town has also staked a claim: the town of White River, where Winnipeg-Bear was originally purchased by Harry Colebourn. A great deal of misunderstanding initially arose from the new claim for Winnie's hometown, due to the bear's name. In a 1987 Canadian Broadcasting Corporation (CBC) television interview, Fred Colebourn, Harry's son, cleared up the confusion when he explained to host Peter Downie the origins of the bear as he knew the story from his father.

> Downie: Now Winnipeg the bear was really an Ontario bear. Didn't your dad
>   get him in White River?
> Colebourn: That's true. Yes, he did, and he picked him up on his way overseas
>   from Winnipeg. He stopped over in White River and by some means or
>   other he ran into the hunter who had killed the mother, and he made a deal
>   with him. For $20 he took the cub, Winnie.
> Downie: 'Cause White-the-Pooh doesn't have the same ring, does it? (CBC 1987)

After the interview aired nationwide, the confirmation that Winnie had been originally purchased from the town's train station began a transformative journey for White River. As a town of only six hundred people, the discovery of such a globally resonant connection immediately launched a push for tourism to the northern community. Interestingly, unlike Winnipeg's focus on the historical bear, White River made the connection with Disney a priority. They lost no time in making White River a visible destination for Winnie-the-Pooh aficionados, including installing a large statue of the Disney bear and opening a museum of Winnie-the-Pooh artifacts. White River also hosts an annual festival in honor of the bear. As explained in the twenty-ninth annual Winnie's Hometown Festival brochure:

> In 1988, some local residents discovered that Winnie the Pooh [*sic*] is originally from White River, and White River proudly proclaims its status as the birthplace of Winnie the Pooh by celebrating with Winnie's Hometown Festival held the third weekend in August every year. (White River Township 2017)

Festival events include rural Canadian activities such as riding lawnmower races, fireworks, a slow-pitch tournament, a parade (with prizes given to "oldest, youngest, cutest, best PJs, Most bears, & Most Canadian"), and a fishing derby. The community also lost no time in asserting its role in the Winnie story internationally.

> The White River Grade Eight Class also went to the London Zoo in 1997 to present another plaque detailing White River's part in Winnie's history. A copy of this plaque is on display at the White River Visitor's Centre. (White River Township 2018)

The distinction between Winnipeg's and White River's celebrations of Winnie is seen in the statues featured at each location. In Assiniboine Park, the Winnie-the-Bear statue presents a handsome Lieutenant Colebourn holding the paw of a small black bear cub and feeding her from a bottle, honoring both the original bear who sparked Milne's stories and those serving in the Canadian army during the Great War. In White River, the statue takes a decidedly different approach, featuring instead the Disney interpretation of the Winnie-the-Pooh character—bright yellow, a red shirt—perched in a tree and holding a pot of "hunny." Even though White River is the "hometown" of the live bear, the advertising, imagery, and focal points all circle around the fictional storybook bear rather than the black bear cub and soldier whom Winnipeg celebrates.

Part of this incongruity between these different portrayals of the same bear emerges from the contemporary relationship between Canadians and black bears. There is an evident tension between conquest and stewardship that comes into play when examining the Canadian relationship with bears, which plays out in Ontario particularly, where the black bear is thoroughly entangled with the history of and shifting attitudes toward hunting. Ontario's cancellation

and then reinstatement of the spring bear hunt is a prime example of this relationship between bears, hunting, tourism, and public sentiment. In 1999, the
provincial government issued an indefinite cancellation of the bear hunt after
reports of orphaned bear cubs led to a public relations disaster (Robinson
2015). The Ministry of Natural Resources "estimated that at least 274 cubs
were orphaned in the . . . spring bear hunt in 1999" with "almost no chance of
survival" (Ontario Spring Bear Hunt n.d.). In 2015, the controversial spring
bear hunt was reinstated in a pilot program that redesigned the hunt with the
intent of reducing the number of "nuisance bears" (bears that disturb human
settlements). Rules were instated to prevent the killing of female bears and
avoid the creation of abandoned litters, although the effectiveness of such rules
in action were (and remain) questionable.[1] The tension between Canadians and
black bears has introduced an attitude toward bears focused on control and
conquest, very unlike that of Colebourn and Winnie and yet in keeping with
the Canadian mentality of being in control of "the North." As White River
has discovered perhaps unintentionally, the easiest way to maintain the public
perception that Canadians love and protect bears while completely avoiding
the issue of contentious black bear hunts is to change the bear from black to
yellow and emphasize the storybook Winnie-the-Pooh over the historical bear.

The color change between the real bear and Disney's interpretation is significant in the White River context because it leads the story of Winnie away
from a context that has to regularly negotiate real black bears and merges
the area's history with the anthropomorphic character of Pooh. Changing
Winnie's color removes a cultural specificity that, while not necessarily iconi-
cally Canadian, is familiar and real in Canadian contexts. Trading a black bear
for a beige or yellow bear inadvertently makes it easier to reconcile the spring
bear hunt to the ethos of stewardship evoked by Winnie's story, without being
confronted with the obvious contradiction in values. The approval and reinstatement of the spring bear hunt is strikingly at odds with the narrative of
the veterinarian soldier buying and caring for a bear cub (from a hunter who
had evidently shot the mother), which has been adopted nationally (particularly in Winnipeg) as an act that exemplifies Canadian values. It is important
to note that while the spring bear hunt came under considerable scrutiny in
Ontario and gave the region a negative reputation with regard to the treatment
of bears when it was eventually reinstated, the province was far from alone in
its policy, as the spring bear hunt was never canceled in adjoining provinces
Manitoba and Quebec.

In an article titled "The History of People and Black Bears in Ontario" (2012), Michael Commito reminds his readers that "[b]lack bears do not play a pertinent role in our ecosystem. We choose to coexist with them because they feed our minds, bodies, and souls. We name our airlines and our sports teams after them; they drive our imagination." Commito goes on to quote bear expert Stephen Herrera, saying: "[T]he decisions about how we will manage bears depends on our attitudes and values related to bears." While the popularity of bears as promotional devices has shifted during the past hundred years from black bears to polar bears (as can be seen by the Canadian military mascot), it appears that Canadian attitudes toward black bears remain contentious. Interestingly enough, it is through the adoption of the Winnie story as a Canadian narrative (and as indicative of Canadian values) that a way forward may be found in the issue of bear stewardship.

Neil Macdonald, a reporter for the CBC, explains that "there are precious few notions that can accurately be described as universally held Canadian values or principles, no matter what our politicians tell us" (Macdonald 2016). However, Canadians are encouraged to celebrate their citizenship by valuing their rights and freedoms and accepting the responsibilities they entail, including obeying the law, voting, serving on a jury, and

> [h]elping others in the community—millions of volunteers freely donate their time to help others without pay—helping people in need, assisting at your child's school, volunteering at a food bank or other charity, or encouraging newcomers to integrate. (Government of Canada 2016)

Lieutenant Colebourn's treatment of the orphaned Winnie exemplifies this sense of responsibility and community. Not only did he assist in the survival of the bear by purchasing her and taking her with him, he took responsibility for protecting her during the war by finding a way to keep her at London Zoo, and then, when confronted with the fact that Winnie had become an important feature bringing joy to the recovering city, he changed his plans to relocate her to Canada. Through Colebourn's efforts, Winnie benefited the many communities around her, from soldiers to children, and, with the reclaiming of Winnie in Canadian contexts, the bear inspires a sense of Canadian patriotism surrounding both bears and Milne's stories. The figure of the soldier dancing with a bear cub models the ideal stewardship, in which the veterinarian takes responsibility for the abandoned black bear cub, thus bettering society first by integrating the bear in the regiment, then by benefiting children in postwar London, and finally, worldwide, through the iconic story of Winnie-the-Pooh. As Commito and Bradley argue: "[T]he ways Canadians used bears as companion animals, promotional devices, and tourist attractions reveal how values and premiums placed on wildlife have changed over time," specifically as "Canadians no longer think of bears as viable candidates for captivity as pets or attractions; most believe their rightful place is in the wilderness, sometimes with protective measures" (2017).

While a Canadian contextualization seems necessary to the origin story of the Winnie figure—and certainly the launching point for the reclamation projects of Winnipeg and White River—transposing the stories to a Canadian landscape by "bringing Winnie home" presents problems in interpretation. If we are to "bring Winnie home," as advertisements for White River's home-town festival suggest, the full consequences of what it means to transplant a story must be negotiated. The real bear and the fictional bear begin to occupy the same space, but the worlds are, to a certain degree, incompatible. The play world offers respite from the Great War in an idyllic pastoral setting. The Canadian boreal forest offers, perhaps no Heffalumps and Woozles, but certainly other animals and elemental dangers—in particular, bears themselves. From this incompatibility emerges a better understanding of the contradictions in Canadian contexts when it comes to the relationship with bears and the natural world, for instance the parallel histories of adopting bear cubs for mascots and promoting the spring bear hunt.

Winnie was never brought back to Canada during her lifetime. If Colebourn had followed through with his plans to relocate her to his home in Manitoba, the landscape of children's literature might very well be unrecognizable. Likewise, the many bearish celebrations in the various Canadian hometowns would be transformed. Bringing Winnie home plays out a fantasy of reclamation, not just of the black bear Colebourn adopted but of the literature, films, and industry she inspired. Through the adoption of Winnie's Canadian origins in places like Winnipeg, there is an increased visibility of bears as symbols and metaphors, which can lead to the protection of bears (as proved through Manitoba's Polar Bear Protection Act) and a celebration of moments of kindness in contexts of war and hostility. Celebrating Winnie's Canadian origins doesn't just leverage a Canadian viewpoint on a global business, it offers a common ground for Canadians to see themselves reflected in the stories of two generous and kindly bears, Winnie and Pooh, while taking on the role of Colebourn to assume responsibility and care for the other. There is a national readiness to once again adopt a bear, but perhaps some reflection on which Winnie—yellow or black—is the best bear to represent Canada is in order.

Notes

1. Killing breeding bears during their most vulnerable time of the year in the interior does not significantly impact those bears who frequent human-inhabited areas. Furthermore, distinguishing a female bear from a male is difficult to do.

Bibliography

Aalto, Kathryn. 2015. *The Natural World of Winnie-the-Pooh: A Walk through the Forest That Inspired the Hundred Acre Wood.* Portland, OR: Timber Press.

Assiniboine Park Conservancy. 2018. "Polar Bear Care." https://www.assiniboinepark.ca /conservation-research-sustainability/polar-bear-care.

Canadian Army. 2017. "Juno the Canadian Army Mascot." December 17. army-armee.forces .gc.ca/en/juno/index.page.

Canadian Broadcasting Corporation (CBC). 1987. "Winnie-the-Pooh's Canadian Connection Video." CBC Digital Archives, June 3. therealwinnie.ryerson.ca/collection /cbcwinnie.

Chaudhuri, Una. 2003. "Animal Geographies: Zooësis and the Space of Modern Drama." *Modern Drama* 46, no. 4 (Winter): 646–62.

Commito, Michael. 2012. "The History of People and Black Bears in Ontario." Network in Canadian History and Environment, May 14. niche-canada.org/2012/05/14/the-history -of-people-and-black-bears-in-ontario/.

Commito, Michael, and Ben Bradley. 2017. "The Bear Facts." Canada's History Society, January 14. www.canadashistory.ca/explore/arts,-culture-society/the-bear-facts.

Gammel, Irene, and Kate Addleman-Frankel, curators. 2018. *The Pooh Gallery.* Pavilion Gallery Museum, Assiniboine Park Pavilion, Winnipeg. https://www.assiniboinepark.ca /park/things-to-do/pavilion-art-galleries/the-pooh-gallery.

Government of Canada. 2016. "Discover Canada: Rights and Responsibilities of Citizenship." October 26. canada.ca/en/immigration-refugees-citizenship/corporate/publica tions-manuals/discover-canada/read-online/rights-resonsibilities-citizenship.html.

Harrison, John Kent, dir. 2004. *A Bear Named Winnie.* Canadian Broadcasting Corporation.

Huizinga, Johan. 1970. *Homo Ludens: A Study of the Play-Element in Culture.* Emeryville, CA: Paladin Press.

Kolbert, Elizabeth, ed. 2007. *The Ends of the Earth: An Anthology of the Finest Writing on the Arctic.* New York: Bloomsbury.

Lockie, Alex. 2016. "Meet the Canadian Army's New "Live" Mascot." *Business Insider,* February 29. businessinsider.com/meet-the-canadian-armys-new-live-mascot-2016-2.

Macdonald, Neil. 2016. "A Very Short List of Canadian Values." Canadian Broadcasting Corporation, September 13. cbc.ca/news/politics/neil-macdonald-kellie-leitch-values-survey-1.3759075.

Mattick, Lindsay. 2015. *Finding Winnie: The True Story of the World's Most Famous Bear*. Illustrated by Sophie Blackall. New York: Little, Brown.

Mattick, Lindsay, and Josh Greenhut. 2018. *Winnie's Great War*. Illustrated by Sophie Blackall. New York: HarperCollins.

Milne, A. A. 1958. *The World of Pooh*. Illustrated by E. H. Shepard. London: Methuen.

Milne, A. A. 1992. *Winnie-the-Pooh*. Illustrated by E. H. Shepard. London: Puffin Books.

Nault, Sheri. 2011. "Military Mascots and the Canadian Black Bear." Prince Albert Right Now, August 18. panow.com/community/news/113549/military-mascots-and-canadian-black-bear.

Ontario Spring Bear Hunt. n.d. "Why the Spring Bear Hunt?" www.ontariospringbearhunt.ca/.

Patterson, David. 2016. "Private #Juno Reporting for Duty with the Canadian Army." Twitter, uploaded by @CanadianArmy, February 25. twitter.com/CanadianArmy/status/702990767216676865?ref_src=twsrc%5Etfw&ref_url=http%3A%2F%2F.

Robinson, Michael. 2015. "Spring Bear Hunt to Be Reinstated in Ontario." *Star* (Toronto), November 3. www.thestar.com/news/gta/2015/11/03/spring-bear-hunt-to-be-reinstated-in-ontario.html.

Ruel, Geneviève King. 2011. "The (Arctic) Show Must Go On: Natural Resource Craze and National Identity in Arctic Politics." *International Journal* 66, no. 4 (Autumn): 825–33.

Shushkewich, Val. 2003. *The Real Winnie: A One-of-a-Kind Bear*. Toronto: Natural Heritage.

Sokoloski, Mia. 1992. *The Romance of the Captain and Winnie the Bear*. White River, Ont., Canada: Self-published.

Solnit, Rebecca. 2005. *A Field Guide to Getting Lost*. London: Penguin.

Travel Manitoba. 2014. "Town of Churchill." Everything Churchill. www.travelmanitoba.com/everything-churchill/about-churchill/.

US Forest Service. 2018. "Story of Smokey." smokeybear.com/en/smokeys-history/story-of-smokey.

Waxman, Olivia B. 2017. "The Bear Who Became a Cigarette-Smoking, Beer-Drinking World War II Hero." *Time*, April 8. time.com/4731787/wojtek-the-bear-history/.

Welchman, Jennifer. 2012. "A Defence of Environmental Stewardship." *Environmental Values* 21, no. 3 (August): 297–316.

White River Township. 2017. "29th Annual Winnie's Hometown Festival!" Brochure.

White River Township. 2018. "The History of Winnie the Pooh, White River Ontario." whiteriver.ca/article/the-history-of-winnie-the-pooh-white-river-ontario-6.asp.

CHAPTER 7

Reading *Winnie-the-Pooh* in Croatian Primary Schools

Nada Kujundžić and Ivana Milković

The canonical value of A. A. Milne's *Winnie-the-Pooh* collection and that of its sequel, *The House at Pooh Corner*, was established almost upon their publication (in 1926 and 1928, respectively). Widely regarded as classics in both their native British setting and in other English-speaking countries (Wozniak 2013, 196), the adventures of the affable toy bear were warmly received by child and adult readers in countries outside the anglophone world as well such as Germany (O'Sullivan 1993), Poland (Wozniak 2013; Wozniak 2014), and Russia (Papusha 2005; Tashlitsky n.d.). The global popularity of Pooh and his friends was further boosted following Walt Disney Studios' acquisition of the rights to Milne's stories, which led to a series of animated adaptations (starting with *The Many Adventures of Winnie the Pooh* in 1977), direct-to-video/ DVD films, TV shows, short films, and video games as well as an avalanche of tie-in products.

The first Croatian translation of *Winnie-the-Pooh* appeared fairly late: sixty years after its initial publication (1986). At that time, Croatia was part of the Socialist Federal Republic of Yugoslavia (SFRY),[2] which also encompassed five other federated states: Bosnia and Herzegovina, Macedonia, Montenegro, Serbia, and Slovenia. At its founding in 1945, the SFRY recognized four official languages: Croatian (Roman script),[3] Serbian (Cyrillic and Roman script), Slovenian (Roman Script), and Macedonian (Cyrillic script).[4] Although at first recognized as separate languages in the SFRY, with the Novi Sad Agreement (1954), which addressed language issues in the new republic, Croatian and Serbian were merged into one language: Serbocroatian or Croatoserbian (see Bašić 2017). Serbocroatian and/or Croatoserbian were treated (in the sociopolitical sense) as one and the same language, which was in fact an artificial construct of two historically, linguistically, and culturally different languages.[5] The Novi Sad Agreement provoked general discontent in Croatia, which was further deepened in the following years, especially with the 1963 constitution of the SFRY, which identified four official languages: Serbocroatian, Croatoserbian, Slovenian, and Macedonian.[6] The dissatisfaction with the language issue in Croatia led to the drawing up of the Declaration on the Name and Status of the Croatian Literary Language (1967), initiated and signed by Croatian scholars, writers, and intellectuals arguing for the equality of the Serbian, Croatian, Slovene, and Macedonian languages in the SFRY. The Croatian Spring (1970–1971) followed, a cultural and political movement that opposed the unitarization of individual languages and cultures (see Batović 2007). Finally, the term "Croatian literary language" was reestablished in the early 1970s and included in the Croatian constitution in 1974. In 1991, Croatia gained independence with Croatian as the official language.

During the described period (until 1992), children in lower grades of primary schools in Croatia were taught to read and write both in the Roman and Cyrillic scripts. In addition to texts in Croatian, textbooks published in Croatia and used in Croatian schools also included texts in Macedonian and Slovenian or their translations. However, Serbian texts (both in the Cyrillic and Roman scripts) were more numerous, and Croatian texts printed in the Cyrillic script were also common.[7] Moreover, Croatian translations were rarely provided for texts already available in Serbian translation, under the guise of the Serbocroatian/Croatoserbian language. This may be due to the fact that permissions to translate and publish were given for a particular language, so if a book was published in Serbian, it was difficult to obtain permission to also publish it in Croatian, since the two were not considered to be two different languages (in contrast, permissions to publish in Slovenian or Macedonian could be obtained). What is more, propaganda and educational practices persuaded the general public that Croatian and Serbian were interchangeable and therefore easily understood by readers speaking either language. The late publication of Milne's book into Croatian therefore does not necessarily mean that Croatian audiences had no contact with the world of the Hundred Acre Wood prior to that; on the contrary, Milne's stories were available through translations into other languages of the former Yugoslavia, such as Serbian (*Vini Pu*, 1951, translated by Luka Semenović; published again in 1966 under the title *Vini zvani Pu* [Vini called Pu]); Slovenian (*Medved Pu* [Bear Pu], 1957, translated by Majda Stanovnik and Gregor Strniša); and Macedonian (*Vini Pu*, 1978, translated by Danica Cvetanovska); all of which belong to the same South Slavic group of languages as Croatian. However, it cannot be stated with certainty whether Croatian audiences actually read Milne's stories in those languages or not.

While its inclusion on required and recommended reading lists for Croatian primary schools points to a recognition and confirmation of its canonical status, the Croatian translation of *Winnie-the-Pooh* met with a fairly lukewarm reception on the part of Croatian audiences. In fact, it might be argued that the underwhelming response to the book is the reason why its sequel, *The House at Pooh Corner*, has never been translated into Croatian.[8] The aim of this chapter is therefore twofold: to explore the possible reasons for the lack of success of *Winnie-the-Pooh* among Croatian readers, and to examine the status and presentation of Milne's book within the framework of Croatian primary education by analyzing special annotated editions explicitly intended for primary school students, as well as guides and companions to required and recommended reading. To accomplish this goal, we use existing studies of the reception of Milne's work in translation—especially the works of Emer O'Sullivan (2005; 1993) and Monika Wozniak (2013; 2014)—as theoretical and methodological models.

The first part of the chapter provides an overview of Croatian translations of *Winnie-the-Pooh* and explores two possible reasons for their relatively marginal status within Croatian translated literature: the change of implied readership present in the first translation of the book and the immense popularity of the Disney version of Milne's stories, which may have overshadowed its literary source. The second part of the chapter analyzes the status, perception, and interpretation of *Winnie-the-Pooh* within the context of primary school education in Croatia. A brief introduction to required and recommended lists in Croatian schools is followed by a discussion of the individual appearances of *Winnie-the-Pooh* on these lists in their historical, cultural, and linguistic contexts. The third part analyzes special editions of the book as well as its appearance in textbooks, guides, and companions to required and recommended reading intended for students and teachers. The chapter ends with a summary of the main findings and suggestions for future research.

Winnie-the-Pooh in Croatian

The immense popularity of the Pooh stories among English-speaking readers, manifested as (among other things) the commercial success of not only the books[9] but also various types of accompanying merchandise such as "games, toys, tea sets, clothes, and all kinds of pop-culture items" (Kidd 2011, 36), quickly led to their translation into foreign languages (the first German translation, for example, was published as early as 1928; O'Sullivan 2005, 30). The lengthy list of Pooh translations currently encompasses around forty languages,[10] including Scots, Yiddish, Tajik, Esperanto, and Latin. Croatian was rather late in joining this list, with the first translation of *Winnie-the-Pooh*, entitled *Medo Winnie zvani Pooh* (Teddy bear Winnie called Pooh),[11] published in 1986.

The inclusion of *Winnie-the-Pooh* in required and recommended reading lists for Croatian primary schools predates the appearance of the book in Croatian by twenty-six years. Given the circumstances, it is no surprise that the previously mentioned Serbian translation by Luka Semenović was the first to be included in reading lists for primary schools (grades 1–4) in 1960. The book was written in the Cyrillic script and published in 1951 by the Belgrade publisher Dečja knjiga (Child's book). *Vini Pu* was reprinted in 1963 and 1965, together with Semenović's translation of *The House at Pooh Corner* (*Kuća na Puovom uglu*) in 1952. In 1966, the book was renamed *Vini zvani Pu* (Winnie called Pooh) and published simultaneously in the Roman and Cyrillic scripts. Both editions include the original illustrations by E. H. Shepard. The Serbian translation reappears on reading lists for Croatian primary schools in 1968 (grade 2) and 1972 (grade 2; Narančić Kovač and Milković 2018). It is important to note that the mere inclusion of the title in these lists does not necessarily mean that the Pooh stories were actually read in Croatian schools. In fact, because Milne's book was at the time not available in Croatian and because it was one of many recommended (rather than obligatory) titles, it is possible that many teachers did not actually recommend it, using instead books available in Croatian. With temporary exceptions (the largest being the period between 1972 and 1993),

Winnie-the-Pooh has kept its place in required and recommended reading lists in Croatia to the present time, with Serbian translations giving way to Croatian ones in 1993 (Narančić Kovač and Milković 2018).

There are two Croatian translations of *Winnie-the-Pooh*, which have been published a total of eight times (see table 1). The first, *Medo Winnie zvani Pooh*, was published as the 244th title in the long-lived children's publishing series Vjeverica (Squirrel) in 1986. Launched in 1957 by the Zagreb-based publishing house Mladost, Vjeverica is one of the most popular twentieth-century Croatian book series, which, in the thirty-eight years of its existence, has contributed 318 children's and young adult books (both translations and books written in Croatian) to the Croatian market (Radošević 2016b, 153).[12] Translated by Mia Pervan-Plavec (later Mia Pervan), *Medo Winnie zvani Pooh* contains the original illustrations by E. H. Shepard. The poems for this edition were translated by the famous Croatian children's poet Zvonimir Balog, known primarily for his playful approach to language and use of nonsense (Perić 2012, 254, 258–59). The second edition of Pervan-Plavec's translation appeared in 1991 in the same publishing series.

In 1996, Pervan's translation appeared in the series Pčelica (Little bee), published by Katarina Zrinski, a Varaždin-based publisher primarily focused on required and recommended reading for primary and secondary schools. Pčelica gradually highlighted its profile as a series of children's and young adult books included in recommended reading lists for primary school[13] by adding informative annotations and other types of educational paratext to its editions. All subsequent editions and translations of Milne's book were published by Katarina Zrinski. By acquiring the publishing rights to the Croatian translations of *Winnie-the-Pooh*, Katarina Zrinski remains the only publisher of Milne's stories in Croatia.

A major change brought about by the new publisher is the substitution of Shepard's drawings with black-and-white illustrations by Nevenka Macolić. Missing are the intraiconic texts—such as "words appearing inside pictures" (Nikolajeva and Scott 2006, 118), present, for instance, in Shepard's illustrations showing Pooh sitting under the name of Saunders or the "expotition" to the North Pole—and the map of the Hundred Acre Wood. The seventeen new illustrations have a primarily decorative function, which is not the case in the English original, where the close interaction between the verbal and the visual creates a synergy (Sipe 1998, 98) reminiscent of picture books, which rely on

Table 1. Croatian translations of Winnie-the-Pooh

Year of publication	Translator	Trans-creator of poems	Illustrator	Annota-tions	Publisher/ Place of publication	Edition	Publishing series
1986	Mia Pervan -Plavec	Zvonimir Balog	Ernest H. Shepard	N/A	Mladost / Zagreb	1st	Vjeverica [Squirrel]
1991						2nd	
1996	Mia Pervan	Zvonimir Balog	Nevenka Macolić	N/A	Katarina Zrinski / Varaždin	1st	Pčelica [Little bee]
1998	Marina Leustek					2nd	
2005				Jadranka Županić		3rd	Pčelica. Metodički obrađena lektira. [Little bee. Recommended reading with didactic suggestions.]
2007			Ernest H. Shepard			4th	
2012						5th*	ABC. Metodički obrađena lektira. [ABC. Recommended reading with didactic suggestions.]
2017						6th	

*First in the series

the interconnectedness of words and pictures to create meaning (Nikolajeva and Scott 2006). Moreover, some changes introduced by Macolić create significant semantic shifts, resulting in a changed temporal setting of the story (see Narančić Kovač 2019): for instance, Christopher Robin is dressed in jeans and a T-shirt and looks a bit older than in the original, while all the toys are presented as animals.

The 1998 edition of *Medo Winnie zvani Pooh* brought forth a new translation, the work of Marina Leustek, accompanied by Macolić's illustrations. In 2005, Leustek's translation was reprinted in a new edition of the book explicitly aimed at young primary school readers, and it was included in a series of annotated editions of books featured on required and recommended reading lists for Croatian primary schools. The year 2007 saw the publication of Leustek's annotated translation accompanied by Shepard's original illustrations. Published in 2012, the fifth edition of the book marks the first appearance of *Medo Winnie* in the new ABC publishing series. The sixth edition published by Katarina Zrinski (the eighth edition overall) appeared in 2017.

Seeing that this chapter primarily aims to explore Milne's book in the context of primary education, special attention will be given to editions created with primary school students in mind, namely those published from 2005 onward.

Reception and Popularity in Croatia

As stated earlier, *Medo Winnie* never reached the levels of popularity or canonical status that Milne's work enjoys in numerous other countries. There are several possible reasons for this rather unenthusiastic response: the fact that the first Croatian translation eliminates the dual addressee in favor of an implied child reader, various extratextual factors such as the fairly late publication date, and the popularity of Disney's Winnie the Pooh.

Emer O'Sullivan ascribes the fact that the first German translation of Milne's book "enjoyed nothing like the enthusiastic reception in Britain and the USA" (2005, 30) to the translator's omission of all the elements intended for adult readers (O'Sullivan 1993). In choosing this approach, the overall complexity (Nance-Carroll 2015) and crossover appeal of the book were diminished, and the dual (adult and child) addressee (see O'Sullivan 2005; Tremper 1977) substituted with a child one. O'Sullivan's hypothesis regarding the German translation is also applicable to the Croatian case, as numerous instances of irony and other linguistic elements Milne uses to "wink [...] over the heads of children to the adults lined up in the back of the room" (Cadden 2005, 294) are omitted. Specifically, Pervan-Plavec's translation ignores the adult reader, explicitly identifying children as the intended readership:

> (*source text*) Pooh is the favourite, of course, there's no denying it, but Piglet comes in for a good many things which Pooh misses; because you can't take Pooh to school without everybody knowing it, but Piglet is so small that he slips into a pocket, where it is very comfortable to feel him when you are not quite sure whether twice seven is twelve or twenty-two. Sometimes he slips out and has a good look in the ink-pot. (Milne [1926] 2005)
>
> (*back translation*) Of course Pooh is the hero, there is no doubt about that, nor would I ever try to deny that. However, Piglet is the hero in many adventures in which Pooh is completely irrelevant. *You, children*, know very well that Pooh Bear cannot be secretly taken to school. *Everyone will see him, perhaps even make fun of you*. And Piglet? Piglet is so small you can put him in your

pocket *without anyone noticing it*! *You yourselves* know very well how comforting it is *to squeeze and caress a cherished toy in your pocket*, especially when you are not sure if two times seven is twelve or twenty-two. Sometimes, *Piglet peeks out of Christopher's pocket* and looks into the ink pot. (translated from Pervan-Plavec 1986, 8–9, emphases added)[14]

This type of direct address ("You, children"), absent from the original text, leaves little doubt as for whom (in the translator's view) the text is intended. The alteration of the implied audience from a dual to a singular, child one, may have (at least to some extent) unfavorably affected the reception of *Winnie-the-Pooh* in Croatia. This might be ascribed to the long-lasting marginalization of children's literature within the Croatian literary system, where it has long been labeled as "low" (as opposed to "high") literature (Narančić Kovač 2012, 644). Furthermore, as Smiljana Narančić Kovač points out, Croatian adult readers rarely read children's books, perceiving them primarily as a means of educating children (Narančić Kovač 2012, 645). The erasure of the adult-implied reader and the book's unequivocal association with children may have therefore not only limited its readership but also undermined its perception as canon (i.e., "high" literature). Since the title was already recognized as a classic of world literature and consequently included in required and recommended reading lists in Croatia, it is possible that the retention of the dual address in the Croatian translation might have made *Winnie-the-Pooh* more appealing to teachers who were in a position to choose which titles from the reading list to recommend to students.

Substituting the dual audience with a single (child)-intended reader has influenced a number of translation choices, such as removing the subtle humor that (among other things) makes the text intriguing and interesting for both adult and child audiences. This points to an underestimation of the child reader's capacity to understand implied meanings on the part of the translator, also evident in her use of explicitation and domestication. Lawrence Venuti defines domestication as a process of replacing "the linguistic and cultural differences of the foreign text with a text that is intelligible to the translating-language reader," often by substituting items characteristic of the source culture (e.g., food, customs, names) with their equivalents in the target culture (Venuti 2008, 14). Explicitation is defined as a technique of "making explicit in the target text information that is implicit in the source text" (Klaudy 1998, 80), typically by adding various explanatory structures that highlight or concretize logical connections, remind the reader of previous events, repeat relevant information, and so on. The translator's need to explain ideas, connections, and situations that the source text does not explicitly address points to her own perception of the intended audience, and of their level of comprehension and literacy (Van Coillie 2006, 132–33). Consider the following scene from chapter 2, in which Pooh gets stuck while trying to leave Rabbit's house:

> (*source text*) "Oh help!" said Pooh. "I'd better go back." "Oh, bother!" said Pooh. "I shall have to go on." "I can't do either!" said Pooh. "Oh, help *and* bother!" (Milne [1926] 2005, 27, emphasis in original)
>
> (*back translation*) Help!—*shouted* Pooh. I will have to go *back to the burrow.*—Oh, bother!—he added quickly.—I mustn't go back. I must get out. The trouble is, I cannot go forward or backward. I am stuck!—he *yelled desperately.*—Bother! Help! (translated from Pervan-Plavec 1986, 35, emphases added)[15]

To make sure young readers fully understand the situation and, perhaps, identify with the unfortunate bear's predicament, the translator replaces the verb "said" with verbs and phrases more expressive of Pooh's emotions (shouted, yelled desperately), and adds several reminders of the situation (e.g., that the way back would lead to Rabbit's house) as well as an explicit statement of his problem (being stuck), which the original suggests in the visual discourse (illustrations) but does not identify in verbal discourse until later. The translator often makes assumptions about children as readers and their ability to understand complex stories. She exhibits a need to leave little to chance and to explain everything so that little or no inference is needed on the part of readers. In doing so, she underestimates readers and detracts from the quality of the text.

As previously mentioned, the possible link between the lack of success of Milne's book in Croatia and the first translation's unambiguous identification of children as its target audience is reminiscent of the fate of the first German translation. However, while the second German translation of *Winnie-the-Pooh* (published in 1987) met with considerable success (O'Sullivan 2005, 99), the same cannot be said of the second Croatian translation. The reason for this may lie in its fairly late publication date: appearing in 1998, Leustek's translation had to contend with a growing number of translated Disney books featuring the characters from the two animated Pooh films. Moreover, the numerous literary adaptations of Disney's film adaptations of Milne's work (Oittinen 2008) have steadily been gaining popularity since 1994, when

Egmont Publishing founded its Croatian branch (Egmont Publishing n.d.). A small number of texts featuring the Disney version of Pooh and friends were available in Croatian even before the appearance of Egmont (for example, Disney's Story a Day series, which includes twenty-two stories about characters from the Hundred Acre Wood, was translated in 1990), with at least four Egmont-published books appearing before 1998, and three more in 1998. Since the 2000s, Croatian translations of Disney's Pooh books have seen an increase in both number and types of publications: by the end of 2018, there were 172 titles in total (including first editions and reprints), encompassing a variety of movie tie-in editions, spin-offs, and companion titles such as story collections, encyclopedias and other educational editions, bathing books, interactive music books, readers, and a children's magazine, making Disney's Winnie the Pooh stories the most popular Disney titles in Croatia (Kujundžić and Milković 2018, 125). As was the case in many other countries (e.g., Italy; see Wozniak 2013), the immense popularity and sheer number of Disney's Pooh movies[16] and accompanying merchandise (Pooh and friends consistently top the lists of the most profitable brands in the world; Santo 2015, 207) helped Disney's Winnie the Pooh overshadow Milne's Winnie-the-Pooh, becoming the first (sometimes the only) and therefore definitive version for many audience members (Deszcz 86). In light of the volume of Disney's products, shorter stories, appealing book covers, the omnipresent visual presentation of Winnie in his two-sizes-too-small red T-shirt, and Macolić's "reinterpretation of the narrative" (Narančić Kovač 2019), it may be presumed that the Croatian translation of the original story was not as appealing to children, especially considering its didactic approach to children's literature. As a result, Croatian children widely accepted Disney's versions of the story and its characters (Wozniak 2013) in place of translations of Milne's originals.

Winnie-the-Pooh in Croatian Primary Schools

Because developing literacy and promoting a culture of reading is one of the key aims of the Croatian language school curriculum (Ministarstvo znanosti, obrazovanja i športa 2006; Ministarstvo znanosti i obrazovanja 2019),[17] the standard program for all grades of primary and secondary education includes a list of required and recommended books (the number of titles varies depending on the grade).[18] Required and recommended reading lists, here understood as "institutionally defined requests for independent reading of literary works at home" (Hameršak 2006, 98; see also Leniček 2002), include works of Croatian and international children's literature, the selection of which is largely based on a work's linguistic traits and suitability to readers' needs and abilities (literacy, linguistic competences, age, etc.; see Hameršak 2006, 107) as well as its literary value and artistic merit (Rosandić 2005, 50; see also Gabelica and Težak 2017, 49–54).[19] In other words, the choice of books to be included in the lists relies on both pedagogical and educational, as well as literary and aesthetic, criteria. Furthermore, the selection of books gradually expands from one grade to the next to include more genres and topics.

Depending on the grade, students are tasked with reading one book on a monthly or bimonthly basis. While reading, they are expected to make notes in the form of a reading journal (written in a plain notebook or special workbook that includes various tasks and questions), which they submit as part of the reading assignment. The journal should include students' personal responses; information about the author, characters, setting, and plot; and other details. While such teaching practice has its support in the curriculum, it was never officially prescribed, but it was often promoted by experts until it became almost the only way to read full-length texts. The main goal of this type of assignment is to develop students into independent readers, capable of literary comprehension and interpretation (Leniček 2002). This is connected to the more general aims of reader education, which include the following: "achieving/developing a certain level of literary education; developing a culture of reading, students' creative abilities, and literary taste; promoting a richer, more substantial, and subtle spiritual life; [and] building a holistic worldview" (Rosandić 2005, 52; see also Gabelica and Težak 2017). Furthermore, as Dragutin Rosandić points out, reading-list-based discussions in the classroom enable students to share their thoughts and observations about the books they read, which promotes critical thinking (Rosandić 1976, 99). Ideally, by reading books included in their required and recommended reading lists, students "perfect their reading skills, adopt principles of spelling and grammar, enrich their vocabulary, become familiar with different cultural, historical, and geographical facts, identify with characters, and enter an imaginary world" (Gabelica et al. 2014, 57).

The Croatian translation of Milne's *Winnie-the-Pooh* was first included in reading lists for the second grade of primary school (ages 8–9) in 1993, reappearing in all subsequent lists (1995, 1997, 1998, 1999, 2001, and 2006;

Narančić Kovač and Milković 2018). Prescribed by the Ministry of Science and Education, the reading list for the second grade of primary school includes a total of nineteen books: only one is assigned (a selection of Hans Christian Andersen's fairy tales[20]), while the others are recommended (usually selected by the teacher). The list is dominated by Croatian authors (twelve), while international children's authors include the aforementioned Andersen as well as Karel Čapek (Czech literature), Carlo Collodi (Italian), Ela Peroci (Slovenian), Desa Muck (Slovenian), Charles Perrault (French), and Milne (English; Ministarstvo znanosti, obrazovanja i športa 2006, 29). It is important to emphasize that *Winnie-the-Pooh* is only one of eighteen titles to choose from, which means that while it has been recognized as linguistically and thematically suitable, it is not deemed mandatory. It is therefore difficult to evaluate the actual presence of Milne's work in Croatian schools, as the inclusion of the book in the curricula is mostly left up to teachers, who are often guided by various extratextual factors such as the availability of books in school and local libraries, their own knowledge about and experience of the books in question, consultation with colleagues (often, teachers in the same primary school working with lower grades jointly agree on the reading lists), possibilities for their didactic interpretation in class, and so on.

Whether or not it is actually being read, *Medo Winnie zvani Pooh* continues to sell, enabling a new edition to appear every three to five years. According to the publisher, the book is mainly purchased by parents and other family members for young primary school students: some probably buy it because their children need it for school, while others are likely drawn to the book through its associations with Disney (Ptiček 2018).

Annotations, Guides, and Companions

In this section, we turn our focus to the annotated editions of *Medo Winnie zvani Pooh* (published in 2005, 2007, 2012, and 2017), explicitly intended for primary school students, who read it as part of their schoolwork, as well as various guides and companions to required and recommended reading (including online sources) that discuss Milne's work. The guides and companions are optional resources intended to promote student comprehension of the required/recommended books by providing analyses and basic information about the books. Teachers also use them to prepare for class discussions. The discussion also includes Karol Visinko's book *Dječja priča* (Children's story), primarily aimed at (future) teachers and other readers interested in children's literature. Visinko discusses the different possible uses and interpretations of *Winnie-the-Pooh* in primary schools, suggesting how to motivate children to read, use problem-solving approaches, and develop their language skills with the help of Milne's stories. Identifying play as the main motif, Visinko proposes that students' interaction with the book should be based on playing with toys (Visinko 2005, 79–80).

The annotated editions of *Medo Winnie* include a brief introduction directly addressing the child readers, intended to prepare them for their first encounter with the text. The introduction aims to stimulate readers' interest and enthusiasm for the book by revealing that the text describes "many exciting, imaginative (mis)adventures of animated toys" (Županić 2012a, 4), and by encouraging readers to connect the content of the book with their own lives ("You might find similarities between your own favorite toys that you yourself brought to life while playing, or become inspired to do so"; Županić 2012a, 4). The introduction also provides information about the origin of the book and its genre, popularity and adaptations, style, and characters.

Milne's text is accompanied by informative annotations, which primarily explain the meaning of words that might be unfamiliar to young readers, and is followed by a list of postreading questions, activities, and creative tasks meant to check students' knowledge and comprehension of the text (e.g., "When Pooh visits Rabbit, he gets stuck while exiting the burrow. Why and how did C. Robin and Rabbit manage to get him out?"; "Describe the kidnapping of little Roo"; "What is an expotition?"; Županić 2012b, 137–38), as well as encourage students to explore and express their opinions about the plot and characters ("Which of the animals did you like the most [why?] and which did you like the least?"; "In your opinion, why is Pooh C. Robin's favorite animal?"; Županić 2012b, 137–38). Questions about the characters are largely suggestive, offering individual character traits (students are asked to add the names of Milne's characters to the list of traits) and evaluations of characters' actions (e.g., "Which of the animals' actions did you find somewhat inappropriate, and which did you find bold [brave]?"; Županić 2012b, 138) in advance. Furthermore, the author of the annotations refers to all characters as animals, perhaps because she is not aware that the majority of Milne's characters are based on and meant to be toys, or because she is guided by Macolić's illustrations, which accompany the first annotated edition.

The majority of activities included in the annotated editions are meant to encourage play and dramatization as a means of exploring and developing children's creativity (e.g., "If you are a member of the theater group, perform a play based on your favorite chapter"; Županić 2012b, 138). The edition closes with short biographical notes about Milne and Shepard. Accompanied by all the added educational materials, the literary work itself becomes a textbook of sorts (Rosandić 1986, 83), which can be used not only to read about Pooh's adventures but also to learn something about them and their creator. Thus, the didactic undercurrent that guides Pervan-Plavec's translation choices (e.g., added explanations) is expanded from the text to the paratext in the annotated editions.

The guides and companions to required and recommended reading typically contain a biographical note about Milne, a summary of the book, information about its origin, setting, genre, and style, and a description of the characters. Inga Čajić and colleagues also include a section entitled "What have we read?" and a short list of suggested postreading activities, all of which revolve around children's use of and interaction with plush toys (e.g., "Draw your favorite plush toy"; "Prepare a play at school using your favourite toys"; Čajić et al. 2005, 82). The "What have we read?" section points out that friendship can be formed not only with human beings but also with animals, toys, and other objects. This is illustrated by a story about the relationship between a little girl named Ana and her teddy bear, who feels lonely whenever she leaves him at home. It is unclear where the story comes from or who the author is.

Various Croatian websites providing information on books included in required and recommended reading lists such as Lektire.hr, Super lektire, and Sjedi5 usually reproduce information provided in the guides and companions, as well as the annotated *Medo Winnie*. However, they often also include erroneous information about the characters, which in the websites are primarily based on the Disney adaptations of Milne's stories. Perhaps the most striking example of this practice is found in the website Lektire.hr, which lists Tigger among the characters from *Winnie-the-Pooh*. However, the bouncy inhabitant of the Hundred Acre Wood is first introduced in *The House at Pooh Corner*, which has not been translated into Croatian. Consequently, Tigger exists only as a Disney character in Croatian culture. Descriptions of other characters also point to Disney films as primary sources of information, for instance the statement that Christopher Robin is messy and avoids cleaning his room, or that Rabbit is overconfident and mostly preoccupied with gardening.

Despite their varying lengths, all biographical notes pay special attention to Milne's relationship with his son (notes that are brief only provide information about Christopher Robin's importance for Milne's life and writing; Čajić et al. 2005, 77). Davor Uskoković, for example, points out that after his marriage in 1913, Milne spent "seven years eagerly awaiting a child" and then used his talents to write poems and stories for the boy, "as many fathers wish they could do, if only they were talented and diligent" (Uskoković 2009, 54). Milne's decision to stop writing children's books is ascribed to Christopher Robin's growing up and "developing his own personality, which—of course—had to come into conflict with his father's" (Uskoković 2009, 54). Similar information is found in the annotated *Pooh*: "Milne loved his son very much, which is why he began writing poems and stories for him. [. . .] When the boy started developing his own personality, Milne stopped writing children's books and started writing novels and plays for adults, as well as newspaper articles" ("Bilješka o piscu" 2012, 141). While Christopher Robin certainly played an important role in Milne's career as a children's author, many scholars have pointed to the author's memories of his own childhood as an important source of inspiration for the world of Winnie-the-Pooh (Kuznets 1994, 47). The link between the son's growing up and the father's decision to pursue writing for an adult readership is somewhat misleading, especially since Milne was already an established novelist and playwright before authoring his first collection of children's poetry in 1924. Moreover, he "quite resented critics who focused on him as a children's author" (Nance-Carroll 2015, 73), actively trying to distance himself from his four children's books and "achieve more adult literary fame" (Kidd 2011, 223n18). Karol Visinko is the only commentator who argues against the importance of Christopher Robin in the creation of the book; claiming that Milne never read his own stories and poems to his son, she concludes that *Winnie-the-Pooh* was not written for children but for "the child that lives inside every one of us" (2005, 77).

The annotated *Medo Winnie* also contains a brief note about E. H. Shepard, introducing him as the illustrator of Kenneth Grahame's *The Wind in the Willows* and explaining that the model for his drawing of Pooh was his own son's teddy bear, named Growler ("Bilješka o ilustratoru" 2012, 142). The text also provides information about the fate of Shepard's two children. The emphasis on children in the lives of the two artists and their influence on their creation perhaps serves to further support the idea that Milne's work—inspired by and created for children—is, in fact, intended (solely) for children.

The fact that both the author and illustrator have personal experience with (their own) children is perhaps meant to somehow reinforce the idea of the text's suitability for children, which, in turn, justifies neglecting the adult readers who might enjoy the text.

All the guides and supporting materials identify the book as a story (Uskoković 2009, 58; Županić 2012a, 5), or, more specifically, a children's story (Visinko 2005), divided into ten chapters, each of which can be read independently. The plot itself is described as taking place in a forest surrounding Christopher Robin's house (the name of the forest is not specified) over the course of one year ("from one spring to another"; Čajić et al. 2005, 79; see also Županić 2012a, 4). The plot is retold through brief summaries of individual chapters. Čajić and colleagues do not mention the framing device, while Uskoković mentions it at the very end of the summary, stating that "we finally find out that Pooh is a teddy bear, Christopher Robin's toy, and the whole book is actually a story the narrator tells his son, Christopher Robin" (Uskoković 2009, 57). The framing device is partially ignored, with the identity of the characters presented as a reveal or twist of sorts, even though the book opens with the boy coming down the stairs carrying his toy bear.

The style is consistently described as simple, "appropriate for the age group it was written for" (Uskoković 2009, 58), which once again confirms the notion of children as the implied audience, this time from the perspective of an adult interpreting the text through the lens of education. The sentences are described as short, clear, and humorous (Uskoković 2009, 58; Županić 2012a, 5). However, it should be noted that this statement applies to the Croatian translations of *Winnie-the-Pooh*, but not necessarily to the source text. In fact, Milne often uses lengthy, cumulative sentences, created by the frequent use of the conjunction "and"; these are consistently divided into shorter sentences in both Croatian translations.[21] The same is true of the poems, which the authors of the guides divide into two categories: nonsensical ones and those that make sense (Županić 2012a, 5). However, the latter category is the creation of translators (or rather, transcreators of poems) who, perhaps sharing Pervan-Plavec's view of the child reader as one to whom things need to be explained, introduce sense into Milne's nonsensical verses.

While all the texts mention Christopher Robin's toys as the inspiration for the inhabitants of the Hundred Acre Wood, most of them do not distinguish between the toy and animal characters,[22] referring instead to the characters either as toys (Uskoković 2009) or as animals (Županić 2012a;

Županić 2012b). In contrast, Visinko claims that all the characters are either Christopher Robin's toys or (in the case of Rabbit and Owl) animals that one might meet in the Hundred Acre Wood (2005, 79). Both Uskoković and Županić comment on the characters' lack of education. Uskoković describes them as "neither too wise nor educated" (2009, 58), claiming that their way of thinking is a source of much humor in the book. He proceeds to identify a certain mocking streak in the book, which, while "by no means malicious," is aimed at the individual traits of the characters (58). Županić also notes that the characters are not educated or "very clever," but finds that "the writer does not mock them because of that" (2012a, 5). The lack of education is repeatedly mentioned in descriptions of individual characters, suggesting that the authors of annotations and guides consider it to be an important topic in the book. This type of reading seems to overlook the carefree and childlike quality of Milne's characters, whose lack of formal education may be a point of identification for young readers (Reynolds 2011, 30).

All the texts characterize the titular bear as mostly silly and foolish, but also resourceful at times. Županić describes him as "good-natured, nice, and kind" (2012a, 5) and mentions his tendency to make up poems. Other texts highlight his love of honey, which often clouds his reasoning (Uskoković 2009, 58), as well as his illiteracy (Čajić et al. 2005, 80). Repeatedly highlighted attributes of Christopher Robin include his love of his animals/toys, goodness, kindness, and status of leader. Most authors comment on the special bond between the boy and Winnie-the-Pooh, with Uskoković going so far as to state that the boy is "in love with his teddy bear, despite his silliness" (59). The majority of texts point out that even though the other characters turn to the boy for help and guidance, he himself is not all-knowing. Frequently cited in support of this claim are his spelling errors and statement about the possible existence of an East and West Pole (Uskoković 2009, 59; Županić 2012a, 5), which, seeing that the character is not yet of school age, we do not consider to be glaring gaps in knowledge. On the other hand, we continually find examples that lead us to believe that the "sophisticated irony intended for the adult reading aloud to a child" (Lathey 2011, 203) did not find its way into Croatian translations of *Winnie-the-Pooh*. Piglet is typically described as "naïve, inexperienced, and insecure" (Županić 2012a, 5), and associated with a lack of courage (Čajić et al. 2005, 81) and the practice of making up his family tree (Uskoković 2009, 59). Identified by Županić as a "realist" (2012a, 5), the down-to-earth Rabbit is often characterized as "funny" (Čajić et al. 2005, 81), even a "jokester" (Županić 2012a, 5). Uskoković also provides an illustration of Rabbit's supposedly jocular nature by referring to the episode in which Pooh pays him a visit and Rabbit replies that he is not home (2009, 59). The guides and accompanying texts typically overlook the humor inscribed in the character of Owl, the "pompous schoolmaster [. . .] who turns out to be nearly illiterate" (Lurie 1973, 12). In fact, most authors describe him as "the most literate" (Čajić et al. 2005, 81) and "most educated of all the animals" (Županić 2012a, 5), even though, as Riitta Oittinen observes, the character "pretends to be wiser than he is" (2008, 82). Uskoković is the only one who hints at the ironic attitude toward the character by pointing out that the "know-it-all" Owl fails to realize that his bell-pull is actually a donkey's tail (2009, 59).

Descriptions of Eeyore's character are generally negatively intoned: he is perceived as being preoccupied with "useless things," which prevents him from noticing (and, presumably, enjoying) the world around him (Županić 2012a, 5). Uskoković even calls him "an aimless, useless thinker, who thinks about causes, consequences, relations, and similar nonsense" (2009, 59). This type of interpretation seems rather harsh, especially in light of the fact that Milne's text never criticizes Eeyore's gloomy mood or depicts it as something that should be altered; however, the criticism of the donkey's pessimism may be a reflection of the intended didacticism of Uskoković's text, which aims to present Eeyore as a character children should not identify with. Even though the Pooh stories do not reveal the donkey's age, all accompanying texts included in the present analysis describe him as being old. This interpretive conclusion might be based on his perceived irritability and grumpiness (stereotypically ascribed to the elderly; see Braithwaite 1986, 358). Kanga and Roo are usually discussed only briefly. All authors mention their outsider status and highlight Kanga's maternal role.

The text included in annotated editions of *Medo Winnie* is accompanied by explanations of words that young readers (ages 8–9) may be less familiar or completely unfamiliar with. Words and their explanations appear on the left and right margins of the spread, typically on the same level as they appear in the text. Each word is followed by a short explanation or synonym. The author, primary school teacher Jadranka Županić, compiled the list of words through cooperation with several generations of her second-grade students, who were asked to note unfamiliar words they came across while reading Milne's book (Ptiček 2018).

The list of words has gradually changed with every edition, probably as a direct result of the different feedback acquired from the different generations of students, as the students' knowledge and understanding of the text inevitably changes from generation to generation. The first annotated edition (2005) contains 600 entries; slight changes to the text introduced in 2007 led to the inclusion of 5 and exclusion of 10 explanations, resulting in a total of 595 words. The 2012 edition saw the removal of 118 entries and addition of 4 words, while the latest edition, published in 2017, contains explanations for 427 words (176 entries were removed and 4 added to the original 2005 list). Judging solely by the number of explained words, the part of the book young readers seem to find the least comprehensible is chapter 7, "In Which Kanga and Baby Roo Come to the Forest, and Piglet Has a Bath." The 2005 edition provides explanations for 81 items from this chapter; the following, 2007 edition adds 2 more explanations (*joke* and *misery*) to the list. In 2012, the number of explanations is reduced to 69, and in 2017 to 59.

Words explained in the margins can be roughly divided into three groups: cultural items, wordplay, and general items. Cultural items—from both the target and source cultures—include (among others) a wide range of plant names (e.g., *oak*: "a high deciduous tree whose fruit is an acorn"; Leustek 2005, 22), types of food (e.g., *butter*: "fat extracted from milk"; 28), and geographical names (e.g., *London*: "the capital of England/Great Britain"; 11). In some cases, the explanations intended for young readers may be even more difficult to grasp than the concepts they are describing (e.g., *the Moon*: "Earth's natural satellite that revolves around it"; 69). Some of the annotations are dedicated to clarifying wordplay, which has an effect similar to the unnecessary explanation of jokes. For instance, the phrase "uobličeni poštipak," used to translate Milne's wordplay "Crustimoney Proseedcake," is accompanied by the following clarification: "wrong pronunciation for usual procedure" (Leustek 2005, 44), which might take the fun out of guessing the origin of the unusual words, which can easily be identified as not belonging to the Croatian vocabulary. When Pooh misinterprets Owl's statement about the need to "issue a reward" as sneezing, the translation offers a nonexistent onomatopoetic word *raspcihati*, a blend of the words *raspisati* (to issue) and *apciha* (achoo). The accompanying explanation consists of only one word, "to issue" (Leustek 2005, 44), presented as a synonym.

In addition to wordplay, the annotations occasionally interpret other translation choices, most notably in the case of Heffalump. The basis for Leustek's translation of Milne's nonsense word lies in Shepard's illustration of the imaginary creature, which depicts him as an elephant. The Croatian translation of the word "Heffalump" is therefore a slight modification of the Croatian word *slon* (elephant) into *Slom*. The explanation for the word does not accompany the first appearance of the word in the text; rather, it appears after a few pages and reads as follows: "Pooh and Piglet think this is an animal, when in fact this is a condition in which a person feels dispirited, reluctant, and despondent" (Leustek 2005, 56). While the Croatian word *slom* can be used to signify a disaster, failure, weariness, or despondency, in *Medo Winnie* it is turned into a proper noun and given a new meaning, which remains somewhat hidden due to the misleading explanation. Finally, general items mentioned in the explanations include verbs, nouns, adjectives, and other word types that may be difficult for children to understand, such as a trunk ("front of the head, where the mouth and nose are"; Leustek 2005, 56), riddle ("a phenomenon that is difficult to understand"; 62), and noise ("unwanted, disturbing sound, yelling"; 69).

While the explanations of the unknown words further support the book's educational purpose and might in some cases be necessary for individual or independent students' reading, the sheer number of explained words suggests that children cannot be trusted to find out their meaning by themselves or even guess at them. Explaining wordplay and nonsense words in particular reduces the playfulness and interpretative possibilities of Milne's text, reducing each instance to a single explanation.

Milne and *Winnie-the-Pooh* in Croatian Primary School Readers (Textbooks)

Although the use of textbooks is not prescribed, using a different textbook for each school subject and grade is a common teaching practice in Croatian schools. Teachers are free to choose literary readers (textbooks) among several peer-reviewed titles that are approved by the Ministry of Science and Education almost every year. The choice of texts in readers is not prescribed and depends on the authors' attitudes and preferences. However, certain didactic standards and recommendations, such as literary and aesthetic value, have to be met.

During the twentieth century, there is not a single mention of Milne or his work in Croatian readers for primary school. In contrast, readers published during the first decade of the twenty-first century contain three texts by/

about the British author. Used in the fourth grade of primary school since 2004–2005, *Susret sa suncem 4* (Encounter with the sun 4) (Bikić 2003) is the first Croatian reader to contain a text by Milne—a translation of the poem "At the Zoo" (trans. D. Malović) from the collection *When We Were Very Young* (1924). While the translator relies heavily on domestication, the paratext includes the names of the author and translator, which can serve as a reference to the source culture (see Milković 2015). Milne's poetry is also mentioned in the study of pedagogical and educational uses of poetry, which describes it as appropriate for inclusion in kindergarten teaching (Centar za predškolski odgoj 1995).

The reader *Zlatni dani 2* (Golden days 2) (Centner, Peko, and Pintarić 2005), used in the second grade since 2005–2006, contains a fragment from the first chapter of *Medo Winnie* (trans. Mia Pervan-Plavec). The paratext also includes the name of the author as well as a reference to the book: "You will find out more about the bear and Christopher Robin in A. A. Milne's book *Winnie-the-Pooh*. Look for it in the library and read it" (Centner, Peko, and Pintarić 2005, 74). Although the reader *Cvrkut riječi* (Chirp of words) (Polak and Cindrić 2004) does not include Milne's texts, it nevertheless contains a biographical note about him. The brief text provides young readers with basic information about the author, which is another significant reference to Milne's book.

The inclusion of Milne's texts in the abovementioned textbooks suggests that some authors (both academics and teachers) considered them to be appropriate for children of the twenty-first century, or at least they trusted the official list of titles for recommended reading to inspire them for the selection of texts for their readers. Regardless of the changes made in the Croatian translations, or perhaps because of the changes of didactic nature, the text has been present in the Croatian educational system to a certain extent throughout the years.

Conclusion

The present analysis of the Croatian reception of *Winnie-the-Pooh* shows that the book has so far led "a comparatively marginal life" (Wozniak 2013, 200) in the Croatian literary and academic context. The fairly unenthusiastic response (especially when compared to the status of the book in other cultures) to *Medo*

Winnie may be ascribed to several factors: the first translation's establishment of children as the sole readership; the late appearance of the second edition, published at a time when the Disney version of Milne's characters was gaining precedence in the public imagination; and the overly didactic approach of the translators. While the book's consistent appearance on required and recommended reading lists points to recognition of its canonical status, literary merit, and linguistic and thematic suitability for young readers, the fact that it has so far always found itself in the "recommended" part of the said list means that it is not necessarily read or studied in Croatian schools. Furthermore, individual (mis)interpretations of the text and its Croatian translation featured in annotated editions, guides, companions, and other resources aimed at students and teachers are (re)shaping the collective knowledge about the book and its characters, forming notions that are not necessarily supported by the source text. While the fact that the book has found its place in the Croatian curriculum confirms its canonical status, it is important to bear in mind that its true literary potential surpasses contemporary didactic interpretations and explanations.

A possible next step in future explorations of this topic might be aimed at determining the extent to which *Medo Winnie* is actually read in primary schools and what its reception is among primary school students. Interviews with students and teachers as well as classroom observations could reveal much about students' responses and the ways in which the book is read, interpreted, and taught in class. Comparisons with the Croatian perception and reception of other classics of anglophone children's literature that have been adapted into Disney films such as *Alice's Adventures in Wonderland*, *Peter Pan*, and *The Jungle Book* may also yield interesting results. Finally, additional research on general translation and literary trends in Croatia in the 1980s and 1990s might provide further insight into the possible reasons for the book's status and reception in Croatia.

Notes

This work has been fully supported by the Croatian Science Foundation under the project BIBRICH (UIP-2014–09–9823).

1. Originally, the state was named the Federal People's Republic of Yugoslavia. It was renamed the Socialist Federal Republic of Yugoslavia in 1963.

2. The Croatian language belongs to the group of South Slavic languages, which also includes Bosnian, Bulgarian, Serbian, Slovenian, Macedonian, and Montenegrin. Bulgarian,

Slovenian, and Macedonian each has its own particular dialect that has served as the founda-tion for a separate standard language, while Bosnian, Serbian, and Montenegrin are based on the Neo-Shtokavian dialect, with clearly defined historical, dialectal, cultural, and literary differences. While Croatian was standardized on the basis of the same dialect in the nine-teenth century, in reality it also comprises two additional dialects: Chakavian and Kajkavian. Each of the three dialects is named after its word for "what": 'što' /ʃtɒ/, 'ča' /tʃʌ/, and 'kaj' / kaɪ/, respectively. They are all recognized as variants of literary Croatian, and each of them is predominantly spoken in one of the three regions of Croatia. Croatian has been recorded in Latin documents since the ninth century, with first written records in Croatian dating from the beginning of the twelfth century. The languages standardized on the basis of the Neo-Shtokavian dialect mostly share some basic features (phonology, basic vocabulary, and, partly, grammar), so language users of Croatian, Bosnian, Serbian, and Montenegrin can mostly understand each other in everyday conversation. However, many elements of one of the lan-guages are not applicable or usable in the other three, nor are "any of the active users of those standardized languages, without lengthy and complex preparations, able to produce oral or written texts acceptable in other Neo-Shtokavian standard languages that would be authentic or accepted by their native users" (Hrvatska akademija znanosti i umjetnosti 2007).

3. The new republic's recognition of four official languages was established by the consti-tutional document of Yugoslavia's highest political body (the Anti-Fascist Council for the National Liberation of Yugoslavia) in 1944, during the preparations for the establishment of the SFRY.

4. By using Ferdinand de Saussure's structuralist and Charles Bally's stylistic methods, Petar Guberina proved the autonomy of the Croatian language (Guberina and Krstić 1940). For an overview of the various phonological, orthographical, syntactic, morphological, lexi-cal, stylistic, historical, and other differences between Croatian and Serbian, see, for instance, Babić 2009; Bašić 2017; and Tafra 2012. Due to their historical and cultural contexts, the two languages belong to two traditions: Croatian developed in the context of Western heri-tage (including Latin as the language of international communication), while Serbian, with its Byzantine roots (including Turkish and Old Church Slavic linguistic heritage), was part of the "Eastern tradition" (Šoljan 1988).

5. Slovenian and Macedonian were not affected by the Novi Sad Agreement because they are not directly understood by speakers of other languages, while Montenegrin and Bosnian have just recently (in 2007 and 2017, respectively) been officially recognized as standard languages.

6. Such hybrid literary texts were also a common publishing practice outside of Croatia. Only a few years after the Novi Sad Agreement, in 1957, a Croatian children's classic (*The Strange Adventures of Hlapić the Apprentice* by Ivana Brlić-Mažuranić, 1913) was published for the first time in the Cyrillic script in Bosnia and Herzegovina (Narančić Kovač and Lovrić Kralj 2019).

7. The only other of Milne's work translated into Croatian is his 1922 crime novel *The Red House Mystery* (*Tajna crvene kuće*, published in 2016).

8. O'Sullivan notes that *Winnie-the-Pooh* sold more than one million copies in the year of its original publication (1993, 112).

9. This information is based on author- and title-based searches of UNESCO's Index Translationum (UNESCO n.d.).

10. The choice of title may have been influenced by the title of the revised 1966 Serbian translation, *Vini zvani Pu* (Vini called Pu). Where no published English translation is avail-able, the titles and quotations have been translated into English by the authors.

11. For a complete bibliography of books published in the Vjeverica series, see Radošević 2016a.

12. In their selection of titles for publication, Katarina Zrinski, Mladost, and other publishers of children's literature relied (and continue to rely) heavily on the reading lists for primary schools. Namely, inclusion in the lists meant that there was already a market for a particular book (teachers, parents, librarians, etc.). Therefore, reading lists provided perhaps the biggest incentive for selecting a particular book for publication.

13. The original text reads: "Naravno da je Pooh glavni junak, o tome nema dvojbe, niti bih to htio zanijekati. No Praščić je zato glavni junak u mnogim zgodama gdje je Pooh posve nevažan. Ta vi, djeco, i te kako dobro znate da Medu Pooha ne možeš poskrivečki ponijeti u školu. Svatko će ga vidjeti, a možda vam se čak i rugati. A Praščić? Praščić je tako malešan da ga možeš neopazice gurnuti u džep! I sami znate kako je utješno gnječiti i milovati u džepu neku dragu igračkicu, pogotovo kad nisi posve siguran je li dva puta sedam dvanaest ili dvadeset dva. Praščić ponekad izviri iz Christopherova džepa i zaviri u tintarnicu" (Pervan-Plavec 1986, 8–9).

14. The original text reads: "Upomoć!—viknuo je Pooh.—Morat ću natrag u brlog.—Sto mu gromova!—brzo je dodao.—Ne smijem natrag. Moram izaći. Nevolja je u tome što ne mogu ni naprijed ni natrag. Zaglavio sam se!—vikne očajan. Sto mu gromova! Pomozite!" (Pervan-Plavec 1986, 35).

15. For more on Disney's adaptation of Milne's work, see, for example, Collins Smith and Smith 2016; and Taylor 2005.

16. The course covers the following areas: Croatian language and communication, literature and literary creation, and culture and media.

17. A detailed list of all recommended titles in twentieth-century Croatian primary education is available online (Narančić Kovač and Milković 2018).

18. One should be careful not to overlook a variety of extraliterary factors that have considerable influence on the formation of primary school reading lists, such as school policies, curricula for the Croatian language course, teachers' preferences, and the active role of publishing houses (Hameršak 2006, 103). Moreover, the lists are inevitably influenced by dominant ideologies and changes in the political and social context (Hameršak 2006, 104–5).

19. Andersen's fairy tales were first published in Croatian children's magazines in the form of adaptations. Together with the Brothers Grimm's fairy tales, they are among the first translated texts read to Croatian children and are subsequently included in lists of required and recommended reading.

20. Consider the following example: (*source text*) "Now, if you have a green balloon, they might think you were only part of the tree, *and* not notice you, *and* if you have a blue balloon, they might think you were only part of the sky, *and* not notice you, *and* the question is: Which is most likely?" (Milne [1926] 2005, 13, emphases added). / (*back translation*) "Now, if you have a green balloon, the bees might think you were nothing but some part of the tree, so they won't even notice you. If you have a blue balloon, they might think you are just part of the sky, so again they won't notice you. The question is, which is more likely?" (translated from Pervan-Plavec 1986, 21–22: E sad, ako imaš zeleni balon pčele mogu pomisliti da nisi ništa drugo nego dio stabla, pa te neće ni zamijetiti. Ako imaš plavi balon, mogu pomisliti da si tek dio neba, pa te opet neće zamijetiti. Pitanje je, dakle, što je vjerojatnije?).

21. Owl and Rabbit are not based on Christopher Milne's toys. This difference is highlighted in Shepard's illustrations, which depict the two characters as real animals (Connolly 1999, 205n9).

Bibliography

Babić, Stjepan. 2009. "Hrvatski književni jezik, ponajprije njim samim" [Standard Croatian language, foremost by itself]. *Jezik* 56, no. 5: 161–200.

Bašić, Nataša. 2017. "Deklaracija o nazivu i položaju hrvatskog književnog jezika u povijesti hrvatskoga jezika i jezikoslovlja" [Declaration on the status and name of standard Croatian in the history of the Croatian language and linguistics]. *Jezik* 64, no. 1: 3–14.

Batović, Ante. 2007. *The Croatian Spring: Nationalism, Repression and Foreign Policy Under Tito*. London: I. B. Tauris.

Bikić, Ante Vladimir. 2003. *Susret sa suncem 4* [Encounter with the sun 4]. Zagreb: Alfa.

"Bilješka o ilustratoru" [Note on the illustrator]. 2012. In *Medo Winnie zvani Pooh*, by A. A. Milne, translated by Marina Leustek, illustrated by E. H. Shepard, 142. 5th ed. Varaždin, Croatia: Katarina Zrinski.

"Bilješka o piscu" [Note on the author]. 2012. In *Medo Winnie zvani Pooh*, by A. A. Milne, translated by Marina Leustek, illustrated by E. H. Shepard, 141. 5th ed. Varaždin, Croatia: Katarina Zrinski.

Braithwaite, V. A. 1986. "Old Age Stereotypes: Reconciling Contradictions." *Journal of Gerontology* 41, no. 3 (May): 353–60. doi:10.1093/geronj/41.3.353.

Cadden, Mike. 2005. "Simultaneous Emotions: Entwining Modes in Children's Books." *Children's Literature in Education* 36, no. 3: 285–98. doi:10.1007/s10583-005-5975-y.

Čajić, Inga, Anita Dragičević, Aleksandra Fulgozi-Pavlović, and Snježana Gabelić. 2005. *Lektira na dlanu za osnovne škole 1: Repozitorij književnih djela za niže razrede osnovne škole* [Required reading in the palm of your hand, for elementary schools, 1: A repository of literary works for lower grades of primary school]. Zagreb: SysPrint.

Centar za predškolski odgoj. 1995. *Poezija: Odgojno-obrazovni rad* [Poetry: A pedagogical-educational work]. Osijek: Centar za predškolski odgoj, 1995.

Centner, Sandra, Anđelka Peko, and Ana Pintarić. 2005. *Zlatni dani 2* [Golden days 2]. Zagreb: Školska knjiga.

Collins Smith, Anne, and Owen M. Smith. 2016. "The Tao at Pooh Corner: Disney's Portrayal of a Very Philosophical Bear." In *It's the Disney Version! Popular Cinema and Literary Classics*, edited by Douglas Brode and Shea T. Brode, 165–76. Lanham, MD: Rowman and Littlefield.

Connolly, Paula T. 1999. "The Marketing of Romantic Childhood: Milne, Disney, and a Very Popular Stuffed Bear." In *Literature and the Child: Romantic Continuations, Postmodern Contestations*, edited by James Holt McGavran, 188–207. Iowa City: University of Iowa Press.

Deszcz, Justyna. 2002. "Beyond the Disney Spell; or, Escape into Pantoland." *Folklore* 113, no. 1 (April): 83–101. doi:10.1080/0015587022012546 2.

Egmont Publishing. n.d. "O nama" [About us]. https://www.egmont.hr/o_nama.

Gabelica, Marina, Ana Radmanić, Anita Skrbin, and Ljiljana Varjačić. 2014. "Lektira: Zadnja crta obrane čitanja u digitalnome dobu" [Required reading: The last line of defense of reading in the digital age]. *Književnost i dijete* 3, no. 4: 54–73.

Gabelica, Marina, and Dubravka Težak. 2017. *Kreativni pristup lektiri* [Creative approach to required reading]. Zagreb: Učiteljski fakultet Sveučilišta u Zagrebu.

Guberina, Petar, and Kruno Krstić. 1940. *Razlike između hrvatskoga i srpskoga književnog jezika* [Differences between the Croatian and Serbian literary languages]. Zagreb: Izdanje Matice hrvatske.

Hameršak, Marijana. 2006. "Osnovnoškolska lektira između kanona i popisa, institucija i ideologija" [Elementary school recommended reading between canons and lists, institutions and ideology]. *Narodna umjetnost* 43, no. 2: 95–113.

Hrvatska akademija znanosti i umjetnosti [Croatian Academy of Sciences and Arts]. 2007. Hrvatski jezik [Croatian language]. *Jezik* 54, no. 2: 41–80.

Kidd, Kenneth B. 2011. *Freud in Oz: At the Intersections of Psychoanalysis and Children's Literature*. Minneapolis: University of Minnesota Press.

Klaudy, Kinga. 1998. "Explicitation." In *Routledge Encyclopedia of Translation Studies*, edited by Mona Baker, 80–84. London: Routledge.

Kujundžić, Nada, and Ivana Milković. 2018. "Disneyjeve višestruke intermedijalne adaptacije proznih djela anglofone književnosti za djecu i mladež u hrvatskim prijevodima" [Disney's multiple intermedial adaptations of anglophone children's and young adult literature in Croatian translations]. *Književna smotra* 50, no. 190, issue 4: 121–31.

Kuznets, Lois Rostow. 1994. *When Toys Come Alive: Narratives of Animation, Metamorphosis, and Development*. New Haven, CT: Yale University Press.

Lathey, Gillian. 2011. "The Translation of Literature for Children." In *The Oxford Handbook of Translation Studies*, edited by Kirsten Malmkjær and Kevin Windle, 198–214. Oxford: Oxford University Press.

Lektire.hr. n.d. "Medo Winnie zvani Pooh." https://www.lektire.hr/medo-winnie-zvani-pooh/.

Leniček, Eva. 2002. *Lektira u razrednoj nastavi* [Required reading in the classroom]. Petrinja, Croatia: Visoka učiteljska škola.

Leustek, Marina, trans. 2005. *Medo Winnie zvani Pooh*, by A. A. Milne, illustrated by Nevenka Macolić. 3rd ed. Varaždin, Croatia: Katarina Zrinski.

Lurie, Alison. 1973. "Back to Pooh Corner." *Children's Literature* 2: 11–17. doi:10.1353/chl.0.0566.

Milković, Ivana. 2015. "Prijevodi anglofone književnosti kao kulturna sastavnica hrvatskih čitanki za niže razrede osnovne škole" [Translations of anglophone literature as a cultural component of Croatian readers for lower grades of primary school]. PhD thesis, Učiteljski fakultet Sveučilišta u Zagrebu.

Milne, A. A. (1926) 2005. *Winnie-the-Pooh*. Illustrated by E. H. Shepard. London: Puffin Books.

Ministarstvo znanosti, obrazovanja i športa. 2006. *Nastavni plan i program za osnovnu školu* [Teaching plan and program for primary school]. http://www.azoo.hr/images/AZOO/Ravnatelji/RM/Nastavni_plan_i_program_za_osnovnu_skolu_-_MZOS_2006_.pdf.

Ministarstvo znanosti i obrazovanja. 2019. *Kurikulum nastavnog predmeta Hrvatski jezik za osnovne škole i gimnazije* [Croatian language curriculum for primary and grammar schools].

Nance-Carroll, Niall. 2015. "Not Only, But Also: Entwined Modes and the Fantastic in A. A. Milne's Pooh Stories." *Lion and the Unicorn* 39, no. 1 (January): 63–81. doi:10.1353/uni.2015.0010.

Narančić Kovač, Smiljana. 2012. "Slučaj dječje književnosti" [The case of children's literature]. In *Peti hrvatski slavistički kongres: Zbornik radova s međunarodnoga znanstvenoga skupa, knjiga 2* [The fifth Croatian Slavic Congress: Proceedings from the international conference, vol. 2], edited by Marija Turk and Ines Srdoč-Konestra, 643–51. Rijeka: Filozofski fakultet, Sveučilište u Rijeci.

Narančič Kovač, Smiljana. 2019. "The Status of Illustrations in Croatian Translations of Children's Classics." *Umjetnost riječi* 63, nos. 3–4: 211–30.

Narančić Kovač, Smiljana, and Sanja Lovrić Kralj. 2019. "Prijevodi *Hlapića* na druge jezike" [Translations of *Hlapić* into other languages]. In *Hlapić u bijelom svijetu* [Hlapić in the big wide world], edited by Smiljana Narančić Kovač, 9–41. Zagreb: Učiteljski fakultet Sveučilišta u Zagrebu.

Narančić Kovač, Smiljana, and Ivana Milković. 2018. *Lektira u hrvatskoj osnovnoj školi: Popis naslova* [Reading lists in Croatian primary schools: A list of titles]. BIBRICH. http://bibrich.ufzg.hr/lektira/.

Nikolajeva, Maria, and Carole Scott. 2006. *How Picturebooks Work*. 2nd ed. New York: Garland.

Oittinen, Riitta. 2008. "From Thumbelina to Winnie-the-Pooh: Pictures, Words, and Sounds in Translation." *Meta* 53, no. 1 (March): 76–89. doi:10.7202/017975ar.

O'Sullivan, Emer. 1993. "The Fate of the Dual Addressee in the Translation of Children's Literature." *New Comparison* 16 (January): 109–19.

O'Sullivan, Emer. 2005. *Comparative Children's Literature*. Translated by Anthea Bell. Abingdon, Oxon., England: Routledge.

Papusha, Olga. 2005. "Translation as Adaptation: The *Winnie-the-Pooh* Stories as Children's and Adult Reading." *LiterNet*, November 9. https://liternet.bg/publish15/o_papusha/translation.htm.

Perić, Marica. 2012. "Balogovo blago: pjesništvo Zvonimira Baloga" [Balog's treasure: Zvonimir Balog's poetry]. *Libri & Liberi* 1, no. 2: 253–60. doi:10.21066/carcl.libri.2012-01(02).0044.

Pervan-Plavec, Mia, trans. 1986. *Medo Winnie zvani Pooh*, by A. A. Milne, illustrated by E. H. Shepard. Zagreb: Mladost.

Polak, Sanja, and Darko Cindrić. 2004. *Cvrkut riječi* [Chirp of words]. Zagreb: Alfa.

Ptiček, Mirjana. 2018. Personal interview, July 18.

Radošević, Vesna. 2016a. "Bibliografija biblioteke Vjeverice" [Bibliography of the "Squirrel" publishing series]. *Libri & Liberi* 5, no. 1: 194–236. doi:10.21066/carcl.libri.2016-05(01).0009.

Radošević, Vesna. 2016b. "The Eternal Vjeverica". *Libri & Liberi* 5, no. 1: 153–92. doi:10.21066/carcl.libri.2016-05(01).0008.

Reynolds, Kimberley. 2011. *Children's Literature: A Very Short Introduction*. Oxford: Oxford University Press.

Rosandić, Dragutin. 1976. *Književnost u osnovnoj školi* [Literature in primary school]. Zagreb: Školska knjiga.

Rosandić, Dragutin. 1986. *Metodika književnog odgoja i obrazovanja* [Methods of literary pedagogy and education]. Zagreb: Školska knjiga.

Rosandić, Dragutin. 2005. *Metodika književnog odgoja* [Methods of literary pedagogy]. Zagreb: Školska knjiga.

Santo, Avi. 2015. *Selling the Silver Bullet: The Lone Ranger and Transmedia Brand Licensing*. Austin: University of Texas Press.

Sipe, Lawrence R. 1998. "How Picture Books Work: A Semiotically Framed Theory of Text-Picture Relationships." *Children's Literature in Education* 29, no. 2: 97–108. doi:10.1023/A:1022459009182.

Šoljan, Antun. 1988. "Carrollov 'Jabberwocky' u dvije tradicije" [Carroll's "Jabberwocky" in two traditions]. *Književna smotra* 21, nos. 69–72: 113–16.

Tafra, Branka. 2012. *Prinosi povijesti hrvatskoga jezikoslovlja* [Contributions to the history of Croatian linguistics]. Zagreb: Hrvatski studiji Sveučilišta u Zagrebu.

Tashlitsky, Xenia. n.d. "Lost in Translation: *Winnie-the-Pooh* in Russian and English." http://international.ucla.edu/media/files/Tashlitsky.pdf.

Taylor, Aaron. 2005. "Everybody Wants a Piece of Pooh: Winnie, from Adaptation to Market Saturation." In *Rethinking Disney: Private Control, Public Dimensions*, edited by Mike Budd and Max H. Kirsch, 181–98. Middletown, CT: Wesleyan University Press.

Tremper, Ellen. 1977. "Instigorating Winnie the Pooh." *Lion and the Unicorn* 1, no. 1: 33–46. doi:10.1353/uni.0.0210.

United Nations Educational, Scientific and Cultural Organization (UNESCO). n.d. Index Translationum. http://www.unesco.org/xtrans/.

Uskoković, Davor. 2009. *Vodič kroz lektiru za niže razrede osnovne škole. I–IV. razred* [Guide to required reading for lower grades of primary school, grades 1–4]. 4th ed. Zagreb: Mozaik knjiga.

Van Coillie, Jan. 2006. "Character Names in Translation: A Functional Approach." In *Children's Literature in Translation: Challenges and Strategies*, edited by Jan Van Coillie and Walter P. Verschueren, 123–39. Manchester: St. Jerome.

Venuti, Lawrence. 2008. *The Translator's Invisibility: A History of Translation*. 2nd ed. Abingdon, Oxon., England: Routledge.

Visinko, Karol. 2005. *Dječja priča: Povijest, teorija, recepcija i interpretacija* [Children's story: History, theory, reception, and interpretation]. Zagreb: Školska knjiga.

Wozniak, Monika. 2013. "To Be or Not to Be a Canonical Text of Children's Literature: Polish and Italian Translations of *Winnie-the-Pooh*." In *Adapting Canonical Texts in Children's Literature*, edited by Anja Müller, 195–212. London: Bloomsbury.

Wozniak, Monika. 2014. "The Strange Case of *Kubuś Puchatek* and *Fredzia Phi-Phi*: Polish Translations of Milne's *Winnie-the-Pooh*." In *La Retraduction en littérature de jeunesse / Retranslating Children's Literature*, edited by Virginie Douglas and Florence Cabaret, 179–92. Brussels: PIE Peter Lang.

Županić, Jadranka. 2012a. "Predgovor" [Foreword]. In *Medo Winnie zvani Pooh*, by A. A. Milne, translated by Marina Leustek, illustrated by E. H. Shepard, 4–5. 5th ed. Varaždin, Croatia: Katarina Zrinski.

Županić, Jadranka. 2012b. "Razgovarajmo o djelu" [Let's talk about the book]. *Medo Winnie zvani Pooh*, by A. A. Milne, translated by Marina Leustek, illustrated by E. H. Shepard, 137–39. 5th ed. Varaždin, Croatia: Katarina Zrinski.

CHAPTER 8

Brains and Fluff
Classification, Colonialism, and Childhood in A. A. Milne's Pooh Books

Sarah E. Jackson

It is difficult to read certain children's "classics" in isolation from the colonial contexts in which they were written. Books like Rudyard Kipling's *The Jungle Book*, Hugh Lofting's Doctor Dolittle series, or Jean de Brunhoff's Babar stories—all still widely read—have garnered considerable criticism from academics and lay readers alike.[1] These texts are some of the most prominent examples of colonial influence in children's literature, but as Clare Bradford asserts: "To read children's books of the nineteenth and twentieth centuries is to read texts produced within a pattern of imperial culture" (2001, 196). According to Bradford, *all* books written for children since the height of European expansion respond to imperialism in some way, even those that, on the surface, seem least concerned with the trappings of empire. A. A. Milne's *Winnie-the-Pooh* (1926) and *The House at Pooh Corner* (1928) are two of the most notable examples of stories set in what Humphrey Carpenter (2009) and others have seen as an arcadian, peaceful realm insulated from the pressures and dangers of the adult world. Yet the Pooh stories are not immune from the influence of colonialism. While the books clearly reflect their nature as products of the British Empire, they also present a complicated understanding of colonialism.

In this chapter, I draw on rhetorical theory to examine this complexity. I highlight the ways the characters in the Pooh books use classification, a rhetorical strategy common in colonial discourse, for various purposes. Throughout the stories, they classify each other, themselves, and their environment in order to appear knowledgeable and in control of their surroundings, establish a hierarchy among themselves, and gain power over each other. However, rhetoric can also be a site of anticolonial resistance. At times, the animals and narrator use classification and reclassification to resist and thwart the efforts of the classifying colonizers, a role most characters take on at one point or another. In other words, a focus on classification makes visible both the colonizing and anticolonizing tendencies that coexist and respond to each other in Milne's Forest. There exists in the Forest a remarkable fluidity between colonizer and colonized, between classification and reclassification. Ultimately in the Pooh books, Milne creates a realm wherein dialogic linguistic play can thrive, isolated from and resisting the most monologic forces of the British Empire.

Colonizer and Colonized in Pooh

Daphne M. Kutzer provides the most sophisticated and extensive treatment of colonialism in Pooh in her book, *Empire's Children: Empire and Imperialism in Classic British Children's Books* (2000). She claims that imperialism is at work on three different levels within the texts. First, she aligns herself with Jacqueline Rose and Perry Nodelman, who argue that all children's literature is a colonization of the child by the adult. In the case of Pooh, Kutzer asserts, "Christopher Robin has been colonized by the adult narrator" because the adult narrator maintains control over his stories (96). Second, she notes the colonization of the animal by the human, saying that Christopher Robin acts as a benevolent colonizer toward his toys, controlling their activities. Finally, Kutzer highlights the imperialism "present in the nature of the animals themselves" (98). I am primarily interested in this third category of colonization, in which animals colonize other animals because it is at this level that the most shifting occurs between the roles of colonizer and colonized.

The most obvious examples of imperialism within the stories themselves are the instances when Milne parodies nineteenth-century adventure novels and hunting narratives. Chapter titles such as "In Which Pooh and Piglet Go Hunting and Nearly Catch a Woozle" and "In Which It Is Shown That

Tiggers Don't Climb Trees" are reminiscent of nineteenth-century novels for boys that promised adventure in the uncharted, uncivilized colonies. Indeed, the creatures initially considered to be strange or frightening by the animals in the Forest are those that have connections to British colonies (Kutzer 2000, 99). Kanga, Roo, and Tigger (kangaroos and a tiger—or at least a tiger-like creature) are the only new animals to be introduced to the Forest. As Sune Borkfelt notes, it is not uncommon for nonnative animals to feature in children's books written during this time period, but the reaction that these outsider characters receive from the inhabitants of the Forest is telling (2009, 557). When Kanga and Roo arrive, Rabbit expresses the attitude of an indignant adult encountering immigrants from the colonies: "Here—we—are . . . all—of—us, and then, suddenly, we wake up one morning and, what do we find? We find a Strange Animal among us. An animal of whom we have never even heard before! An animal who carries her family about with her in her pocket!" (Milne 1958, 92). They are "Strange Animals" who look different and behave differently from anyone else in the Forest and as such represent the intrusion of the colonies into Milne's arcadia. Furthermore, because Tigger ends up living with Kanga and Roo, the three outsiders in the books effectively create a foreign ghetto in much the same way that immigrants did in various cities across Europe and the United States. In short, Pooh can be seen as a prime example of what Donald E. Hall calls the "colonial project at home"; despite the theme of domesticity that runs throughout the books, it becomes clear that the proverbial sun that shone over the entire British Empire casts shadows in Milne's Forest as well (Hall 1991, 52).

Some characters in the Pooh stories are consistently more colonizing than others. Christopher Robin leads the expedition to the North Pole, and he sometimes spends his mornings "indoors going to Africa and back" (Milne 1958, 170). Rabbit is behind both the plan to kidnap Roo and the attempt to change Tigger's wild nature by "unbouncing" him (256). Kanga literally whitewashes Piglet to the extent that he is given a new identity. A handful of scholars note what Peter Hunt calls an "interesting tension between characters who are essentially 'adult-like' [. . .] and those who are essentially childlike," although none agree completely on how the categories should be drawn (Hunt 2001, 101). Typically, the characters who are more consistently designated adults are also the ones who behave most like European colonists. This pairing would seem to confirm Nodelman's argument that the relationships between adults and children involve an "inevitable imperialism" (1992, 34). However,

Kutzer's second category of imperial activity—Christopher Robin colonizing the animals—positions *all* the animal characters as colonized, even those who most frequently adopt colonial language and behaviors.

In the Pooh books, therefore, the lines between adulthood and childhood on the one hand and colonizer and colonized on the other are not as clear-cut. While certain characters in the Pooh stories seem to be the worst offenders in terms of their colonizing actions, a more careful study reveals that their roles as colonizers are relative to each other. Rabbit's consideration of himself as second only to Christopher Robin indicates that, like the other animals, he thinks of the boy as their benevolent ruler. Likewise, Kutzer's argument that Christopher Robin is both colonizer (of his toys) and colonized (by the narrator within the story and his father outside of it) demonstrates how slippery the binary can be.

Similarly, even those who are not the primary perpetrators of the most objectionable colonizing actions in the stories still occasionally move in and out of the position of the colonizer. When readers first encounter Pooh, for instance, he is in the process of invading a beehive in order to get honey. Upon hearing some bees, he says to himself: "[T]he only reason for being a bee that I know of is making honey . . . And the only reason for making honey is so as *I* can eat it" (Milne 1958, 18). His characteristic narcissism is often benign, but in this case, it can be understood as colonial: Pooh believes that the bees' sole purpose is to provide honey to satiate his cravings, and he goes to great lengths to obtain the honey. He even acknowledges that he needs to "deceive . . . the Queen Bee" (27). From the bees' perspective, Pooh is an invader, and they are rightfully "*suspicious*" (26). At other points in the books, Pooh and Piglet may not initiate colonial schemes, but they play central roles in them, nevertheless. Each is essential in Rabbit's schemes against Kanga, Roo, and Tigger. Rather than a colonizing/colonized binary, it is helpful to consider a spectrum along which characters move fluidly in relation to each other and their environment. Hunt claims that "[s]ome of the best moments" in the Pooh books "are generated by the contrast between adult solipsism and childhood innocence" (Hunt 2001, 101). I argue that part of the enduring fascination with the Pooh stories comes from a similar tension between the colonizing and anticolonizing attitudes within and among the individuals in the Forest. Through the language of classification, which I discuss next, the characters can both colonize *and* resist colonization; when language is flexible, the binary of colonizer/colonized is not fixed.

Classification as Colonial Rhetoric

Rhetoric is key to success as a colonizer. While Kutzer's reading of the Pooh books is helpful in highlighting the presence of imperialism at work on multiple levels in the texts, her analysis leaves out the role of rhetoric in the colonial process, a significant omission, since, as Bradford says, "[r]elations of colonial power were constructed through language" (2007, 19). In *The Rhetoric of Empire: Colonial Discourse in Journalism, Travel Writing, and Imperial Administration* (1993), David Spurr lists a number of rhetorical concepts found in writing about the colonies. In the remainder of this chapter, I demonstrate how characters in the Pooh stories use one of these rhetorical concepts—classification—to both colonizing and anticolonizing ends. First, I provide examples of how the characters classify for three different purposes: to appear knowledgeable and therefore in control of their environment; to establish a hierarchy; and to exert power over others. Next, I demonstrate that classification and reclassification can also indicate instances of anticolonizing resistance, albeit sometimes unintentionally. I conclude with the final story in the Pooh books, which provides an example of how colonial classification and anticolonial reclassification can occur in a single character simultaneously. I hope to show that, although true, it is insufficient to say that the Pooh stories are colonial, as Kutzer and others have argued. A close focus on rhetoric reveals Milne's complex and, at times, contradictory narrative world in which readers can encounter a range of perspectives on colonialism as characters shift in and out of the role of colonizers through their language.

Classification as Colonization

In his insightful investigation into rhetorical modes employed by colonial writers, David Spurr devotes one chapter to classification. All language can be seen at some level as classification, and "humans have an innate ability to classify" (Borchers 2006, 313). However, at the same time that European colonialism was on the rise in the eighteenth century, classification became a particular "system of ordering that allowed for a hierarchy of characters depending on their relative complexity of organic structure and for classification according to certain key functions: how a species reproduces or what it eats" (Spurr 1993, 63). Spurr demonstrates how classification was therefore a way for colonial writers not merely to organize information about the colonies and the people who lived there, but to establish "hierarch[ies] based on internal character" (63). To classify is to justify domination and power over those further down in the hierarchy.

The Pooh books are filled with mock classification, often indicated by Milne's characteristic capitalization of words normally written in lowercase. Pooh is famously known as a "Bear of Very Little Brain" (Milne 1958, 56). When he goes for a walk to find Piglet, he classifies it as a "fast Thinking Walk" (163). When he and Piglet "go Hunting," he classifies the tracks they spot in the snow: "Three, as it were, Woozles, and one, as it was, Wizzle" (49). Much of the time, this organizing functions largely as a wink from Milne to the reader. At other times, though, characters classify to gain control or power over each other or their environment, and it is here that Spurr's discussion of colonial classification is especially salient. The characters in Pooh use classification to appear knowledgeable and to gain control of a confusing or potentially threatening environment. From plants to people, Europeans classified everything they could in the territories they invaded. Bernard S. Cohn notes that classification was one of the most crucial methods Europeans used to create and control knowledge in a colony (1996, 7). Similarly, when they encounter something new in their environment, be it a creature or some words, the characters in the Pooh books employ the language of categorization to create and control (usually fabricated) knowledge about it. When Owl and Rabbit are concerned about the meaning of Christopher Robin's mysterious note, "Gon out. Backson," Owl "gave a great sigh of relief" when he decided that it meant their friend has gone out with a creature called a "Backson." Owl feels the need to further classify this newly invented creature; although he admits he doesn't "know what they're like," he knows enough to call it "the Spotted or Herbaceous Backson" (Milne 1958, 232). This layer of specificity adds order and "relief" in what might otherwise be a confusing and alarming situation.

The animals in Milne's books classify other creatures—even when they don't exist—in order to appear knowledgeable and in control of their surroundings. In some cases, this can allow them to manipulate each other. In another story, when Kanga and Roo arrive in the Forest, Piglet explains that, according to Christopher Robin, "a Kanga was Generally Regarded as One of the Fiercer Animals" (Milne 1958, 94). Rabbit imitates Christopher Robin's attempt at scientific parlance when he reassures Piglet that "Kangas were only Fierce during the winter months, being at other times of an Affectionate

Disposition" (95). Rabbit uses this classifying language not out of kindness to Piglet (whom he tells bluntly, "you haven't any pluck") but in order to convince him to join him in kidnapping Roo (94). Spurr says that classification is a form of "enframing," relying on Heidegger's term meaning "the process by which the mind transforms the world into an object" (Spurr 1993, 71). Rabbit uses classification to transform Kanga into an object to expel from the Forest and in the process turns Piglet into an object, a "very small animal that . . . will be Useful" to his plan (Milne 1958, 95).

Of all the characters in the books, Rabbit is the most concerned with classification, largely because it allows him to establish a hierarchy among the animals in the Forest. As Bill Ashcroft, Gareth Griffiths, and Helen Tiffin note: "Language becomes the means through which a hierarchical structure of power is perpetuated, and the medium through which the conceptions of 'truth,' 'order,' and 'reality' become established" (2003, 7). Rabbit uses classifying language to establish what he believes to be the true hierarchical order in the Forest. He demonstrates the connection between power and categorization when he wakes up feeling "important, as if everything depended on him. It was just the day for Organizing Something" (Milne 1958, 226). He relates organization to "feeling important," because as he establishes a hierarchy of animals in the Forest, he places himself near the top: "After all," says Rabbit to himself, "Christopher Robin depends on Me. He's fond of Pooh and Piglet and Eeyore, and so am I, but they haven't any Brain" (227). Later, Rabbit describes the kind of day in which the other animals in the Forest might respond to him by saying, "'Yes, Rabbit' and 'No, Rabbit,' and waited until he had told them," as "Captainish" (226). His use of this military term demonstrates how he positions himself over the other animals through classification. He then proceeds to describe why the other animals are also inferior in their own ways. Rabbit views himself as a captain, second only to Christopher Robin in the hierarchy he invents.

Indeed, Rabbit is the one in whom Christopher Robin confides during the North Pole expedition and the character who initiates the efforts to rid the Forest of the three foreign animals. Spurr notes: "Colonial discourse [. . .] finds a natural justification of the conquest of nature and of primitive peoples, those 'children of nature'" (1993, 156). Rabbit describes and organizes his world according to what he sees as natural qualities in his friends, such as Tigger's bounciness, Piglet's small stature, or Kanga's and Roo's strangeness. Rabbit tells Owl, "[Y]ou and I have brains. The others have fluff," and considers them to be the only ones in the Forest capable of any real *thinking*" (Milne 1958, 230). In colonial writing, there is a clear "hierarchical classification of humanity along a series of gradations ranged between the two poles of civilization and savagery" (Spurr 1993, 67). Rabbit's designations of those with "brains" and those with "fluff"—those who "must do" the "thinking to be done" and those who must not—parallels this classification (Milne 1958, 230).[2] Rabbit accounts for his "Captainish" behavior and language through these arbitrary comparisons; as in colonial writing, classification in the Pooh books simultaneously reveals and justifies hierarchy (226).

Classification in colonial writing both results in and is caused by a distinctly linear understanding of governments and cultures, one that draws on the science of evolution (Spurr 1993, 62). In response to his classification, Rabbit's understanding of the world is likewise linear. On the "Expotition to the North Pole"—the most explicitly colonial activity the animals engage in together—"[f]irst came Christopher Robin and Rabbit, then Piglet and Pooh; then Kanga, with Roo in her pocket, and Owl; then Eeyore; and, at the end, in a long line, all Rabbit's friends-and-relations" (Milne 1958, 114). While the animals may have arranged themselves in this fashion on their own after Christopher Robin defined expedition as "a long line of everybody," Rabbit is invested in preserving this line (111). When his "friends-and-relations" show up, he makes it clear that they are the least important animals present: "I didn't ask them," he says. "They just came. They always do. They can march at the end, after Eeyore" (114). Rabbit treats his unnamed family members as insignificant, "carelessly" brushing them aside, to the place farthest from the center of power. Rabbit has stepped out of the line only to organize it further, and once the call comes down the line that the expedition is starting, he rejoins the visible hierarchy. He "hurried off to the front of the Expotition" to rejoin the center of power with Christopher Robin (115). Although the text says that Christopher Robin was at the head of the line, both of the accompanying illustrations show Rabbit ahead of even him. Christopher Robin may have initiated the expedition, but Rabbit is seen as a primary leader. His position of power is reinforced when Christopher Robin takes him aside to ask if Rabbit knows what the North Pole actually looks like. Neither does, of course, but their posturing and seclusion separate them as the leaders of the expedition, and though Pooh ends up finding the pole, they are the ones with the linguistic authority to name it as such. Rabbit's "friends-and-relations," on the other hand, are not mentioned after the discussion of their place in line. They exist, it seems, simply to provide Eeyore with creatures to say "Hush!"

to as the instruction goes down the line. It is telling that there is a group less significant than the character known for reveling in his insignificance. No one in the party seems to notice when the very last member, Alexander Beetle, "was so upset to find that the whole Expotition was saying 'Hush!' to *him* that he buried himself head downwards in a crack in the ground and stayed there for two days until the danger was over" (117). A linear, hierarchical world view privileges those in power and ignores those at the end or the bottom.

Because it establishes hierarchies, classification justifies the exertion of power of those at the top of the hierarchy over those lower down. Classification is, according to Spurr, a "value-positing activity" that "always takes place within a sphere of relations marked by the presence of power" (1993, 71). This connection between power and classification is highlighted in one of the most concerning episodes in the books. When Kanga and Roo arrive in the Forest, Rabbit classifies Kanga as a "Strange Animal." Piglet, "fidgeting a bit," expresses concern that "a Kanga was Generally Regarded as One of the Fiercer Animals," a designation he learned from Christopher Robin (Milne 1958, 92, 94). Rabbit, having already made up his mind about his plan to rid the Forest of the two immigrants, responds to Piglet's concern by classifying Piglet as "[u]seful in the adventure before us" because of his size (95). Likewise, Pooh is deemed essential to the mission and, in response, he classifies himself. "Impossible without Me!" he marvels to himself. "*That* sort of Bear!" (95). Piglet and Pooh both relish the designation Rabbit gives each of them, but neither is aware that Rabbit is in the process of enframing, to return to Heidegger's term, objectifying them so they can provide labor in the service of his scheme.

As the plan to kidnap Roo is unfolding, Pooh attempts to distract Kanga from Roo by sharing a poem he has written, but when she studiously ignores him, he uses classification instead. He points to a tree behind her to get her to look away from Roo, but her eyes remain fixed on her child. In response, and encouraged by Rabbit, Pooh raises the stakes, with Piglet joining in:

> "I can see a bird in [the tree] from here," said Pooh. "Or is it a fish?"
> "You ought to see that bird from here," said Rabbit. "Unless it's a fish."
> "It isn't a fish, it's a bird," said Piglet.
> "So it is," said Rabbit.
> "Is it a starling or a blackbird?" said Pooh.
> "That's the whole question," said Rabbit. "Is it a blackbird or a starling?"
> And then at last Kanga did turn her head to look. (Milne 1958, 102)

After multiple attempts, what finally distracts Kanga enough so that Rabbit can steal her child from her is a question about classification: "Is it a blackbird or a starling?" Colonial classification is inherently distracting, "a misrecognition that allows interpretation to pass for objective truth" (Spurr 1993, 71). In their use of classification, colonial writers connected the visible signs and functions of an object with its "invisible character," thereby justifying subjective valuations with seemingly objective truths; perceived defects in character could be explained through physical differences, and vice versa (Spurr 1993, 64). Pooh, Rabbit, and Piglet may not even be talking about a real bird, and they do not seem to ascribe any moral qualities to it based on its category; however, this instance nevertheless illustrates the distracting nature of classification. They point to something (potentially) visible in order to distract from their secret plan to exert power over Kanga and Roo.

At times, characters justify their actions through emotional and relational classifications in additional to physical ones. When Rabbit plans to "lose" Tigger because the strange new creature is too "Bouncy," he insists that "he'll be a different Tigger altogether . . . he'll be a Humble Tigger. Because he'll be a Sad Tigger, a Melancholy Tigger, a Small and Sorry Tigger, an Oh-Rabbit-I-am-glad-to-see-you Tigger" (Milne 1958, 259). By describing not just how his actions will affect Tigger but how Tigger will become a "different Tigger altogether," Rabbit demonstrates a disregard and disdain for Tigger's personhood. He desires that Tigger become a *fundamentally different being*. When Piglet questions Rabbit's system of classification, saying that he "should hate [Tigger] to go on being Sad," Rabbit replies with another flurry of pseudoscientific jargon: "Tiggers never go on being Sad . . . They get over it with Astonishing Rapidity. I asked Owl, just to make sure, and he said that's what they always get over it with. But if we can make Tigger feel Sad and Small just for five minutes, we shall have done a good deed" (259). Rabbit cites Owl, the other creature in the Forest who has "Brain," and connects his plan with moral duty. Through classification, Rabbit manipulates Pooh and Piglet into following his scheme, making it seem to be not only the intelligent but also the *right* thing to do; Rabbit's plan is the Forest's equivalent of the White Man's Burden.

Throughout the stories, many of the colonizing impulses the various characters experience and attempt to act upon are expressed through classification in order for the characters to appear in control of their environment, to establish a hierarchical ordering of a group, or to exert power within those hierarchies. The position of the characters within these hierarchies is contextual, however, and shifts as characters move in and out of the roles of the classifying colonizer and the classified colonized.

Resisting and Reclassification

Wherever there is colonial activity, it is essential to look for anticolonial resistance. In the Pooh books, this resistance is subtle but not insignificant. As Ashcroft, Griffiths, and Tiffin claim, a "discussion of post-colonial writing" is "largely a discussion of the process by which the language, with its power [...] has been wrested from the dominant European culture" (2003, 7). Rhetoric, in other words, can construct power, but it can also deconstruct and reconstruct it. Although the Pooh books are more appropriately considered colonial rather than postcolonial texts, Ashcroft and colleagues' point about the "wrest[ing]" of control of "dominant European [...] language, with its power" is nevertheless fitting. Because so much of the colonizing in Pooh happens through classification, it follows that some of the anticolonial attitudes in the Pooh books occur in response to it. At times, characters use classification to question or expose the folly or the darker motives of the colonizer. At other times, *re*classification thwarts the plans of the classifying colonizer. Because the role of colonizer in the Forest is not stable, colonial power is also insecure. Through classifying language, characters can both attempt to exert power over others and resist those attempts.

One of the ways the characters resist the colonizing tendencies they encounter is by exposing them as foolish. In response to Rabbit's sinister plan to kidnap an immigrant child, Piglet questions the logic behind the plan. Piglet uses the categorizing language Christopher Robin initiated about Kanga and Roo: "I am not frightened of Fierce Animals in the ordinary way," Piglet says, "but it is well known that, if One of the Fiercer Animals is Deprived of Its Young, it becomes as Fierce as Two of the Fiercer Animals. In which case, '*Aha*!' is perhaps a *foolish* thing to say" (Milne 1958, 93–94). While Rabbit uses classification to control other creatures, Piglet uses it to demonstrate the foolishness of Rabbit's scheme, even if he is clearly doing so out of his own fear of the new arrivals. When Rabbit chastises Piglet for his cowardice, the latter classifies himself, saying, "It is hard to be brave . . . when you're only a Very Small Animal" (94). Piglet points out the illogic of Rabbit's criticism; if Rabbit insists on categorizing his friends along seemingly natural lines,

Piglet cannot be blamed for the natural side effects of his category. It is true that immediately following this exchange, Rabbit is able to manipulate his classification system enough to keep Piglet on board with the plan, causing Piglet to become "so excited" at the prospect of being designated "Useful" (95). However, his small moment of resistance to Rabbit's plot should not be underestimated, especially for a "Very Small Animal" who admits to struggling with bravery (94). Moreover, one of the animals Rabbit criticizes for having "fluff" rather than "brains" has exposed his lack of logic. Rabbit's reasoning, based on his invented hierarchical belief in their superiority over the "Strange Animal[s] among [them]," has been shown to be explicitly *foolish* (94, 92).

At times, the animals in the Forest actually use *re*classification to halt colonial plans. Although a handful of episodes in the Pooh stories revolve around colonial attitudes or actions, perhaps one reason they have not garnered more colonial criticism is that most of the more colonizing plans are not ultimately successful. In each case, the plans disintegrate, and the stories resolve with relative contentment partly because the characters, including the narrator, reclassify each other or objects from their environment. As noted above, the first story in the books involves Pooh as a colonizer attempting to take honey from a hive. His creative efforts to access the honey are ultimately resisted by the bees themselves. Pooh, disguised as a rain cloud, is concerned that the bees are becoming "suspicious" (Milne 1958, 26). After some time, one bee sits down "on the nose of the cloud for a moment" and stings Pooh (29). In response to his difficulty, Pooh concludes that "[t]hese are the wrong sort of bees" who "would make the wrong sort of honey" (29). Before this point, Pooh can think of bees in only terms of his own desire for honey, but he now concludes that there are bees who make honey that isn't meant for him. His reclassification of the bees as the "*wrong sort of bees*" provides enough of a justification for him to abandon his plan; the bumbling colonizer returns with a few reminders of his troubles, but not too much the worse for wear.

The kidnapping episode ends with a mock reclassification. Piglet takes Roo's place in Kanga's pouch, and after discovering the change, Kanga plays along, pretending that Piglet is Roo. After she gives him a bath, Christopher Robin arrives, and when Piglet tries to make his identity known, the boy argues that this couldn't be Piglet because "he's *quite* a different colour" (107). Kanga and Christopher Robin then declare that Piglet must be "some relation of Pooh's," and Kanga says that "they would have to call it by some name." Christopher Robin decides to call him "Pootel . . . Henry Pootel for short" (108). To play a joke on Piglet (and possibly to get back at him for his role in taking Kanga's child), Kanga and Christopher Robin reclassify him; he is no longer himself until he can escape and roll in the dirt "so as to get to his own nice comfortable colour again" (108). The relationship between colonizer and colonized is especially complex and fluid in this story. From Piglet's perspective, Kanga and Christopher Robin act as adults colonizing the child, particularly in light of the forced change of his skin color through bathing. However, if Kanga is seen as the colonized, as the immigrant whose new neighbors have conspired to steal her child, then she can be read as successfully negotiating a position of power within her new community, partly through her use of mock classification. From this point on, she and Roo are accepted in the Forest, and all the characters return to their proper classifications and are "happy again" (108).

At other times, reclassification in the face of colonial attitudes is more profound. Perhaps the most significant reclassification in the stories occurs during Rabbit's other plot against a newcomer, the plan to "unbounce" Tigger. Spurr notes the "tension which sees humanity as historically capable of improvement, but which also reifies the existing hierarchy of human societies" (1993, 65). This tension can be seen in Rabbit's desire to change Tigger into "a different Tigger altogether," "a Humble Tigger," "a Sad Tigger, a Melancholy Tigger, a Small and Sorry Tigger, an Oh-Rabbit-I-am-glad-to-see-you Tigger" (Milne 1958, 259). While Rabbit views Tigger as capable of changing, Pooh can offer no help in the planning stages other than an impromptu poem, which reveals the arbitrariness of Rabbit's mode of reasoning:

> If Rabbit
> Was bigger
> And fatter
> And stronger,
> Or bigger
> Than Tigger,
> If Tigger was smaller,
> Then Tigger's bad habit
> Of bouncing at Rabbit
> Would matter
> No longer,
> If Rabbit
> Was taller. (258)

Pooh understands that Tigger is a problem to Rabbit only because he is bigger. In other words, Pooh reveals the limitations of Rabbit's natural category: Rabbit may have more "Brain" and administrative skill than anyone in the Forest, but he cannot truly control the other animals as long as he is smaller and weaker than the unpredictable and bouncing Tigger. With this rhyme, Pooh both acknowledges and complicates the hierarchy that Rabbit establishes and predicts the reversal at the end of the episode. Despite Rabbit's professed knowledge of Tiggers, one crucial fact he neglects is that "Tiggers *never* get lost" (267). This means that Tigger is the only one who does not get lost in the mist, and as such he is able to rescue Rabbit. The narrator reclassifies Rabbit from being the proud and competent captain to the "Small and Sorry" Rabbit (271). Rabbit himself is forced to completely reclassify Tigger because he himself has been humbled. From Rabbit's newfound perspective, Tigger has become "Friendly" and "Grand," and his bounces have become "beautiful" (271). The irony, of course, is that while Tigger has been reclassified, Rabbit is the one whose has actually changed, and *he* is the one telling Tigger emphatically, "I *am* glad to see you," as he had originally planned for Tigger to say (271). The colonizing plan to tame Tigger is foiled, as Rabbit has to readjust his categorization of the members of the Forest according to their natural and moral value.

At times, reclassification can be the result of a disruption of the colonial order. The only colonial plan in the books that can be read as successful is the "Expotition" to the North Pole, though even this success relies on reclassification and an abandonment of the hierarchical "long line of everybody" (111). When the party stops to eat, the line falls apart, and though Christopher Robin and Rabbit continue to act like the leaders, the strict chain of command they had established earlier through the line dissolves. When Roo falls in the river, "[e]verybody was doing something to help" in uncoordinated and ineffectual ways (121). Christopher Robin and Rabbit attempt to take control of the situation and call out "to the others in front of them" (122). No longer "in front," they have momentarily lost their authority. Rabbit does suggest the idea that ultimately saves Roo, but the narrator makes clear that Pooh had already thought of it: "*But* Pooh was getting something" to hold across the river for Roo to grab (122, emphasis added). Moreover, this "something" that Pooh found ends up being reclassified as the North Pole, making their "Expotition" a success. When the hierarchical line, which is so important to Rabbit, is disrupted by the crisis with Roo, Christopher Robin's youthful linguistic flexibility allows a reclassification of the word "pole" to become the object of their search. Pooh—decidedly not at the top of Rabbit's hierarchy—not only rescues Roo but also finds the North Pole in the process. The reclassification of the word "pole" mirrors Pooh's reclassification from being a "silly old Bear" to one who becomes a double hero. If words can have different effects in different contexts, Milne suggests, then so, perhaps, can people; in the Forest, neither are fixed.

The Pooh books end with an example of reclassification that does not stick. In the final story, as Christopher Robin is preparing himself and Pooh for his upcoming departure from the Forest, it becomes clear that he is heading into a world of both increasing classification and increasing awareness of his role as a child of the British Empire. He is aware that he will be learning, among other topics, about "People called Kings and Queens," "a place called Europe," "an island in the middle of the sea where no ships came," "when Knights were Knighted," and "what comes from Brazil" (312). It is significant that Christopher Robin will learn about these various subjects, laden with colonial connotations, by learning what they are "called." In other words, he is aware that he is entering a world in which there is a sanctioned and monologic classification system; where he is going, the meaning of "North Pole" cannot accommodate a long pole one stumbles upon in the woods.

Pooh attempts to join Christopher Robin by entering this system of classification, but ultimately, he and the other animals must remain behind in the Forest, separated from the inevitability of colonization. After listening to Christopher Robin describe what he will learn at school, Pooh wants to know if being a knight is "as Grand as a King and Factors and all the other things [Christopher Robin] said" (313). In response, Christopher Robin lays out a simple hierarchy: "it's not as grand as a King... but it's grander than Factors" (313). Pooh immediately asks to become a knight, and Christopher Robin performs a knighting ceremony, dubbing Pooh "Sir Pooh de Bear, most faithful of all my Knights" (313). Pooh tries to imagine himself into this new position within the hierarchy as he drifts into a dream "in which he and Sir Pomp and Sir Brazil and Factors lived together with a horse, and were faithful Knights (all except Factors, who looked after the horse) to Good King Christopher Robin" (314). However, he acknowledges, "I'm not getting it right," and he returns to his most frequently used name throughout the stories: "a Bear of Very Little Brain" (314). In the end, Pooh is not a knight, and as earnest as his motivations may have been, the ceremony serves as a parting ritual more than an initiation into a hierarchical system of service to the king.

This final story highlights the discrepancy between the Forest and the world Christopher Robin will enter. Outside the Forest, Brazil is not a knight but a colony, and he is not a king but an imperial subject. Pooh and the other animals, however, can remain behind in their world where language is permanently fluid. Because words can have multiple meanings in the Forest, the animals can classify and reclassify themselves, each other, and their environment. In the last line of the stories, Milne makes it clear that they are fundamentally depicting a "little boy and his Bear [. . .] playing," and one of the main ways Christopher Robin and especially the animals play is through language (316). They use language, and classification in particular, to play at being colonizers, but also to play at resisting that colonization. The Forest is a space where colonial and anticolonial impulses exist alongside each other and where colonial plans get tried out, amended, and even abandoned because of the highly flexible and dialogic nature of children's linguistic play.

Notes

1. For discussions of imperialism in *The Jungle Book*, see John McBratney's "Imperial Subjects, Imperial Space in Kipling's *Jungle Book*" (1992) and M. Daphne Kutzer's chapter "Kipling's Rules of the Game" in her book *Empire's Children* (2000). Ariel Dorfman's *The Empire's Old Clothes* (1996) is necessary reading for understanding imperialism in Babar. Isabelle Suhl discusses imperialism in Lofting's work in her chapter "The 'Real' Doctor Dolittle" in *The Black American in Books for Children: Readings in Racism* (1972).

2. While Rabbit is likely referring to the fact that he and Owl are the only animals in the Forest who were not inspired by Christopher Milne's stuffed toys, his distinction here is meaningless in two important ways. First, within the narrative world, there is no other difference between the "real" characters and the toy characters. There are no barriers to communication, and their ways of living and being in the world are not noticeably different. Second, although Rabbit and Owl are both regarded as wise and intelligent, the stories are replete with examples of their folly and naïveté.

Bibliography

Ashcroft, Bill, Gareth Griffiths, and Helen Tiffin. 2003. *The Empire Writes Back: Theory and Practice in Post-Colonial Literatures*. 2nd ed. London: Routledge.

Borchers, Timothy. 2006. *Rhetorical Theory: An Introduction*. Belmont, CA: Thomson Wadsworth.

Borkfelt, Sune. 2009. "Colonial Animals and Literary Analysis: The Example of Kipling's Animal Stories." *English Studies* 90, no. 5 (October): 557–68.

Bradford, Clare. 2001. "The End of Empire? Colonial and Postcolonial Journeys in Children's Books." *Children's Literature* 29: 196–218. doi:10.1353/chl.0.0796.

Bradford, Clare. 2007. "Language, Resistance, and Subjectivity." In *Unsettling Narratives: Postcolonial Readings of Children's Literature*, 19–44. Waterloo, Ont., Canada: Wilfrid Laurier University Press.

Carpenter, Humphrey. 2009. *Secret Gardens: A Study of the Golden Age of Children's Literature*. London: Faber and Faber.

Cohn, Bernard S. 1996. *Colonialism and Its Forms of Knowledge: The British in India*. Princeton, NJ: Princeton University Press.

Dorfman, Ariel. 1996. *The Empire's Old Clothes: What the Lone Ranger, Babar, and Other Innocent Heroes Do to Our Minds*. London: Penguin.

Hall, Donald E. 1991. "'We and the World': Juliana Horatia Ewing and Victorian Colonialism for Children." *Children's Literature Association Quarterly* 16, no. 2 (Summer): 51–55. doi:10.1353/chq.0.0784.

Hunt, Peter. 2001. *Children's Literature*. Oxford: Blackwell.

Kutzer, M. Daphne. 2000. *Empire's Children: Empire and Imperialism in Classic British Children's Books*. New York: Garland.

McBratney, John. 1992. "Imperial Subjects, Imperial Space in Kipling's *Jungle Book*." *Victorian Studies* 35, no. 3 (Spring): 277–93. www.jstor.org/stable/3828034.

Milne, A. A. 1958. *The World of Pooh*. London: Methuen.

Nodelman, Perry. 1992. "The Other: Orientalism, Colonialism, and Children's Literature." *Children's Literature Association Quarterly* 17, no. 1 (Spring): 29–35. doi:10.1353/chq.0.1006.

Rose, Jacqueline. 1992. *The Case of Peter Pan; or, The Impossibility of Children's Literature*. Philadelphia: University of Pennsylvania Press.

Spurr, David. 1993. *The Rhetoric of Empire: Colonial Discourse in Journalism, Travel Writing, and Imperial Administration*. Durham, NC: Duke University Press.

Suhl, Isabelle. 1972. "The 'Real' Doctor Dolittle." In *The Black American in Books for Children: Readings in Racism*, edited by Donnarae MacCann and Gloria Woodard, 78–88. Lanham, MD: Scarecrow Press.

CHAPTER 9

Seeing Past Cuteness
Searching for the Posthuman in Milne's Pooh Books

Perry Nodelman

The Forest A. A. Milne describes in his books about Winnie the Pooh might be a utopia like the ones Donna Haraway defines as posthuman: places "where the clean lines between traditional and modern, organic and technological, human and nonhuman, give way" (2008, 8). At once animals, toys, and beings with human personalities who then simultaneously represent all three groups and thus occupy all three categories, Milne's characters might well be read as exemplars of a view of life that crosses restrictive lines and thus moves beyond what Rosi Braidotti calls "the humanistic arrogance of placing Man at the centre of world history" (2013). Understood in that way, they might offer one possible answer to Haraway's question, "[W]ho will 'we' become when species meet?" (2008, 5). But a closer look at the world Milne imagines reveals why it is unlikely to please thinkers like Haraway and Braidotti.

In posthumanist thought, the arrogance of humanism emerges from its insistence on hierarchical relationships between the categories it creates. For Haraway, as a result, "[t]he discursive tie between the colonized, the enslaved, the noncitizen, and the animal—all reduced to type, all Others to rational men, and all essential to his bright constitution—is at the heart of racism and flourishes, lethally, in the entrails of humanism" (2008, 18). The marginalization of anyone perceived specifically to be animal or animallike is at the heart of this sort of discourse, which has traditionally either viewed women, children, and colonizable humans as more animallike than rational men or else urged woman, children, and racialized others to evolve beyond their current "animal" nature into something more admirably human. As Lindsay Lerman says, then, "humanity is a situation, a project, created and maintained only through a constant striving to separate from animality. This, despite the fact that humanity is animal. Humanity (co)exists with, and in the face of, animality. To cultivate humanity, then, is to cultivate a discontinuity with the world" (2011, 303). Posthumanism is an effort to rejoin what humanism has put asunder.

In bringing together the characteristics of differing species—rejoining what humanism disconnects—the many children's stories that, like the Pooh books, describe creatures who look like animals but talk and think like human beings might suggest how we might do that. But while Pooh and Piglet are animallike in appearance, there is little about them that seems like a realistic evocation of animal behavior. There is, of course, an excellent reason for that: as the widely publicized connection between the characters Milne invented and the stuffed toys belonging to his young son Christopher suggests, they are representations of representations of animals—not so much bears or pigs as they are an attempt to imagine the lives of stuffed versions of bears and pigs provided with something like human thoughts. The description in the first chapter of *Winnie-the-Pooh* of a child named Christopher Robin asking for a story about the small-scaled bear the accompanying illustration shows him dragging down a flight of human stairs makes that project clear.

But that these creatures are toys then adds another dimension to their potential to challenge humanist views. As manufactured versions of living creatures, Milne's characters are not just somewhat like animals but also somewhat like cyborgs—what Haraway identifies as "creatures of mixity or vectors of posthuman relationality" (2008, 8). While Zoe Jaques suggests that "Winnie-the-Pooh might seem an odd choice in the context of a discussion of the cyborg" (2015, 209), she goes on to argue that "[t]oys trouble the boundaries of being: in a child's play, the toy becomes imbued with 'life' via the imagination," and in children's fiction like the Pooh books, "toys are frequently (and paradoxically) imagined as possessing a different kind of life, in which they are 'real' beings" (212).

Pooh and his friends are neither human, animal, nor cyborg. But what they are and how they act represents a point where human, animal, and cyborg intersect and therefore, presumably, interact. They might well represent an answer to Haraway's question about what forms of existence might emerge "when species meet." But do they?

More Than Human—or Less?

Being more than human sounds like an expansion, an opening into less restrictive possibilities. But the ways in which Milne represents his characters tend to diminish rather than enlarge them—to make them less rather than more than merely toy, merely animal, or merely human. Paradoxically, the diminishment is signaled by the addition of yet another intersecting species—or in this case, not so much a separate species as a subset of what we consider to be most completely human: human children. One of the creatures, Roo, is represented as being in a parent/child relationship with one of the other characters, Kanga. Furthermore, the inhabitants of the Forest include not just humanized kangaroos, bears, and owls but also, at times, one other creature defined as being more directly human: the child named Christopher Robin.

Furthermore, many readers of the Pooh books assume that, as in the life of the author's son, the real Christopher Robin, the space the animals come to life in is actually the imagination of the one young human being who visits there—or more exactly, the imagination of that young human being as imagined by the adult human author, or at least by the "I" of the first chapter of *Winnie-the-Pooh*, who, asked to tell a story about the child's bear, says, "I'll try" (Milne 1992a, 4). As happens in many stories produced for and often read to or by children, the Pooh books then offer an imagined version of childlike—that is, not yet completely human—thinking. In my book *The Hidden Adult*, I describe how theorists of children's literature focus on the assumption that adults produce a special literature for beings other than themselves because those other beings are understood to be less capable, less advanced, less sophisticated than adults—or if not exactly lesser than, at least significantly different enough from adults not only to need a special literature but to need people older than themselves to produce that literature (Nodelman 2008, 146–56). More often than not, literature of this kind, often accused of didacticism, concerns itself with educating its less than completely human audience into becoming more like the adults doing the educating—that is, more completely human.

Merely in existing, then, literature like the Pooh books that identifies itself as stories told to and for children is problematic in relation to posthumanist ideas. Its foundational assumptions are inherently humanist. Consider, for instance, the extent to which children as conventionally understood in the contemporary world might be accurately characterized by Braidotti's description of how humanism defines itself and what it excludes and perceives to be Other:

> Subjectivity is equated with consciousness, universal rationality, and self-regulating ethical behaviour, whereas Otherness is defined as its negative and specular counterpart. In so far as difference spells inferiority, it acquires both essentialist and lethal connotations for people who get branded as "others." These are the sexualized, racialized, and naturalized others, who are reduced to the less than human status of disposable bodies. We are all humans, but some of us are just more mortal than others. (2013)

While the size of children specularly marks their difference from adults, widespread assumptions about the nature of childhood mean that most people do not think of children as being sexualized or as having disposable bodies. It is, instead, a desire to protect their fragility and specifically, often, to deny them knowledge of or access to their own sexuality that requires them to be protected in a way that justifies the existence of a "safe" literature for children—a literature that then marks them as being different and "other" from less protected and more permissibly sexual—more fully human—adults.

Meanwhile, though, and as Jaques argues, "[i]t is perhaps no accident that children and animals share a rhetorical and restrictive linguistic stereotype; the expressions 'behaving like an animal' or 'acting childishly' operate as negative, regulating metaphors in everyday speech, applicable only to (adult) human behavior which operates outside of the civilized or socially acceptable" (2015, 26). Whatever else they are, children are often assumed to be more like animals than socialized adults are. Socialization is almost by definition the diminishment of animality.

As it happens, furthermore, the most obvious interpretation of Milne's Forest is that it represents a colonialist view of the delightful and therefore desirable limitations of children and childlike thinking. Jaques speaks of "the posthuman potential encoded within mixed modes of being" (153) like that of Pooh and his friends, and of "the disorder that arises from contaminated, vexed, challenged and even re-established identities, the confusion—as it were—that accompanies 'all the things being alive'" (237). A first look at the Pooh books tends to emphasize how that potential has actively been thwarted.

The addition of human consciousness to Milne's characters seems to make them less capable of actual animal behavior, less dangerous, as do the ways in which they represent harmless toys. As toys, their existence as representations of specific animals mechanically reproducing a limited range of supposedly animal character traits apparently based on their animallike appearance— chubby Pooh's insatiable greed, sad-faced Eeyore's eternal pessimism, child-encumbered Kanga's obsessive mothering—equally limits their potential to engage more widely imaginative responses in those who interact with them. On the other hand, though, the addition of either or both an animal nature and the qualities of a toy to something like a human consciousness diminishes the rationality and the ability to make choices that usually define, for humanists at least, what it means to be human. Pooh and the others are, then, something like human beings living something like human lives in ways that make them less than animals, less than toys, and less than human.

As I suggested earlier, the diminishment relates significantly to the fourth kind of being the animals intersect with: children. Depicted as a safe place, for the most part uncontaminated by the troubles and trauma of the world beyond its borders, the Forest is easily read as a representation of what childhood is, or more likely, should be. While the real Christopher Robin acknowledges the more traumatic aspects of his connection to his father's fictional characters, most of his memories of his childhood and his father's reinvention of it accurately reflect the utopian title he gave his memoir: *The Enchanted Places*—a pluralization of his father's description of the most essentially utopian spot in the Forest, the high spot where "a little boy and his Bear will always be playing" (C. Milne [1974] 2016, 180). While the enchanted places include this one that Christopher Milne describes as "an enchanted spot before ever Pooh came along to add to its magic" (55), it also significantly includes the privileged country life of his father, "who had derived such happiness from his childhood" (141), and his own similar life in a country house with loving parents, a loving nanny, and a number of other servants—an upper middle-class vision of utopian childhood. Indeed, Paula Connolly suggests that the Forest is protected from the woes of adult life much as the middle-class nurseries of Milne's time were meant to protect their child inhabitants: "[T]he Forest is an Arcadia, a pastoral world or innocence, play and peace—a place where a child can adventure without the constraints of close parental control but with the certainty, insulation, and protection of the nursery" (1995, 104). According to Niall Nance-Carroll, furthermore: "The domesticity and 'middle-classness' of these stories reflect not sentimentality but an attention to life as it is—or perhaps how it could be. The focus on the middle class . . . refers to the specific level of comfort and security associated with an English turn-of-the-century upper-middle-class household" (2014, 98)—a security especially represented by the household's nursery. The Forest then mirrors the ideal childhood Europeans and people in European settler societies have envisaged for the past few centuries—a safely limited utopian place whose utopianism is based on adults rich enough to sustain it and actively working to prevent anything perceived to be less than ideal from contaminating it.

As childhood itself is understood to be ideally limited enough to be free from sources of woe, free from too much knowledge of potentially disturbing things, so, then, we tend to assume, are the thoughts of children. Because we keep them from experience, they are innocent of it, safely limited in their knowledge of it. So, too, in their diminishment, are the residents of the Forest innocent. As dwellers in a place clearly intended to represent a childlike imagination—as animallike toys bought to life as Milne and many of his adult readers assume a child might imagine it for them, and as child readers might enjoy having Milne imagine it for them—Milne's characters are themselves childlike, innocent, a diminished (or more positively, perhaps, a not yet fully expanded) form of being human. Milne's characters are less than adult, less than animallike, even less than toylike, because they are essentially perceived as being childlike. They resist posthumanist interpretations because, in terms of humanism as defined by writers like Braidotti and Lerman, they are prehuman—that is, preadult.

Milne establishes their childlikeness primarily by focusing on their ineptitude. As Pooh himself often insists, he is a bear of "little brain." Owl also lacks brains, though unlike Pooh he is egocentrically convinced of his own wisdom and comically unable to live up to his conviction. Piglet's sense of himself revolves around his perceptions of his childlike smallness and fragility, his physical ineptitude. Tellingly, however, Milne presents these various inabilities not as unfortunate or off-putting liabilities, but as endearing—what makes both Christopher Robin and, ideally, readers of the books love these characters. As all too often happens to human children, their limitations come to be viewed as positive assets—examples of the inherently demeaning category of cuteness.

Cuteness is inherently childlike, at least insofar as widespread cultural assumptions about children define childlikeness. The cultural theorist Sianne Ngai speaks of "the formal properties associated with cuteness—smallness, compactness, softness, simplicity, and pliancy"—and suggests that they "call forth specific affects: helplessness, pitifulness, and even despondency" (2005, 816). As toys, Milne's characters are small, compact, simple, and soft; and as characters they tend to be helpless, often pitiful, and in at least one case, despondent. They are decidedly cute, in ways that children are often considered to be cute.

Ngai goes on to suggest that cuteness is a quality imposed on objects by means of a special way of looking at them: "a special kind of attention paid solely to an object's appearance or 'aspect' (as opposed to its origin, identity, or function) accompanied by an appraisal based on the positive or negative feeling that its apperception elicits" (813). While the nature of cute beings allows a view of them as being cute, it is the viewer's perception that imposes the idea of cuteness upon them—a perception that is inherently limiting. As Daniel Harris says: "The process of conveying cuteness to the viewer disempowers its objects, forcing them into ridiculous situations and making them appear more ignorant and vulnerable than they really are" (2000, 6). The cuteness of the imaginary inhabitants of the Forest does not so much disempower them as it imagines them as disempowered in the first place, as inherently ignorant and vulnerable—as beings who are other from and less than completely human (and, as toys, less than completely animal). Again and again throughout the Pooh books, the focus is on "ridiculous situations" that emerge from the characters' ignorance and inadequacy: not knowing what a Heffalump or the North Pole might be, confusing an animal's tail with a bell pull, not considering that the footprints one is following might be one's own, not being aware that eating too much might prevent one from leaving a friend's home. Furthermore, and as Piglet rightly says, "Pooh hasn't much brain, but he never comes to any harm" (Milne 1992a, 131). Nor do any of the others. Because the animals' inadequacy is never actually dangerous in the protected world of the Forest, it is safe to view it as lovably cute—the kind of childish weakness that engenders a protective affection.

The invitation to readers to think of the characters as cute arrives by means of the way Christopher Robin thinks about them. He is consistently aware of their limited skills, thoughts, and so on, and while he spends much of his time helping them out of the problems their limitations create, his attitude toward them is centered around what can easily be read as his pleasure in their cuteness—his awareness that it is their inadequacy that makes them loveable. When Pooh gets stuck in Rabbit's doorway, Christopher Robin calls him "Silly old Bear" in "a loving voice" (Milne 1992a, 29), and when Pooh gets his head stuck in a honey jar, Christopher Robin tells him, "How I love you" (71). Clearly, Christopher Robin loves Pooh for his adorable inadequacies—just as many adults love children for theirs. The human child Christopher then becomes something like an adult in relation to the bear's adorable childlikeness. For Humphrey Carpenter, Christopher Robin represents the "only true adult in Pooh's world" (1985, 203–4). While Robert Hemmings points out that Carpenter forgets about the narrator's presence, he also rightly suggests that "Christopher Robin's authority in Pooh's forest, similar to an adult's authority over a child, reveals a reconstruction of childhood that serves the interests of adults, not children" (2007, 72).

But while readers are clearly being invited to accept and share Christopher Robin's perception of the animals' cuteness, what Peter Hunt identifies as the "intrusive adult voice of the adult narrator" (1992, 115) might seem especially intrusive because the narrator invites a simultaneous awareness of Christopher Robin as cute himself, adorably childlike in his act of imagining himself a grown-up adult in relation to his toys. The extent to which the Pooh books operate as a representation of what Milne imagines his son might be imagining when he plays with his toys then transforms the Forest into an adult vision of the son's cuteness; and Christopher Robin's imagining of the creatures he interacts with as being more limited than himself and thus in need of his supervision and care reads as an endearingly childlike way of coming to terms with his own limitations and his own need for adult supervision.

For an adult reader like me, outside the Forest and looking into it, the human child Christopher appears to be just as cute as the toy animal characters whose cuteness he purports to be imagining, all the while, it seems, endearingly unaware of his own cuteness. The perception of Christopher Robin as cute might well disrupt what Hunt identifies as the "enchantment of the world of the Pooh books" (1992, 114) by requiring a consciousness of and pleasure in the limitations of the childlike mind that purportedly created it—thus, possibly, preventing younger readers outside the book from being enchanted by drawing attention to the limitations of the childlikeness they share and inviting them to celebrate their own inadequacy. I suspect, though, that the child readers the text implies are expected simply to accept the accuracy of

Milne's depiction of childhood, to identify with Christopher Robin, understand events as he does and share his childlike pleasure in being in a position of potential protectiveness to creatures more childlike than himself. However readers respond, then, Pooh and the other animals, as creatures imagined by Christopher Robin as Milne imagines Christopher Robin, are then doubly Othered, doubly colonized, held within a limiting framework that focuses on the pleasure they offer to those thinking of them as cute—not just the child imagined to be imagining them and the author who imagines that childlike imagining, but also the readers being invited to share in the child's and his author's vision.

All that sounds depressingly bleak—and a long way from nostalgia for a utopian childhood, or at least from an uncritical perception of utopian views of childhood. As Nance-Carroll says, "While there are nostalgic elements in the Pooh stories—and while Milne does recount happy times associated with childhood—some critics emphasize these selectively, interpreting the Pooh stories as defined by nostalgia and implying that sentimental recollections have here overridden the satiric style that characterizes Milne's other writing. . . . The Pooh stories are not wholly nostalgic, even though they inspire nostalgia in some readers" (2015, 69, 72). There is a real possibility that the stories might be too bleak to reveal any of the "posthuman potential" Jaques suggests is inherent in depictions of mixed modes of being like Pooh and his friends.

Waiting for Christopher Robin

The potential bleakness of the world Milne imagines becomes particularly easy to discern if we assume for a moment that the Forest is a real place and try to consider what it might seem like if we could access how it would look outside the positive, nostalgia-inflected view of it offered by Christopher Robin and by Milne. That the Forest might in fact exist without their presence in relation to it is first implied by the fact that Christopher Robin can go away from it, apparently for good, at the end of *The House at Pooh Corner*—and yet leave it still existing outside his involvement with it. But even before then, many of the stories describe moments in the lives of Christopher Robin's presumably imaginary friends when he is not present. Admittedly, Milne is still there as author doing the imagining that allows readers to know of events in their lives Christopher Robin is unaware of. But what if he were not? In a discussion of

Lewis Carroll's *Alice in Wonderland*, Jaques speaks of "Alice's desire to escape into a universe in which she can understand, and ultimately dominate, the unruly natural world. . . . Alice imagines 'a world of my own' peppered with flowers 'that would sit and talk to me for hours' and a 'babbling brook' which sings a song 'that I can understand.' . . . [T]he narrative quest for dominion is absolute and discloses Alice's sense that nature speaks a language that can only be understood once owned" (2015, 73). What would the Forest look like if Milne and Christopher Robin did not similarly own it?

As *The House at Pooh Corner* nears its end, Christopher Robin says: "[W]hat I like doing best is Nothing" (Milne 1992b, 172), and is sad that he is not going to be allowed "to do Nothing any more" (178). Much of what Milne describes throughout the Pooh books is little more than nothing: sitting around, chatting, worrying about things that might happen but usually don't, inventing endearingly silly games to pass the time. Deprived of its framework of cute childlikeness, the ongoing depiction of the characters doing nothing is surprisingly like what happens in Samuel Beckett's play *Waiting for Godot*, which begins with one of its two central characters trying unsuccessfully to take off his boots, giving up, and saying, "Nothing to be done" ([1956] 2010, 5). The rest of the play involves Vladimir and Estragon sitting around doing nothing as they wait for the mysterious Godot, who never comes. *Waiting for Godot* is usually understood to be a tragic parable about the meaninglessness of existence, the absurdity of being alive in a world with no purpose but waiting for a purpose to reveal itself. Divorced from the assumption that Pooh and the others are cute and their lives a utopian idyll, Milne's books seem to offer an equivalent sense of absurd futility and existential angst.

Like Beckett's Vladimir and Estragon, Milne's characters are weirdly disconnected from other people, other places, and even, surprisingly often, from each other. Except for Christopher Robin, they never leave the woods. While Piglet mentions his grandfather, Pooh responds by "wondering what a Grandfather was like" (Milne 1992a, 39); and while he remembers having an uncle (62), the uncle seems to have left Pooh's current life, as apparently has the Uncle Robert whose portrait Owl has hanging in his house (Milne 1992b, 135). While Kanga and Roo have a parent/child relationship, they are a single-parent family and appear to have no other relatives. Only Rabbit has a number of friends and relations, but there is little evidence that there is any significance in his relationship to them except insofar as there are enough of them that they are hard for him to keep track of; and since Rabbit might well be not a toy but possibly an actual pet rabbit as humanized by Christopher Robin, his connections might simply be whatever other small animals and insects inhabit the actual garden that Christopher Robin imagines as the Forest, merely the background for Rabbit's realer, or at least more human, relationships with the other main characters. Except for Kanga, Roo, and later Tigger, the central characters live as disconnected adults often do, alone in separate dwellings—and seem to spend much of their time alone in or near those separate dwellings. Unlike human adults, though, they have no jobs and no other responsibilities. And while they do have problems, they are minor ones: no serious conflict, no threat of violence or war, not even all that much in the way of suspense or drama, just as in *Waiting for Godot*. Pooh and his friends fill in the time much as Vladimir and Estragon do, daydreaming or engaged in idle conversation, turning small decisions like which carrot or jar of honey to eat into big dilemmas. As Christopher Robin suggests, what they do is not much more than nothing.

Beckett's characters find themselves doing nothing because they are waiting for something to happen—the arrival of the mysterious Godot. While Milne's characters do not specifically wait for visits from Christopher Robin before they do anything important, they do tend to think of him as something like Godot—someone whose arrival will inevitably lead to good things happening and the solution to all problems. And at the end of *The House at Pooh Corner*, finally, it becomes clear that Christopher Robin is gone from the Forest for good—as absent from the known world as Godot turns out to be. All that prevents readers from responding to the emptiness and futility of this world as being a bleak vision of the meaninglessness of life is its colonization by the perceptions of Christopher Robin and Milne that the emptiness of Pooh and his friends' lives is in fact evidence of a utopian state of being childlike. As a result, Pooh and the rest's unquestioning acceptance of the limitations of their own state of being merely confirms their childlike cuteness.

I suggested earlier that in limiting rather than expanding the boundaries between species, the childlikeness of Milne's characters prevents their inter-sectional qualities from developing into a more enriched posthuman understanding. Having attempted to see beyond that colonial act of limitation, I am tempted to add that even beyond it, the world Milne describes is too bleak and hopeless to offer much in the way of positive posthumanism, too much a vision of human angst and solitude to offer much in the way of a celebration of animal- or cyborg-like otherness. Milne simply has too much invested in

the endearing charm of the childlike limitations of the creatures he has imagined to allow them to open pathways to a larger and less humanistic vision.

Anxiety in the Forest: Childlike and Adult

Once more, however, we might see the world Milne created in ways he did
not himself intend. As Jaques says, "To suggest . . . that an animal can simply
be (mis)represented in order to peddle (or obscure) specific human agendas is
a denial of the fact that animal representation automatically stimulates reflection upon, and potential anxiety about, real animals and their relations with
human viewers" (2015, 77). It seems equally easy to assume that any depiction
of humanlike objects like cyborgs or toys might have the same implications. If
that anxiety is automatic, it must be happening in the Pooh books.

In a fairly obvious sense, it is. Milne's characters do have animal and toy
characteristics, and the ways in which those characteristics affect them might
suggest something larger and more uncontrollably inhuman about them. Like
Pooh, real bears are known for their voracious and dangerous appetites, and
like Tigger, real tigers can perform prodigious and dangerous acts of leaping.
Real toys represent a much larger than human, indeed infinite, capacity for
and patience in response to doing nothing; properly stored in the right conditions, they could easily wait for Godot forever. The toy/animal surrogates of
the Forest then act or do not act in ways that might well elicit anxiety about
their actions or inactions. The human personalities are attached to bodies
that imply their potential for disturbing capabilities beyond more ordinary
human bodies.

But I suspect it is their existence as childlike beings that most suggests
a potentially thought-provoking form of anxiety. For while everyone who
appears in the book is childlike at least in some ways, almost all of them also
act at times in ways understandable as adult. The shifting perspectives that
define them as either or both child and adult open a pathway beyond the very
act of colonization that defines them as acceptably childlike in the first place.

As Christopher Robin's request for a story about Winnie in the first chapter
of *Winnie-the-Pooh* makes clear, Milne (or at least the adult he has imagined
to represent someone like himself in the book) makes up everything that follows to entertain the fictional Christopher Robin (and so, presumably, the real
one). What he describes appears to be his adult conception of what a childlike

Christopher Robin might make up himself about his own imaginary life with his toys—or, perhaps, Milne's version of what an ideally childlike child might imagine. One way or the other, the introductory acknowledgment that an adult is making up the story underlines the degree to which what follows represents a specifically adult conception of childhood. Milne stands outside the world he creates and seems to be defined, even just in his adult ability to make up the story, as both significantly beyond the boundaries of childhood and significantly capable of access to it. He is an adult who, if we accept the authenticity of his vision of childhood, possesses a childlike imagination. Although he is not in the childlike world of the Forest, he is able to have knowledge of it. But while he may not be in it, it is very much inside him, inside his imagination. Paradoxically, then, the very fact that as an adult he imagines a childlike existence means that he is a disturber of categories, a leaper of the boundary between adult and child that defines childhood as limitation.

Since Christopher Robin appears within the stories, he is part of what Milne has imagined—and as a depiction of human child, the most direct evidence of what Milne imagines children and childlike imagination to be like. Intriguingly, then, the essence of what Christopher Robin imagines is that he relates to the other characters in much the same way as Milne relates to him. Christopher Robin is the adult presence within the Forest, the one who comes and goes from a world outside, the one the others go to and depend on in times of trouble. That tends to define him as being something of an outsider, and he does seem to be significantly outside the lives of the other characters. He is not always there in the Forest as they are always there. In *The House at Pooh Corner*, he is there less and less often, and the stories come to an end as he leaves the Forest permanently. Unlike the others, he has a life elsewhere, apparently a more complex one about which the others know nothing. They never even seem to get past the outside door of his house in the Forest.

What most distinguishes Christopher Robin from the others is that he can change into something else—become an adult. As the "Contradiction" that begins *The House at Pooh Corner* says, "[T]he Forest will always be there . . . and anybody who is Friendly with Bears can find it" (Milne 2012b, n.p.), an idea reiterated at the end of the novel: "[I]n that enchanted place at the top of the Forest, a little boy and his bear will always be playing" (180). The Forest represents a place outside of ordinary time, eternally the same, a version of the ideas about children and childhood thinking in which, as Paul Wake suggests, "childhood is placed outside of the temporal in a space that is clearly demarcated as being somehow *extra*-temporal, at least in the sense that it belongs to an instant that stands outside of the progression of time" (2009, 31). Suggesting that the Forest occupies what Maria Nikolajeva identifies as "mythic time," where there is "no linear progress whatsoever, or the linear development rounds back into the circular pattern" (2000, 31), Danielle O'Connor points out that "the mythic nature of time for Pooh and his friends is emphasized by the clock on Pooh's wall, 'which had stopped at five minutes to eleven some weeks ago' and 'was still saying five minutes to eleven when Pooh and Piglet set out on their way half an hour later.' . . . Time does not matter for Pooh; it is repetitive and everlasting" (2018, 31). Pooh does, however, have a clock: the idea of time is still present. Pooh also has a human friend, a child indulging in the timelessness of the mythic who is nevertheless simultaneously changing into something else—something outside the mythic, for as O'Connor says, "In order to grow and mature, the child must move away from the safety of mythic time into the harsh reality of linear time" (29). The mere fact that Christopher Robin can change in this way suggests, to the other characters and potentially to readers, that the Forest itself and the childlike state it represents is not so mythically changeless after all.

A closer look reveals a surprising amount of change already present in this theoretically changeless place. Weather happens, in serious rainstorms and snowstorms. New inhabitants like Kanga, Roo, and Tigger suddenly find themselves there, arrived from places unknown; Tigger is so disconnected from whatever life he might have led earlier that he does not even know what animals like himself eat. Most revealingly, there is the stream that runs through the Forest: "By the time It came to the edge of the Forest the stream had grown up, so that it was almost a river, and, being grown-up, it did not run and jump and sparkle along as it used to do when it was younger, but moved more slowly. For it knew now where it was going, and it said to itself, 'There is no hurry. We shall get there some day'" (Milne 1992b, 92). While the Forest might always be there, its unchanging youthfulness encompasses a movement toward growth, toward adulthood, beyond the border of the Forest of youthful running and jumping and into the less playful adult world outside.

While Christopher Robin can enter and be in this space, he must also, like the stream, leave it; as Wake says, "Temporality pulls Christopher Robin, and the child in general, into a continuity with adulthood that paradoxically demands that it must engage in a temporality that is premised on the fact of its own passage" (2009, 28). Simply in being represented as a human child, then—as a being who will gradually and eventually turn into something not a child and not childlike—Christopher Robin introduces a potential for time passing and adulthood emerging in the theoretically ongoing timelessness of the Forest and of the childhood it represents, a potential already present in the stream. Furthermore, what pulls Christopher Robin away from the Forest is, as Eeyore says, "Learning . . . Education" (Milne 1992b, 88)—the process of becoming equipped with what takes the place of the limiting unknowingness that sustains this sort of vision of childhood innocence. Like Milne, then, Christopher Robin is also a disturber of categories, and of the boundaries between child and adult—as, perhaps, all children who are enmeshed in adult conceptions of their cuteness but also engaged in the business of growing up always are.

But then what about the animal inhabitants of the Forest? Milne tells us that they are eternally unchanging—always there and the same whenever we might choose to visit them (as is, of course, true not only of them but of all the characters whose stories are recorded within the pages of any novel). In relation to Christopher Robin, furthermore, they are childlike, endearingly limited creatures who call upon him to fill the role an adult might play in the life of a child. But while they relate to Christopher Robin as children relate to adults, and while he relates to them as adults relate to the endearing cuteness of children, they are generally described as living the lives of adults, away from whatever parents they might have once had. Indeed, many of the characters seem more like caricatures of overly adult adults than they read like children: Owl, who pretends to possess a body of information identifiable as characteristically adult because it is neither interesting nor fun enough to be childlike; Eeyore, who lacks the exuberance and joie de vivre usually considered to be characteristically childlike; Rabbit, who acts with an authoritarian bossiness of the sort children often accuse parents and teachers of expressing; and Kanga, who is never anything other than purely and completely maternal. These characters are all childlike satires of the silliness of adulthood.

But the lives of these characters would not seem so significantly adult if there was not also another character that they were able to think of as a child and therefore as definably different from and requiring different treatment than they do themselves. That character is Roo; and later, Tigger plays a similar role. That these thoughtless, exuberant characters are defined as inherently and eternally children means that the other animals, while equally childlike but not placed in the social world of the Forest in the role of being children, must be viewed as childlike adults—much as Milne as he appears in the text is an adult with childlike qualities, and not much different from Christopher Robin as he appears in the Forest and in his absences from it as an adult-like child. Intriguingly, then, Roo and then later Tigger are the only characters defined as being exclusively and only childlike, and it seems that they can be so only because there are more adult figures in the Forest for them to be children in relation to. That Roo and Tigger are primarily childlike then reveals the degree to which all the other characters, including Christopher Robin and Milne and/or the narrator he imagines, are unstable entities combining childlikeness and adulthood in ways that challenge the separation and thus the validity of those categories. In being nothing more than childlike and in being that unlike all the other characters, Roo and Tigger confirm the extent to which adulthood contaminates and explodes the vision of childlike utopia.

Intriguingly, furthermore, the contamination of childlike characters and values by adult ones occurs in a way that mirrors the act of its creation. Milne's envisioning of the childlike Christopher Robin is shaped by and therefore limited by his adult ideas about what it means to be childlike and what the limitations of childhood require from adult supervisors. Not surprisingly, then, the fictional child Milne imagines is himself depicted as imagining fragile childlike beings in need of his help with the childlike troubles they cause for themselves—he is an adult in relation to them. But then the childlike animals this adult-like child has imagined are frequently understood to be adults, especially in their relationship to Roo and Tigger, so that the adult mind outside the childlike creation penetrates to its very heart in a way that destabilizes conceptions of childhood and adulthood. The safe place is riddled by what it considers to be dangerous, primarily because the limitations it imposes on its characters are inevitably too restrictive to define or contain them.

Always Posthuman Already

In describing the characters of the Pooh books as destabilized animal/toy/ child/adults, Milne offers a telling example of what Jaques identifies as "a kaleidoscope of fractured, hybrid, shifting and powerfully unstable identities that pollute the boundaries by which the human and the non-human are constructed" (2015, 237). Like all the boundaries that human thought and language impose on the world, both the boundaries between the human and the nonhuman and the boundaries that separate the Forest from the world outside it are always artificial, always an imposition of limited categories and definitions on something larger and less easily graspable. Milne's act of imagining a childlike space representative of childlike thinking is contaminated in the very act of conceiving it as different from the mind that made it up—the mind that therefore remains active within it in ways that undermine its separateness and its supposed limitations. Most significantly, then, what a posthuman analysis of the Pooh books reveals is that they were always posthuman already.

Bibliography

Beckett, Samuel. (1956) 2010. *Waiting for Godot*. London: Faber and Faber.

Braidotti, Rosi. 2013. *The Posthuman*. Cambridge: Polity Press.

Carpenter, Humphrey. 1985. *Secret Gardens: A Study of the Golden Age of Children's Literature*. London: George Allen and Unwin.

Connolly, Paula. 1995. *"Winnie the Pooh" and "The House at Pooh Corner": Recovering Arcadia*. Woodbridge, CT: Twayne Publishers.

Haraway, Donna J. 2008. *When Species Meet*. Minneapolis: University of Minnesota Press.

Harris, Daniel. 2000. *Cute, Quaint, Hungry, and Romantic: The Aesthetics of Consumerism*. New York: Basic Books.

Hemmings, Robert. 2007. "A Taste of Nostalgia: Children's Books from the Golden Age—Carroll, Grahame, and Milne." *Children's Literature* 35, no. 1 (January): 54–79.

Hunt, Peter. 1992. "Winnie-the-Pooh and Domestic Fantasy." In *Stories and Society: Children's Literature in its Social Context*, edited by Dennis Butts, 112–24. New York: Palgrave Macmillan.

Jaques, Zoe. 2015. *Children's Literature and the Posthuman: Animal, Environment, Cyborg*. New York: Routledge.

Lerman, Lindsay. 2011. "Lovingly Impolite." In *Philosophy in Children's Literature*, edited by Peter Costello, 301–14. Lanham, MD: Lexington Books.

Milne, A. A. 1992a. *Winnie-the-Pooh*. London: Puffin Books.

Milne, A. A. 1992b. *The House at Pooh Corner*. London: Puffin Books.

Milne, Christopher. (1974) 2016. *The Enchanted Places: A Childhood Memoir*. London: Pan Books.

Nance-Carroll, Niall. 2014. "A Prosaics of the Hundred Acre Wood: Ethics in A. A. Milne's *Winnie-the-Pooh* and *The House at Pooh Corner*." In *Ethics and Children's Literature*, edited by Claudia Mills, 89–100. Abingdon, Oxon., England: Routledge.

Nance-Carroll, Niall. 2015. "Not Only, But Also: Entwined Modes and the Fantastic in A. A. Milne's Pooh Stories." *Lion and the Unicorn* 39, no. 1 (January): 63–81.

Ngai, Sianne. 2005. "The Cuteness of the Avant-Garde." *Critical Inquiry* 31, no. 4 (Summer): 811–47.

Nikolajeva, Maria. 2000. *From Mythic to Linear: Time in Children's Literature*. Lanham, MD: Scarecrow Press.

Nodelman, Perry. 2008. *The Hidden Adult: Defining Children's Literature*. Baltimore: Johns Hopkins University Press.

O'Connor, Danielle A. 2018. "Frozen Rivers, Moving Homes, and Crossing Bridges: Liminal Space and Time in Neil Gaiman's *Odd and the Frost Giants* and A. A. Milne's *The House at Pooh Corner*." *Children's Literature Association Quarterly* 43, no. 1 (Spring): 28–46.

Wake, Paul. 2009. "Waiting in the Hundred Acre Wood: Childhood, Narrative and Time in A. A. Milne's Works for Children." *Lion and the Unicorn* 33, no. 1 (January): 26–43.

CHAPTER 10

"There's Always Pooh and Me"
The Reality of Edward Bear in a Posthuman World

Tim Wadham

Wherever I am, there's always Pooh,
There's always Pooh and Me.
—A. A. Milne, "Us Two," from *Now We Are Six*

While on a trip to New York City, my wife, daughter, and I entered the children's room of the New York Public Library's Donnell Library Center with hushed anticipation. Quickly, we found what we sought—a glass museum case in which sat some old and ragged children's plush toys. A kangaroo, a donkey, a small pig, a tiger, and at the center of them all, a teddy bear. I don't recall how my then four-year-old daughter reacted to the toys—we had read all the Pooh books out loud together, so she knew who they were. What I remember is the sense of awe I felt—these were the actual toys that Christopher Robin Milne played with! Eeyore's tail was really tacked on with something resembling a nail! However, there was also the predictable letdown. The enclosure in which Pooh and his friends were posed was nothing really special. The toys themselves looked rather old, tattered, and entirely ordinary. In fact, Pooh did not look much different from the teddy bear I had and loved as a child, a teddy bear with patches where the fur had been rubbed off with all that love. What was missing was the magic—the spark of imagination that turned these toys into real sentient beings with personalities that have enchanted both children and adults since their creation.

Of Winnie-the-Pooh, Christopher Robin Milne said, "Pooh was the oldest, only a year younger than I was, and my inseparable companion. As you find us in the poem 'Us Two,' so we were in real life." Indeed, A. A. Milne's poem "Us Two" celebrates the inseparable and bucolic relationship of the real Christopher Robin and his companion teddy bear, Winnie-the-Pooh: they are always together, but can one make a distinction between the two? Which of them is "real"? Or are they both real, and in what sense? Is Pooh still relevant in a world of intelligent, interactive playthings? Children have interacted with representational playthings since those playthings have existed, and fictional narratives have been written about these interactions for children. Children have named their plush toys and projected human characteristics on them. They have engaged in imaginative play with these playthings, creating worlds that exist only in their own minds. However, these interactions *require* a human to happen. In this chapter, the application of a posthuman theoretical lens to the Winnie-the-Pooh texts forces a reconsideration of the foundational assumptions of posthumanism, which in its antihumanist incarnation rejects the traditional understanding of the human condition, taking the idea of human superiority and relegating it to the level of biocentric, nature-based inquiry. The Pooh texts, on the other hand, are profoundly humanist, exalting human children and their ability to create reality.

"That's What It Is," Says Pooh: Posthumanism, Children's Narratives, and God

Winnie-the-Pooh's statements in the poem "Us Two"—"That's what it is," "That's who they are," and "That's how it is"—represent a rejection of relativist thinking. In Pooh's simple, incontrovertible declarations of fact, we find the certainty that posthumanism lacks. One of the leading posthumanist theorists, Neil Badmington, has shown how, in fact, posthumanism has an unstable foundation. For the purposes of this discussion, posthumanism can be seen, as Badmington suggests, as a reaction to humanism (2000, 9). More specifically, it is a philosophical and theoretical result of the crisis in humanism. Badmington states that "posthumanism arises from the theoretical and practical inadequacy—or even impossibility—of humanism" (2014, 374). The backward appeal to humanism yields similarly unspecific results. Massimo Lollini says that "[h]umanism has no fixed meaning" (2008, 14), and in the introduction to his *Posthumanism* volume of essays, Badmington notes that his contributors do not all use the term to mean the same thing (2000, 10). Therefore, if neither of these "isms" has a solid foundation, it is impossible to unlink them, and they must be considered in tandem. Posthumanism in some iterations is simply a rejection of humanism, or in other words the centrality of the human being with his/her function of being a rational being, capable of independent thought. Humanism can in one sense be seen as an expression of secularism, which is itself a reaction to and indeed a rejection of a previous episteme that focused on the human as a product of the divine—in other words, as a child of God. But the rejection of humanism does not mean a return to religion, spirituality, or belief in the supernatural. Instead, one flavor of posthumanism focuses on the rise of a new God—technology and with it, artificial intelligence, which now threatens humanism with the notion that machines will be able to reason and perhaps take jobs once performed by humans.

It is this "AI Will Supplant Humans" variety of posthumanist thought that is of particular relevance in understanding how Pooh demonstrates the necessity of humans and human superiority. A valuable expression of the posthumanist theory of the coming superiority of AI can be found in Dan Brown's 2017 thriller *Origin*, in which he posits an evolutionary scenario in which humans and machines will be merged and indistinguishable. "Human beings are evolving into something *different*," Brown's billionaire futurist character Edmond Kirsch declares; "We are becoming a hybrid species—a fusion of biology and technology. The same tools that today live *outside* our bodies—smartphones, hearing aids, reading glasses, most pharmaceuticals—in fifty years will be incorporated into our bodies to such an extent that we will no longer be able to consider ourselves *Homo sapiens*" (Brown 2017, 411). Essentially, the question that Brown is asking is, "[W]ill God survive science?" (Tuohy 2017). Many would feel that posthumanism has already answered that question and that the answer is "no." As reviewer Wendy Tuohy writes, Dan Brown believes that "humans will replace their supernatural God with artificial intelligence (AI), which will produce a 'collective consciousness' to replace the major faiths." Brown further says: "We will start to find our spiritual experiences through our interconnections with each other. . . . Our need of that exterior God that judges us . . . will diminish and eventually disappear" (qtd. in Tuohy 2017). Equally, it may be the case that we will still need an "exterior God," but rather than an all-powerful spiritual entity that judges us, we will turn to an AI god to whom we can speak and who speaks to us, answering our questions and constantly reminding us what we need to do next. Stephen G. Post posits that there already "exists a religion of technology that promotes the uncritical and irrational affirmation of unregulated technological advance. In essence, technological advance is *always deemed good*" (2005, 1459; emphasis added). It is worth noting here that this new religion of technology is bereft of anything remotely spiritual and derives its morality from the fact that it simply *exists*. By extension, this episteme gives its acolytes no compelling reason to be concerned about the moral implications of technological advance, the ultimate result of which will be "transforming life," most likely by technologically enhancing humans (Post 2005, 1461). How this worldview relates to children, their essential humanness, and their interaction with stories is cause for concern.

The seismic cultural changes that have occurred over the past century in the realities of our understanding of what it means to be human correlate directly with the evolving relationship between children and their narratives during the hundred years since *Winnie-the-Pooh* was first published. The philosophical shifts that led to posthumanism are quite clearly mirrored in the development of what we define as children's literature, the roots of which can be found in the literature of folklore and myth, which attempted to explain the divine and the relationship of humans to forces they could not understand. While in many cases mythmaking was an attempt to explain phenomena that later received rational, humanistic, and scientific explanations, there was still a belief in or appeal to some higher power or order in the cosmos. There was to the mythmakers a childlike sense of wonder in the contemplation of the stars and the movement of the planets. This is also the feeling one gets from the earliest myths, which were stories for everyone, from the young to the aged. There was no such thing as "children's literature." It was simply the magic of storytelling.

Just as the humanists reacted against the dialectic of magic and supernatural explanations, the episteme of childhood and children's literature shifted from a construct of sheltered innocence to one of experience. Scientific, humanistic explanations of the world led to the notion of stories written with children as the intended audience. These stories initially had a didactic rather than artistic purpose. Focusing on the "scientific" process of raising small humans to behave appropriately, these stories taught children to be obedient to their parents and to use proper manners. Consider the story "The New Mother" penned by Lucy Clifford in 1882. "The New Mother" reaches the heights of motivating children to behave by presenting a scenario in which two children are promised by a "strange wild-looking girl" that, if they will be naughty, she will show them two dancing figures that she claims are enclosed in a box she carries, and that she shows only to naughty children. The children return three times to the girl, and each time they are told they have not been naughty enough. Blue-Eyes' and Turkey's mother tells them that if they continue to misbehave, she will be forced to leave them and "send home a new mother, with glass eyes and wooden tail." This is, in fact, what happens, and at the end of the story the children are left looking into their house from outside. Their mother is gone, and "[n]ow and then, when the darkness has fallen and the night is still, hand in hand Blue-Eyes and the Turkey creep up near to the home in which they once were so happy, and with beating hearts they watch and listen; sometimes a blinding flash comes through the window, and they know it is the light from the new mother's glass eyes, or they hear a strange muffled noise, and they know it is the sound of her wooden tail as she drags it along the floor" (Clifford [1882] 2011).

By the 1920s, children's book creators had jettisoned these sometimes horrific lessons and begun to write a new type of humanistic literature for children. These were books that celebrated childhood innocence, portraying children at the center of their own universe. Since toys are inextricably linked to childhood, many of these books also celebrated play and playthings. A common concern among all of them is what makes toys "real." Preceding *Winnie-the-Pooh* were Johnny Gruelle's *Raggedy Ann Stories* (1919) and *Raggedy Andy Stories* (1920). These rag dolls take on a life of their own when their mistress, Marcella, is out of the room, and their adventures with the other toy room occupants are dutifully chronicled by Gruelle. Perhaps the most well-known fictional plush plaything is the Velveteen Rabbit of Margery Williams's book of the same name (1922). The Velveteen Rabbit is tossed aside by her owner, a small boy, for more up-to-date and mechanical playthings. At the beginning of the story, the Velveteen Rabbit asks the question, "What is real?" The Skin Horse, the oldest toy in the nursery, replies that it is "something that happens to you." The Skin Horse goes on to say that "[w]hen a child loves you for a long, long time, not just to play with, but REALLY loves you, then you become Real" (Williams 1922).

There is a key thematic difference between these early twentieth-century texts and A. A. Milne's Pooh books. Through the act of anthropomorphizing toys, Gruelle and Williams actually prefigured posthumanism in children's literature. Raggedy Ann and Andy and the Velveteen Rabbit are portrayed as absolutely, indisputably *real* or as having the potential to become real. On the other hand, even with the element of what I will call, for lack of a more precise term, magical realism, the Winnie-the-Pooh books are ultimately humanist texts. Pooh and his friends are not concerned about becoming real; they just *are*. To adapt Descartes, they are acted upon by a human child; therefore, they are. The human child is the actor as opposed to the notion that toys have their own secret lives, can act independently of the child, and thus are on the same level as the child.

Supporting the argument for the Pooh books as humanistic texts is the fact that Pooh and his friends are subject to Christopher Robin, who always shows up to sort things out. Pooh is a self-described bear of "Very Little Brain," with the implication that Christopher Robin's physical organic brain is superior. Christopher Robin, and by association a child reading or having read to them the Pooh books, knows that Owl cannot write Happy Birthday properly and that Pooh cannot spell, despite the fact that they are confident that they can. The child reigns supreme in the Hundred Acre Wood because the child knows that he or she is superior in intelligence and learning to the playthings. As Milne says of Pooh, "because when you are a bear of Very Little Brain, and you Think of Things, you find sometimes that a Thing which seemed very Thingish inside you is quite different when it gets out into the open and has other people looking at it" (Milne 1928, 102).

As we read and reread *Winnie the Pooh, The House at Pooh Corner*, and Milne's books of poetry, we are transported into a world of unfettered imaginative play, with a child at the center having adventures in a forest with no adult supervision and with no didactic lessons to be found. There is only Christopher Robin and Pooh, and no sense that Pooh and the other toys' sentience comes from any outside source, whether divine or technological. The Pooh books appeal to the "wisdom of literature," which is a reliance on literature itself for meaning (Lollini 2008, 14). In his autobiography, Christopher Robin Milne describes his father as agnostic. As for himself, while he was a believer for much of his young life, he later became agnostic as well. Christopher Robin concluded: "There was no God. God had not created Man in His own image. It was the other way round: Man had created God. And Man was all there was." It is ironic, then, that the Pooh stories portray Christopher Robin as the "God" of his hundred-acre domain. The toys look to him for solutions to their problems. It is this view of "Man as God" that will unwittingly lead us back to the spiritual, prehumanistic world.

But before we circle back to the beginning, it is important to remember that the Pooh books were received in a much different way by children at the time of their publication than they are one hundred years later. Just as posthumanism leads to the possibility of having to redefine the term "human being," children's books have been sufficiently transformed by technology to the extent that the definition of what constitutes "literature" for children must be rethought. Mobile app and other multimedia versions of picture books to be consumed on screens have become the "posthuman" iteration of children's literature. Books for older children now also include "bonus content" available on the internet, where children are directed to continue their interaction with the story. The Disney acquisition of the Pooh properties and "brand" has resulted in a plethora of consumer products based on Milne's characters; however, it is interesting to note that there are no AI Pooh plush toys. Pooh toys, in other words, still require a child and an imagination. The most "technologically" advanced Pooh spinoff book currently offered by Disney is a personalized book entitled *Pooh Loves You*, with the child's name appearing on the cover and used throughout the text of the book. No electronics are required for a child to enjoy and interact with these toys, and a child's relationship with them can be the same as it was for Christopher Robin Milne and his plush bear.

"That's Who They Are": Children, Toys, and Narrative

Toys have always been an intrinsic part of children's literature, particularly for younger children, and even from the days of the Velveteen Rabbit and Raggedy Ann and Andy, physical toys based on these characters have been available for purchase. Once they acquire such a toy, children can use their imagination to turn it into something not necessarily "human," but sentient nonetheless. The relevance, then, of posthuman thinking to children's literature, and specifically to the plush toy known as Edward Bear now sitting in the New York Public Library, can be found in the idea of toys themselves, and the narratives created around those toys with children as the intended audience. All toys can be seen as "technology" in the sense that they represent the application of processes derived from scientific methods applied to the creation of children's playthings. Of course, plush toys in and of themselves are decidedly "low-tech." However, even as early as the second decade of the twentieth century, manufacturers were using the technology of the time to give "life" to their products. Indeed, the Gund Company, one of the earliest manufacturers of stuffed, plush toys, notes on the "History" page of their website that by 1912 Adolf Gund was responsible for several patents that "brought life to his creations." The accompanying illustrations show diagrams of internal mechanisms that would cause toys to move in a lifelike manner.

From this point of view, then, using posthumanism as the theoretical lens through which to examine the continued relevance (or nonrelevance as the case may be) of the Winnie-the-Pooh stories is thus quite apropos. As Neil Badmington has suggested, posthumanism "emerges from a recognition that 'Man' is not the privileged and protected center because humans are no longer—and perhaps never were—utterly distinct from animals, machines, and other forms of the 'inhuman'" (2014, 374). I would argue that there is an utter distinction between humans and other forms "of the inhuman" that can be found through an examination of child and plaything relationships as portrayed in literature. Taking into account the fallibility of memory, here is how Christopher Robin Milne describes it:

> The bear [Winnie-the-Pooh] took his place in the nursery and gradually he began to come to life. It started in the nursery; *it started with me.* It could really start nowhere else, for the toys lived in the nursery and they were mine and I played with them. And as I played with them and talked to them and gave them voices to answer with, so they began to breathe. But alone I couldn't take them very far. I needed help. So my mother joined me and she and I and the toys played together, and gradually more life, more character flowed into them, until they reached a point at which my father could take over. Then, as the first stories were written, the cycle was repeated. ([1974] 2016)

Stefan Herbrechter eloquently articulates the more general role of toys in children's literary narratives:

> There is indeed nothing more closely associated with "narrative" than a toy. Toys always "tell stories." They are like little story machines, narrative catalysers,

objects that help make sense of the world. There is something utterly "realist" even about the fanciest of toys. Toys always refer to reality even if they are of the order of complete fantasy and thus completely unrealistic. . . . In this sense, the "postmodern condition" seems to have a close affinity with the nature of the toy in general. (2004, 152)

This theory supports the view of the Pooh books as humanist. The toys assist in the creation of narrative. Their presence invites the child to create a narrative. But the human, the child, remains the creator.

The teddy bear plush toy, inspired by a *real* exploit of President Theodore "Teddy" Roosevelt with a *real* bear, first appeared in 1903, putting it within two decades or so of the advent of Winnie-the-Pooh. This means that teddy bears and other plush toys were readily available for purchase, and a very popular type of toy at the time Alan Milne began to write poems and stories about his son. Although contrary to Christopher Milne's memory, it is plausible that A. A. Milne observed his son's relationship with his plush bear and, with his writer's eye, saw immediately that therein lay a story. In his autobiography, the adult Christopher Robin describes his relationship with the plush bear toy: "When a child plays with his bear *the bear comes alive* and there is at once a child-bear relationship which tries to copy the Nanny-child relationship. Then the child gets inside his bear and looks at it the other way round: that's how bear feels about it. And at once sympathy is born and egotism has died" ([1974] 2016). There is a great deal to unpack in this rather profound statement. The real Christopher Robin here confirms that Pooh Bear was *alive* to him. We recall that Pooh's contemporaries, such as Raggedy Ann and Andy and the Velveteen Rabbit, were also portrayed as sentient toys. In her remarkable Arbuthnot Lecture on the role of (real) animals in children's literature, the late Ursula K. Le Guin made brief mention of Pooh and other stuffed toys that have become part of the children's literary canon:

Some of our animal friends are stuffed. One of them is covered with velveteen. The most famous of them are Pooh and Piglet and that lot. . . . As one who lived for years with stuffed animals, dear friends and active companions, far more autonomous, adventurous, and unpredictable than any doll I ever met, *I will only say that the borders of reality are less defined than some believe.* (2004, 27; emphasis added)

Christopher Robin interacted with his bear in real life much the same way he is depicted as interacting with them in the books, blurring the borders of reality. As the relationship between toy and boy developed, Christopher Robin also developed the ability to see things from Pooh's point of view, developing a sense of empathy. As Christopher Milne told it:

> Every child has his favourite toy, and every only-child has a special need for one. Pooh was mine, and probably, clasped in my arms, not really very different from the countless other bears clasped in the arms of countless other children. From time to time he went to the cleaners, and from time to time ears had to be sewn on again, lost eyes replaced and paws renewed. ([1974] 2016)

Herbrechter very articulately describes the world of Christopher Robin and Pooh in a more general sense in this passage:

> Children are supposed to live in a world of their own, which is clearly confined and marked out as the space and time for play, and in which toys are the main objects and controlling devices of socialisation. This miniature world, at once infinitely remote and utterly inseparable from the "real" and "serious" world of adults, in which play is a mere pastime and toys are mere consumables, has always served as a kind of significant "other" space and time which, through certain discursive practices, exists only to guarantee the precarious order of social organization as a whole. (2004, 142)

The notion of socialization is particularly relevant to the story of Christopher Robin and Pooh, because Christopher Robin was an only child. The humans with whom he primarily interacted were most importantly his nanny, and then his parents. There is no question that Pooh and the other toys were the main objects of Christopher Milne's socialization. The bucolic and pastoral life lived by Christopher wandering through Ashdown Forest, playing in the hollows of trees, was made social because his toys accompanied him. When Christopher Milne went off to school, his socialization was less successful. Known by that time as the "Christopher Robin" of the immensely popular Pooh books, he was teased and bullied by his unsympathetic or perhaps jealous peers. In his autobiography, Christopher Milne describes a visit to the Milne home by a journalist whom he calls "Mrs. Brown." Using her voice and perspective, and without contradicting her, Christopher Robin clearly tells us that school was difficult: "It can't be too pleasant to have that ['That' referring to Milne's then-ubiquitous poem 'Vespers' with the refrain, 'Christopher Robin is saying his prayers'] hanging round your neck when you are at school, however good you are at sums. Boys, after all, can be pretty beastly to each other when they try."

Since this is a consideration of Pooh, let us focus on the teddy bear. Edward Bear is certainly not the only sentient teddy bear immortalized in children's books: he has many descendants. One of the most well known, Paddington Bear, is not a stuffed toy but an anthropomorphized real bear from "darkest Peru." However, the Paddington character was inspired by a teddy bear author Michael Bond purchased for his wife. Don Freeman's Corduroy is another notable Pooh descendent. Corduroy is a teddy who comes alive when the lights in the store where he is for sale go out. A young girl and her mother come by the store. The girl wants to buy Corduroy, but her mother notices that a button is missing from the bear's overalls, and the disappointed girl leaves the store without the imperfect toy. That night, Corduroy goes on a search throughout the department store for his missing button, feeling that he would be purchased—and loved—if he was whole. The following day, the girl returns, buys Corduroy, takes him home, and makes him whole again, sewing on the button. Unlike Pooh, characters such Corduroy posit a posthuman interpretation in which the "realness" of the toys is not dependent upon human interaction. The fact that Corduroy can act on his own is presented as a form of unexplained magic, or fantasy, that is now passé with the advent of technologies that make what formerly inspired awe into mundane reality.

"That's How It Is:" Posthuman Bears

We have followed the path of children's literature as it has moved from a mythic, prehumanist literature that acknowledged the spiritual, to a humanist literature that insists upon human reality. However, in the posthuman world, the increasing intelligence of toys profoundly based on AI technology alters children's relationships with both the toys themselves and their own reality. The question of "what is real?" or "am I real?" becomes one of supreme importance and echoes the much older question the Velveteen Rabbit asked the Skin Horse. Descartes said that reason is the only thing that distinguishes men from beasts. What happens to this hypothesis now that plush toy "beasts" can actually reason? Can we distinguish between what is human and not human?

And what of these plush stuffed toys that became sentient and real in the mind of Christopher Milne, and are portrayed as such in his father's books? One might classify the Pooh books as very early precursors of magical realism. Now we arrive at the point where we find the Posthuman Pooh, Edward Bear, in a new world that is barely comprehensible to him. He remains sentient, but the toys around him have long since surpassed the intelligence of this Bear of Very Little Brain.

The definition of "sentient" blurs with the availability of "smart" playthings for children. When an intelligent AI plaything can interact with a child, which is the more real? Toys can now provide meaningful answers. What does it mean when a toy is responding in a "human" way? Now not only can toys speak and hold intelligent conversations with children, but they can also record what children say to them. The more real toys become, the less imagination needs to be exercised. Or is it simply a different kind of imagination? To understand the relevance of these more posthuman toys in understanding Winnie-the-Pooh—Christopher Robin's teddy bear, the character in the books brought to life through Ernest Shepard's illustrations, and the animated Pooh of the Disney films—I would like to appeal to two other bears. First, Teddy the "Super-Toy," first of Brian Aldiss's 1969 short story "Super-Toys Last All Summer Long," who was later visualized in Steven Spielberg's film adaptation, *AI Artificial Intelligence*. Then, the evil purple Lots-o'-Huggin' Bear from Disney/Pixar's *Toy Story 3*.

In his short story, Brian Aldiss foresaw the implications of artificial intelligence in the characters of the child robot "mecha" David and the "Super-Toy" Teddy. David is a perfect simulacrum of a human boy with a connection imprinted to his "mother" that allows him to love her just as her "real" son loves her. But David is a machine, created and manufactured by human beings. In his conversation and actions, David, though mechanical, is indistinguishable from a real human boy. Bert Olivier argues: "Ironically, if being human consists in a specific, utterly distinguishing mode of action, he [the mecha David] is human already for all intents and purposes" (2008, 34–35). Using this logic, David is to his "mother" Monica what Pooh is to Christopher Robin: a nonhuman entity seen as absolutely and incontrovertibly human by the human "owner."

But what of the Super-Toy, Teddy? Aldiss describes Teddy as being activated by the "speech pattern of his master's voice," the phrase recalling the image of the RCA Victor dog listening to an unspecified recording with the implication that the dog cannot distinguish between the recording and its real master's voice, or in the terms of a later advertisement for magnetic recordable cassette tapes, "Is it live or is it Memorex?" ("Memorex Cassette Commercial 1982" 2013). In Aldiss's story, the mecha boy, David, is trying to write a note to his "mummy" but does not quite know what to say. David's natural instinct is to ask his Super-Toy. Aldiss states that "[i]nside the bear, a small computer worked through its program of possibilities" to provide an answer, which ends up being for David to try it again with crayons, a highly unsatisfactory answer that demonstrates a limit (at least at the time Aldiss was writing) in the power of AI. Aldiss acknowledges this limit, given the nonhuman nature of technology—Teddy must work through his programming before responding. David thinks and then asks Teddy, "How do you tell what are real things from what aren't real things?" This conversation begins to sound a great deal like the much older conversation between the Velveteen Rabbit and the Skin Horse.

When responding to David's question about real things in "Super-Toys," Teddy shuffles his alternatives to arrive at a satisfactory answer for David. "Real things are good," is his response. David is not finished with his questions. He asks, "You and I are real, Teddy, aren't we?" Aldiss writes that in response, "[t]he bear's eyes regarded the boy unflinchingly." Finally, Teddy replies: "You and I are real, David." Then Aldiss notes of Teddy: "It specialized in comfort." Ironically, at the end of the story, Teddy says just the opposite. David asks, "Teddy—I suppose Mummy and Daddy are real, aren't they?" Teddy replies, "You ask such silly questions, David. Nobody knows what 'real' really means. Let's go indoors." Teddy's last comment clearly echoes Lollini's statement quoted earlier that humanism (or in this case, the word "real") has no fixed meaning. The key here is that the progression from humanism to posthumanism neglects the reality that there can be no posthumanism without humanism in that humans and human intellect create the technology and tools that could potentially lead to a posthuman future.

In their Toy Story films, Pixar Studios imagined that toys have secret lives when their owners are not present, a trope that can be traced back to Raggedy Ann and Andy and the toys in the Velveteen Rabbit's nursery. The films present a reality in which toys are terrified of no longer being needed by their owners and being forgotten and discarded—consider the bitter, purple, evil Pooh doppelgänger; the benignly named Lots-o'-Huggin' Bear (Lotso, for short) in *Toy Story 3*.

Toy Story 3 begins with a scene reminiscent of the Pooh stories in that it takes place completely in the imagination of Andy, the grown boy who owns the toys, and shows Andy's imaginative play with his toys as if that were what is real and really happening. This is an anomaly, however; in the world of Toy Story, unlike the world of Pooh, the toys only become "alive" when children are not there. It is, in effect, a story of the secret life of toys. The *Toy Story 3* screenplay describes what the toys do when a child appears: "They lie frozen, smiling, forever eager to play" (Arndt 2010, 19). Notice here that even in a world where toys have a life of their own outside the context of their human owner, the human owner is still in command. In *Toy Story 3*, Andy has grown up and is ready to go off to college. He has to determine what to do with his childhood toys, and when his mother suggests that he donate them, Andy replies, "No one's going to want these old toys. They're junk!" (Arndt 2010, 19). Andy's toys end up at the Sunnyside Day Care Center, where they find themselves part of a prison-like social structure lorded over by Lotso, who, according to the screenplay, "exudes an easy, cheerful persona" (33). Lotso fashions himself as the lord of misfit toys, the toys that have been forgotten, misplaced, and discarded. He assures the Toy Story gang that they don't have to worry about children growing up and deserting them in the day care, because the children there are always replaced by new ones (34). Therefore, they never have to deal with owners. "We own ourselves!" Lotso says. "We're masters of our own fate . . . ! We control our own destiny!" (37). They have a chance to make kids happy again (40). As the story unfolds, it is revealed that while Lotso is "plush and huggable on the outside," inside "he's a monster!" (72). Flashbacks reveal that Lotso's bitterness comes from being abandoned by his owner, Daisy, while on an outing. When he finally finds Daisy again, she is playing with another Lots-o'-Huggin' Bear that her parents have given her to replace him. That day, "something snapped," says Lotso's right-hand stuffed clown toy, Chuckles (74). Chuckles focuses on the loss of love: "We were lost," he says, "[c]ast off. Unloved . . . Unwanted" (74). As Lotso says bitterly, "We're all just trash, waitin' to be thrown away. That's all a toy is!" (107). Certainly, children's toys are consumables, meant to be used and then discarded. Few are the toys that retain such fame that they are preserved and displayed like Pooh and his friends. Regardless, whether in stories or in memory, toys can transcend the limits of their physical existence when the memory of the joyous interactive play remains. But this is still a humanist construct, as it takes a human to write about toys and a human to remember playing with their toys.

"What Would I Do . . . If It Wasn't for You?"
A Return to Prehumanism

The recent Disney live action film *Christopher Robin* takes Pooh and his friends to a place that A. A. Milne might never have imagined. The film takes place in an alternative reality in which A. A. Milne died when Christopher Robin was young, the Pooh books apparently never existed, and Christopher's last name is Robin and not Milne. This film reinforces that the toys were, in fact, real, but not in the way that the real Christopher Milne made them real. Using CGI for the first time to visualize the Pooh toys as real and sentient, the film forces a posthuman interpretation of the stories. In the rules of this alternative Christopher Robin world, everyone can see the toys speaking and moving, and everyone is equally alarmed by this reality. What the aesthetic of the film actually demonstrates is that posthumanism is an ineffective way to approach the interaction of Christopher Robin and Pooh. It portrays Pooh and his friends existing without any human intervention, which circumvents the entire point of Milne's books. We have reached a point where, as Istvan Csicsery-Ronay observes, "the boundary between theory and fiction has been breached beyond repair" (qtd. in Badmington 2000, 8). The Disney film fiction replaces the humanistic core of the Pooh books and replaces it with a contemporary posthuman theoretical interpretation that negates Christopher Robin's centrality and, like Williams with her Velveteen Rabbit and Gruelle with his Raggedy Ann and Andy, places Pooh and his friends as equals. But they are not equals, as Milne is not writing about plush toys that come alive of their own accord, nor about toys that exist as sentient outside of their relationship with a child.

The magic in the relationship between child and toy is metaphorically related to the inevitable journey of a child from innocence to experience (and from religion to humanism), which is reinforced in the narrative of *Toy Story 3* with Andy's departure for college. The beginning of the *Christopher Robin* film re-creates the final chapter of *The House at Pooh Corner* almost word for word, as the toys give a party for Christopher Robin, who is going off to boarding school and will soon leave childish things behind. This leads to a montage showing how the film's fictional version of "Christopher Robin" becomes an adult pressed by his work to cut costs at a luggage company, unable to spend time with his wife and daughter even on a long-promised vacation. This Christopher Robin has virtually forgotten his childhood toys.

Despite its faithful re-creation of *The House at Pooh Corner*'s final chapter, the film seems to have neglected the substance of the conversation between Christopher Robin and Pooh in the book. Christopher Robin asks, "Pooh, when *I'm—you* know—when I'm *not* doing Nothing, will you come up here sometimes?" Pooh asks, "Just me?" Christopher Robin replies affirmatively, and Pooh then asks for reassurance that he won't be alone: "Will you be here too?" Christopher Robin gives Pooh his promise, but then asks something of Pooh: "Pooh, *promise* you won't forget about me, ever. Not even when I'm a hundred." Milne then creates an image that connects the human with the spiritual: "*Still with his eyes on the world* Christopher Robin put out a hand and felt for Pooh's paw (Milne 1928, 178–79; emphasis added). At this moment, Christopher Robin sees his future in school and ultimately in the world, while at the same time keeping one hand on the magic, innocence, and belief of childhood. Even with the knowledge that he is growing up and will reach the age where he will put his toys aside, Christopher Robin wants to somehow hold on to that connection with Pooh. The final words of the last Pooh story read, "So they went off together. But wherever they go, and whatever happens to them on the way, in that enchanted place on the top of the Forest, a little boy and his Bear will always be playing" (Milne 1928, 181–82). The film fails in its essential misunderstanding of what constitutes the "realness" of Pooh. When the toys become sentient for all to see, presented in a realistic, live-action film, they are no longer the toys of Christopher Robin's imagination.

Through the omnipresent media and technology to which children today are exposed, the poignant moment Milne describes—a moment common to all children—happens earlier and earlier. Children can no longer experience the freedom and innocence so central to the Pooh books. With each passing year, *Winnie-the-Pooh* and *The House at Pooh Corner* become further removed linguistically and contextually from the truth of modern children's lives. Where, then, can children find what is real? Where can we find hope in the midst of this posthuman crisis?

Is it possible that we could see the answer in the light of a young boy with his bear trailing behind him going "bump—bump—bump" (Milne 1926, 161) up the stairs? When A. A. Milne (or at least the father character in the book) finishes the evening's story, Pooh and Christopher Robin are still together, inseparable for the moment, just as in the poem "Us Two." At the end of *Winnie-the-Pooh*, Christopher Robin asks his father if he can tell him and Pooh another story sometime. Milne says, "If you wanted it very much."

Christopher Robin replies, "Pooh does" (160). What he really means is, "I do." The Pooh stories help Christopher Robin know who he is, and who he is is the creator of Pooh, which leads us back to the essential humanism portrayed in Milne's books, where a child is free to create his own imaginary worlds, independent of technology.

And so come back full circle to the lifeless toys in the museum case in the children's room at the New York Public Library. The "real" Pooh toys were there, but the magic was not. As Christopher Milne said, "If you saw them today, your immediate reaction would be: 'How old and battered and lifeless they look.' But of course they are old and battered and lifeless. They are only toys, and you are mistaking them for the real animals who lived in the forest. Even in their prime they were no more than a first rough sketch, the merest hint of what they were to become" ([1974] 2016).

This is the great key—Christopher Robin refers to the "real animals" who lived in the forest. He refers to their potential, their "being," which came initially through his relationship with the real Pooh, Piglet, Eeyore, and the rest. Yes, they were inanimate plush toys, but they were his creations, made real through the gift of his imagination and that of his Father. Brian Aldiss's character Henry Swinton says, "It seems like a paradox that in this day and age we can create life but not intelligence" (Aldiss [1969] 1997). He is wrong. We can't create life, but at the same time we can. We are creators in the image of our own creator who mimic our own creation with those things that we *can* create: art, literature, and the inner lives of our plush toys. Edward Bear is not real because he is a tangible object. Pooh is real because Christopher Robin made him so.

Bibliography

Aldiss, Brian. (1969) 1997. "Super-Toys Last All Summer Long." *Wired*, January 1. https://www.wired.com/1997/01/ffsupertoys/.

Arndt, Michael. 2010. *Toy Story 3*. Screenplay. https://www.raindance.org/scripts/toy-story-3.pdf.

Badmington, Neil. 2000. "Introduction: Approaching Posthumanism." In *Posthumanism: Readers in Cultural Criticism*, edited by Neil Badmington, 1–10. Basingstoke, Hants., England: Macmillan.

Badmington, Neil. 2014. "Posthumanism." In *The Routledge Companion to Literature and Science*, edited by Bruce Clarke and Manuela Rossini, 374–84. Abingdon, Oxon., England: Routledge.

Brown, Dan. 2017. *Origin*. New York: Doubleday.

Clarke, Bruce. 2008. *Posthuman Metamorphosis: Narrative and Systems*. New York: Fordham University Press.

Clifford, Lucy. (1882) 2011. "The New Mother." *Weird Fiction Review*, November 3. http://weirdfictionreview.com/2011/11/creepy-classic-lucy-cliffords-the-new-mother/.

Duvall, John N. 1994. "The (Super)Marketplace of Images: Television as Unmediated Mediation in DeLillo's *White Noise*." *Arizona Quarterly* 50, no. 3 (Autumn): 127–53.

Forster, Marc, dir. 2018. *Christopher Robin*. Walt Disney Pictures.

Herbrechter, Stefan. 2004. "Toying with the Postmodern: 'To Infinity and Beyond.'" In *Post-Theory, Culture, Criticism*, edited by Ivan Callus and Stefan Herbrechter, 141–65. Leiden: Brill.

Jess-Cooke, Carolyn. 2006. "Virtualizing the Real: Sequelization and Secondary Memory in Steven Spielberg's *Artificial Intelligence: AI*." *Screen* 47, no. 3 (Autumn): 347–65.

Le Guin, Ursula K. 2004. "Cheek by Jowl: Animals in Children's Literature." *Children and Libraries* 2, no. 2 (Summer–Fall): 20–30.

Lollini, Massimo. 2008. "Humanisms, Posthumanisms, and Neohumanisms: Introductory Essay." *Annali d'Italianistica* 26: 13–23.

"Memorex Cassette Commercial 1982." 2013. YouTube, uploaded by Joe Bob Tarheel, November 8. https://www.youtube.com/watch?v=mEf6dNXZ3uI.

Milne, A. A. 1926. *Winnie-the-Pooh*. Illustrated by Ernest Shepard. London: Methuen.

Milne, A. A. 1928. *The House at Pooh Corner*. Illustrated by Ernest Shepard. London: Methuen.

Milne, A. A. 1988. "Us Two." In *Now We Are Six*. Illustrated by Ernest Shepard. New York: E. P. Dutton.

Milne, Christopher. (1974) 2016. *The Enchanted Places: A Childhood Memoir*. Kindle ed. London: Pan Books.

Olivier, Bert. 2008. "When Robots Would Really Be Human Simulacra: Love and the Ethical in Spielberg's *AI* and Proyas's *I, Robot*." *Film-Philosophy* 12, no. 2 (September): 30–44. http://www.film-philosophy.com/2008v12n2/olivier.pdf.

Post, Stephen G. 2005. "Posthumanism." In *Encyclopedia of Science, Technology and Ethics*, edited by Carl Mitcham, 1458–62. New York: Macmillan Reference USA.

Strong National Museum of Play. 2010. "A Brief History of Raggedy Ann." News Release, June 17. https://www.museumofplay.org/sites/default/files/press/releases/pdf/Raggedy history.pdf.

Tuohy, Wendy. 2017. "Dan Brown's New Book 'Origin' Challenges the Concept of God and Suggests Humans Will Worship AI." *Courier Mail* (Brisbane), October 28. https://www.couriermail.com.au/news/queensland/qweekend/dan-browns-new-book-origin-challenges-the-concept-of-god-and-suggests-humans-will-worship-ai/news-story/14e8e4ef97e4d9c3592f094c37f0662c.

Williams, Margery. 1922. *The Velveteen Rabbit; or, How Toys Become Real*. Digital Library, University of Pennsylvania. http://digital.library.upenn.edu/women/williams/rabbit/rabbit.html.

Bonus Chapter
Pooh, Poohing, and Other Verbal Time Bombs

Nicholas Tucker

When A.A. Milne's poem with its line "Pooh is poohing in the sun" appeared in *The House at Pooh Corner* in 1928, the word "poo" was not associated with feces. But by 1960 or so it had passed into common use in Britain and increasingly in America. This invests the poem in particular but also every other mention of Pooh in Milne's stories with an extra meaning never intended by its author. Publishers faced with the existence of these sorts of verbal time bombs in children's literature have often quietly changed texts over the years. But this has never been the case for Pooh Bear, who has become such a genuinely iconic figure that any proposal to change his name would have been controversial in the extreme.

This unquestioned survival of Pooh as a named character is linked with other instances in British children's literature where double entendres were often allowed to stay however incongruous they may have seemed in later years. By contrast, adult literature during the last and this century has been quicker to protect itself from potential ridicule in this area. Paul Fussell, in his fine study *The Great War and Modern Memory*, has drawn attention to what he calls the "[c]urious prophylaxis of language" existing before 1914 in which "one could use with security words which a few years later, after the war, would constitute obvious *double extenders*. . . . Even the official order transmitted from British headquarters to the armies at 6.50 on the morning of November

11, 1918, warned that 'there will be no intercourse of any description with the enemy.' Imagine daring to promulgate that at the end of the Second World War!" (1975, 23).

Although "intercourse" had been used to refer to sexual activity as long ago as 1798, after 1918 or so there seemed less hope of staring down a now less-malleable audience and forbidding it to laugh at any unfortunate double meaning arising from its use. Henry James and E. M. Forster could happily make use of the word in their prewar novels, and White Star officers at sea as late as 1912 could still be warned to "avoid at all times, convivial intercourse with passengers or each other" (Oldham 1961, 40). But most postwar writers for adults soon learned to avoid such pitfalls.

Yet this new awareness took much longer to take root in contemporary children's literature. In Christine Chaundler's school story *Jan of the Fourth*, published in 1923, the hot-tempered pupil of the title is advised by her head-mistress that "I do not wish you to have intercourse with anybody" (152). Later on, the same girl is "too surprised to put on the armour of lofty disdain she usually donned when she was obliged to hold an intercourse with Joey" (178). Both passages still appeared when the story was reprinted in 1940.

The headmistress and popular children's writer Elinor Brent-Dyer provides two more examples of the sort of cultural blindness affecting interwar children's writers and publishers. In her 1930 school story *The School by the River*, "the Principal allowed the girls much liberty, but intercourse with the men from the Academia was strictly forbidden, and any girl who transgressed this rule, and was found out more than once, was sent away" (86). Twenty years later, the same author unwittingly ran into more potential problems in her *The Chalet School and the Island*. As fiery fifteen-year-old Annis exclaims at one point, "That doesn't seem to have occurred to Aunt Margaret. I suppose she thinks that all that matters is a decent screw and holidays. Well, I can have a go at the screw in another way, but I *won't* teach! That's definite" ([1950] 1967, 153). Brent-Dyer's publisher, Collins, waited until 1999 and a new edition before finally changing "screw" to "decent salary."

Following a similar pattern, Enid Blyton's occasional use of "frig" as youthful slang for "refrigerator" was eventually quietly dropped by her publishers. In her best-selling Famous Five series, the names Dick and Aunt Fanny were also later changed to Rick and Aunt Frannie. Arthur Ransome's brave young character Titty still retains her name in the published version of his classic

1936 story *Swallows and Amazons*. But she was later renamed, first as "Kitty" on a television series and then as "Tatty" for a 2016 film version.

This suggests that while publishers might have felt they had little to fear from silent readers enjoying a story on their own, they became less confident when faced by a mass film or television audience reacting together and at the same time. The Disney studio still stuck to the name Pooh in various cartoon films made about this favorite toy bear, taking advantage of the fact that what British children describe as "poo" is more commonly referred to as "poop" by their American counterparts. Had A. A. Milne called his great character Winnie-the-Poop, there would surely have been more of a problem.

"Cock" is another word with which British children's writers have sometimes had problems. H. L. Mencken quoted in his magisterial study *The American Language* as an example of American squeamishness the way that the term *rooster* "had come into use in place of cock as a matter of delicacy, the latter word having acquired an indecent significance" (1919, 149). But numbers of interwar British writers and their publishers once again continued to display an equal determination to preserve tradition and not let sleeping cocks lie. When their books were reprinted, some of the unfortunate sentences that resulted were often left unaltered.

One memorable example of an inability to come to terms with this particular loss of innocence in adult fiction can be found in Angela Thirkell's best-selling 1939 light romantic novel *The Brandons*. In this, a well-heeled group of young unattached adults on holiday come to take some rides on a merry-go-round at a country fair. We then read how "Mr. Grant, really glad of an excuse to dismount, offered his cock to Lydia, who immediately flung a leg over it, explaining that she had put on a frock with pleats on purpose" (268). A page later, she observes, "I say, someone's on my cock!" As another character, Mr. Merton, puts it later, "Once Lydia is on her cock nothing will get her off" (270). This novel was reprinted without changes in 1945, this time in large print, and several times after that.

Editors at the time clearly failed to notice anything potentially unfortunate in what they saw before them, even though "cock" as slang for the male member had been in use since 1610. But in the generally feminized prewar publishing world of romantic novels, staff dealing with these manuscripts would almost invariably have been women drawn from the respectable middle classes. These would often have been promoted from secretarial jobs in order to deal with branches of literature that their better-paid male colleagues initially never took seriously. Some of these women evidently also shared in the same sorts of verbal unawareness that enabled their authors to ignore occasional double meanings in what they wrote.

This type of cultural myopia lasted much longer in children's books. Enid Blyton's short story "The Chocolate Cock," for example, written for her magazine *Sunny Stories* in 1930, begins with this sentence, surely startling for some children and parents even at the time: "Once there was a piece of chocolate in the shape of a cock." Ten years later, this sentence is repeated verbatim in Blyton's collection *The Talking Teapot and Other Tales* (1940, 53). Another best-selling children's writer, Richmal Crompton, had similar problems with this word, long after the 1893 edition of the *Oxford English Dictionary* had described it and what it referred to as "[t]he current name among the people, not permissible in polite speech or literature" (*OED* 1893, s.v. "cock," 77).

In the chapter headed "Aunt Jane's Treat" in her 1924 novel *William the Fourth*, Crompton describes how one of William's respectable maiden aunts accompanies him to a fairground. Once there, the excitement of the occasion overcomes her, and she finally takes a ride on a merry-go-round, mounting—as the author puts it—"[a] giant cock. It began. She clung on for dear life. It went faster and faster. There came a gleam into her eyes, a smile of rapture to her lips. . . . She seemed to find the circular motion anything but monotonous. It seemed to give her a joy that all her blameless life had so far failed to produce" (79).

This passage still appears in the 1983 reprint. Crompton's William books are less read by children now, but audiotapes with choice stories narrated by the actor Martin Jarvis remain hugely popular, both with those older readers for whom the William stories were originally intended and with newer, younger audiences. Jarvis has so far left the above story unselected. But he has recorded another story, "William and the Black Cat," also appearing in the 2005 reprint of *William the Fourth*. This still contains the following contributions from two middle-aged lady cat-lovers, each time directed at William: "You must call and see my pussy again soon, little boy" (145); and "You admirin' my pussy, little boy?" (151). It seems the publishers were right to take a risk here by fielding an unaltered text, since no one to my knowledge has since raised any questions about the presence of a double entendre some might think might now be better avoided.

There is also this extract from Angela Brazil's 1917 story *The Madcap of the School*. "'Oh!' Raymonde's sudden ejaculation was caused by a vision of no less a person than Miss Gibbs, who was standing in the doorway of the dormitory regarding the sewing party in some astonishment" (152–53). The same passage is reprinted in an edition published by Blackie in 1972. Raymonde is one of the lead girl characters, so anyone reading the text would not be thinking about her in terms of such a quintessentially male reaction. But it is still surprising that this passage got through so late in the day.

Captain W. E. Johns also makes extensive use of this term in his Biggles adventure stories, featuring an ever-audacious British pilot and his small group of equally heroic friends. The 2003 paperback edition of *Biggles: The Camels Are Coming*, originally published in 1932, still contains "'Good Lord!' ejaculated Biggles suddenly" (270). Going forward seventy years, the American edition of J. K. Rowling's *Harry Potter and the Order of the Phoenix* has a moment when Ron Weasley, Harry's close friend, "ejaculated 'We're not going to use magic?'" (2004, 242). In the British edition, he merely "exclaimed." Could this be one of the last times that "ejaculate" appears in children's literature as a manner of speech?

Other children's titles, caught out by time once words have changed their meaning to something less appropriate than as originally defined, have simply been allowed to fade away. Brenda Girvin's 1912 novel *Queer Cousin Claude* has never been reissued, and Enid Blyton's story *The Queer Adventure* is also now out of print, although its final edition was published as late as 1961. Bessie Marchant's spirited 1929 adventure story for girls, *How Nell Scored*, also ran to a reprint in 1952, but Ethel Talbot's 1925 school story *Fellow Fags* did not. *The Gay Way Reading Scheme*, once popular in British schools, has now turned into *The New Way Readers*, with the formerly popular character Fat Pig more safely renamed Pat the Pig.

Over in America, *Boners*, *More Boners*, and *Still More Boners*, all written by the young Dr. Seuss in the 1930s (Geisel), are also unlikely to be republished today without editorial change, although the same author's *The Pocketbook of Boners* (Geisel 1932) was reprinted in 1945, having already sold over a million copies. This was still a time when the term "boner" referred to a stupid mistake; it was only after 1950 that it acquired its current priapic meaning. A few defiant titles have tried to cling on to formerly innocent meanings, as in Charles A. Pemberton's illustrated *My Big Book of Pretty Pussies* (1965). But on Amazon lists today his book stands out like isolated island of good taste surrounded by modern titles now aiming for deliberately obscene effects.

Yet changes in addressing child audiences in both countries were on the way. As the children's literature historian Brian Alderson put it, "For well over 150 years, the print-runs of children's books were governed by expectations of sales to a largely middle-class public, or to schools and Sunday Schools where unthreatening convention prevailed" (2010, 39). But the post–Second World War advent of school and children's libraries and the arrival of cheap paperbacks led to a far wider social base for child readers. The image of a middle-class child being read to by his or her mother now had to broaden to accommodate the existence of less-protected children from more diverse backgrounds, possibly being read to at school. This new awareness helped sharpen both subject matter and vocabulary in children's books. Previously overlooked double entendres, of the type that a perceptive and socially confi-dent parent at home may once have glossed over, might now be greeted with mirth on all sides.

No experienced schoolteacher today would ever choose to read aloud to a class from a text once thought to be safe but that now, in a generally more relaxed classroom atmosphere, could turn out to be decidedly more risky. As a young teacher myself I once found a battered copy of Cecily Marianne Rutley's 1951 story *Little Blue Tit* in a school's stock cupboard. The word "tit" in the title and in the subsequent story had in every case been firmly altered in ink to "bird." I took this as a warning from a previous teacher, possibly aris-ing from painful personal experience, never to read this story aloud without careful editing beforehand.

A similar new awareness could be found in postwar radio programs. BBC radio used to broadcast *Music and Movement* in the mornings, to encourage small children listening at home to take part in simple games and dances. In one particular episode in 1947, recorded but never transmitted, the announcer began, "Pretend that you've got some balls, and I'm going to hide them." She closed, accompanied by a jolly accompaniment played on the studio piano, with "Run lightly around, looking everywhere for your balls." When the pro-ducer was told this was unacceptable, she accused her (clearly more worldly) colleagues of having dirty minds. This recording, still available, is now a col-lector's item (Ash 2010, 35).

In this new atmosphere, readers could sometimes be uncertain whether double entendres in children's books continued to be accidental or were possibly intended. In 1991, the respected British author and illustrator John Ryan won libel damages from two newspapers when they published stories claiming that the BBC had taken his popular animated picture book series *Captain Pugwash* off the air with no plans for any repeats. The reason for this, it was claimed, was because of the deliberate insertion of risqué names for some of the crew aboard the fictional pirate ship, the *Black Pig*. These, it was said, included Master Bates, Seaman Staines, and Roger the Cabin Boy. In fact these names never existed, and the BBC had not taken the series off air as a result. In 2009, the singer and comedian Richard Digance stated that it was he who had originated this story in a 1970s sketch. A twenty-five-year injunction preventing Digance from making any further references to *Captain Pugwash* followed (Ash 2010, 211).

Up to this point, it had generally been assumed that double entendres in children's literature were merely oversights on the part of otherwise innocent authors and publishers. That so many continued to believe this false story years after it was exposed is an indication of changing views about what could now appear in print, even when an author was writing for a very young audience.

As it is, except in the case of famous classics, it has been reasonably common for children's texts from the past to be altered over the years by publishers to better suit modern circumstances. References to old money, for example, are routinely changed to decimal coinage in reprints occurring after 1971, and illustrations are often brought up to date in similar fashion, with jeans and anoraks replacing shorts and blazers. So, how do we account for the persistence of genuine double entendres from the past of the type already quoted even well into modern times?

There are a number of possible explanations. Children's publishers, having once let a text go through for printing, would have hesitated to risk alienating a respected author by later on drawing their attention to certain important social changes in vocabulary usage. Enid Blyton, for example, was notoriously self-regarding and prickly as well as immensely profitable for her publishers. It would have been a brave, even foolhardy editor who would dare to advance reasons for changes to an author long used to taking the moral high ground, and resentful of any criticism. Venerable texts that had long proved popular might not even have been reread before reissue. If any of the more alert editors had noticed something untoward, more evident in later reprintings in less innocent times than they might have been in the original texts, there was always the expense and bother of having to reset the offending page. Young readers would not be expected to make any particular fuss. Potential adult protesters who might in later years have objected to passages containing racist or other incendiary mixed messages would have been more likely to smile at inadvertent double entendres rather than send complaints. So why not, they might reason, just reprint an old favorite in its entirety and hope for the best?

It is noticeable, too, that some of the most spectacular double entendres occurred in literature at its most child-centered. Adult readers who were once happy to share classics like *Treasure Island* and *The Wind in the Willows* with younger audiences might still enjoy Richmal Crompton's William series. But there was much less for them in the growth of books very much written for children of the type epitomized in the works of Enid Blyton. So without the expectation of any determined adult postpublication scrutiny, editors in their turn also sometimes failed to read texts with adequate care.

Once discerning adults became more closely involved, however, things could be very different. Josephine Pullein-Thompson, author of many successful pony stories for girls, contributed with her two sisters to a collective autobiography, *Fair Girls and Grey Horses*, in 1996. In it, she recalls writing her first novel while still a prewar child, naming her hero, in all innocence as she had never come across the term before, Edwin Pisspot. Because this particular name was absent from her local telephone directory, she believed that she would therefore run no risk of a libel suit. Her mother, who was a professional writer, gently suggested that another name might be more appropriate. Neither she nor her daughter lived to witness an age in which a character called Edwin Pisspot in a children's book could pass more or less without notice, as it surely would today.

The only threat to lax editorial control back in the publisher's office would be if any offending passage was later picked up for comic effect. The popular British humorist Arthur Marshall was always on the lookout for choice ambiguous passages in girls' school stories. His annual surveys of such fiction in the weekly *New Statesman* magazine, starting in 1935 and continuing intermittently for the next four decades, were eagerly anticipated.

The writer Dorita Fairlie Bruce was one of his regular victims, with many verbatim quotations from her works reproduced for adult enjoyment. "Tits, lassies!" was one such, uttered by way of a gentle admonition by kind old Miss Peters to fellow pupils Primula and Anne in *Prefects at Springdale*. She goes on, "We mustn't let ourselves grow gloomy over troubles that have been with us for close on four hundred years" (1938, 123). Elsie Oxenham was also one of his favorites. From *Schoolgirl Jen at the Abbey*, he quotes one Lavinia Page complaining about her current treatment at school. "'Mrs. Jaikes, she calls me Vinny. The boys call me Lav. I hates it.' And Lavinia flushed resentfully" (1950, 18). Given this sudden spate of inadvertent cloacal imagery, it seems only fitting that Lavinia's home address is announced as King's Bottom Farm.

From Marshall's affectionately mocking contributions, however, other British critics up to 1960 and often beyond generally ignored girls' school stories and indeed most other children's literature. With little fear therefore of any critical comeback, otherwise alert editors were under little pressure other than to make money for their firms. But while this was often the case, it still cannot explain away the existence and subsequent persistence of every double entendre in children's literature, particularly the more egregious examples. A Freudian approach would suggest that such occasional slips point to the existence of an Unconscious occasionally breaking through with its own agenda of otherwise suppressed darker thoughts and emotions. Psychoanalytic interpretations of all aspects of children's literature have been common for many years now, and there will doubtless be many who look to them when considering the phenomenon of double entendres in children's books.

Another possible explanation can be found in the work of the American psychologist Leon Festinger. In 1957, he coined the term "cognitive dissonance," developing this concept after studying how groups of cultists behaved after their various predictions of the forthcoming end of the world due to a massive flood failed to materialize. From this, he theorized that when two cognitions become inconsistent with each other, in this case a belief that the world would end on a certain date and the fact that it did not, the most extreme cultists simply argued for the existence of another date in the future. Facing up to the fact that everything they had previously believed in had just been proved wrong generally appeared not to be an option, such was the desire to avoid experiencing mutually contradictory thought processes or, as Festinger put it, a state of cognitive dissonance. This inner drive to hold attitudes and behavior in a state of constant harmony was described by Festinger as the principle of cognitive consistency.

In terms of reacting to double entendres in literature, the wish to avoid a state of cognitive dissonance might help explain how many readers could ignore any troubling double meaning and simply push on to the next page. And if the double entendre was eventually identified, letting it stand in future editions would seem like an assertion by the publisher that the audience they were looking for would never spot this sort of thing until they were well out of the children's book market anyway. Harmless entertainment in print can always cast something like an escapist spell over everyone involved, from author and publisher to parent and child, particularly at a time when reading books as opposed to comic strip magazines was seen as an essentially safe, domestic activity.

Younger children are also not quick to understand ambiguities. Up to the age of seven or so, the idea that any particular phrase can have two diverse meanings can be quite a challenge to a child's more literal state of understanding. This was the defense put up by Poundland, a major British shopping chain, after they were criticized for some suggestive advertisements issued around Christmas 2018. One caption to an illustration including an elf and a donkey ran: "Don't tell Rudolph I've found a new piece of ass." Poundland defended their campaign, claiming that it was based on "humour and double entendres" that were not intended to be understood by children (Sweney 2018). They lost the case, but the assumption they made about small children's limited understanding of textual ambiguities was a common defense. The fact that this defense was thrown out suggests that, by that time, any assumption of innocence even in the very young could no longer be taken for granted.

Before this time, however, parents in general would commonly look to children's books as upholders of values they shared themselves. In these circumstances, occasional double entendres could easily pass unnoticed or else simply appear as unimportant accidents that most children and some less-worldly adults would not have recognized anyway. Only a critic like Arthur Marshall out for the kill, or a class of disrespectful pupils, might still insist on spotting and then enjoying such unintended comic moments.

Could this general desire to avoid potential states of cognitive dissonance brought about by certain passages in literature also help explain why children and perhaps some adults over time failed to react to the growing fact of a double meaning for Pooh? Have publishers and readers for years entered into a state of denial about the existence of a second, embarrassing reading? Or is it more a case of publishers realizing what has happened but being unwilling to do anything about it, at least in the first instance? Banking on the existence of a prolonged state of childhood innocence among their young readers could have further buttressed the comfortable expectation that all such double meanings would never have been noticed. Believing this was certainly easier and cheaper than resetting pages. And if young readers did spot any double entendres that have become more obvious with time, the hope could have been that they would forgive the slip knowing that it was never intended.

But while some other texts and titles have been changed and some characters given different names over time, Pooh Bear was always going to be too big and famous to risk any thought of rebranding. From a time when his name had no improper connotations to years where he had become synonymous with a normally taboo subject, his survival against these odds, while never becoming an object of ridicule, is impressive. However basic the name "Pooh" might sound, at least to British children when read aloud, there is that potentially saving "h" at the end of his name in print, very often preceded by "Winnie-the." He has also been around since 1926. Parents and children reading about Pooh once his name had become more problematic could reassure themselves that they were continuing to celebrate part of a valued literary heritage.

Cognitive dissonance describes a state of mind in which competing thoughts vie with each other for ascendance. The ability to read stories aloud featuring a character whose name is synonymous with feces suggests an altogether milder process perhaps best described as cognitive supertolerance. In this state, whatever exists in the status quo must be acceptable because it has always been there. If there were anything wrong, this would surely have been put right some time ago. Like the proudly phallic Cerne Abbas Giant, dating from at least the seventeenth century and still happily inscribed on his hill in Dorset, it was for a long time easier to accept leftover improprieties from the past once they bore the stamp of unquestioning tradition.

But that attitude was changing, too. Potentially embarrassing British street names, from Pissing Lane in the City of London to Bell End in the West Midlands, have now been replaced, although Minge Lane in Worcester and Grope Lane in Shrewsbury still survive. On the book front, anecdotal evidence suggests that modern children were beginning to giggle at the name of one of our most famous literary characters. Lines describing how Christopher Robin "walked off to the door, trailing Pooh behind him" (Milne 1926, 18), or even the very title *The House at Pooh Corner*, increasingly challenged any teacher or parent anxious to stem disrespectful laughter.

Those who might once have wished that Milne had chosen another name for his favorite character, however, can now relax. Beginning early in the twenty-first century, "poo" has become a favorite topic in picture books, with this once taboo word appearing both in titles and regularly in various would-be humorous texts. Representative examples include Taro Gomi's *Everybody Poos*

(2004), Steve Smallman and Ada Grey's *Poo in the Zoo* (2015), and Stephanie Blake's *Poo Bum* (2012). Poo, poop, or Pooh in a title for children no longer seems quite so bizarre, at least to some. Marlene Brown's picture book *Cooking with Pooh* uncontroversially appeared in 1996, followed by Isabel Gaines's *Pooh Gets Stuck* in 1998. It is a commentary on how far public taste has traveled since Milne first wrote that it is not certain whether these two titles now consciously aspire to the sort of double entendre that even the author's original publishers might have done their best to avoid.

Other forms of double entendres are also beginning to appear more deliberately in contemporary texts. The Cifaldi Brothers' 2015 venture *Do You Want to Play with My Balls?* uses its ambiguous title for deliberate, would-be comic effect. Intended for adults but written and illustrated as if for children, every page contains contrived double entendres. This is one of many spoof titles taking a well-known children's book format as a new vehicle for sometimes extreme adult jokes. In Britain, the cartoonist Simon Thorp found the same type of humor in his long-running comic strip *Finbarr Saunders and His Double Entendres*, appearing in the satirical magazine *Viz*. His hero's delight is to spot and then laugh at every conceivable double entendre uttered by others within his hearing.

A few inadvertent examples still occur from time to time, as in the veteran British writer Geoffrey Trease's 1995 children's adventure story *No Horn at Midnight*. This was published forty-five years after the American film *Young Man with a Horn*, starring Kirk Douglas and with its hit song "Get Happy," was renamed *Young Man of Music* when released for UK audiences. But in general the days when otherwise respectable children's publishers could still be caught out have now drawn to a close or are even going into reverse. Instead, artificial and contrived double meanings have become a going concern, given today's greater tolerance for what goes into print for any age.

Double entendres from the past seem even extra naïve by comparison, so indicative of times when verbal taboos were more numerous and therefore more at risk of being unintentionally flouted. Their survival in print often for many years after first appearing is testimony to a convenient if untested residual belief in a still surviving basic state of childhood innocence. But once more generally liberated children in the 1960s and after started not just chuckling at inappropriate passages but also sharing the source of their amusement with parents and teachers, the game was up. Former days of shared adult and child innocence were numbered.

Comic stereotypes of unworldly vicars or hypersheltered women uttering phrases rich in unintended undesirable double meanings no longer fit into a post-1945 world. Cheerfully vulgar music hall humor once aimed only at limited audiences now started to feature in mass broadcasting, first on radio and then more particularly on television. The hugely popular BBC television comedy series *Are You Being Served?*, first screened in 1972 and later running into ten seasons, constantly included quite frankly sexual double entendres without ever receiving significant complaints. Editors back in the publishing houses, faced by this new tide of heightened awareness, were now therefore forced to scrutinize texts as never before while going some way to correcting some of the former double entendres they had allowed to survive. No longer could they rely upon an audience hopefully oblivious to double meanings that only some adults would quickly recognize.

Ironically, though, this new state of editorial awareness arrived at a time when double entendres were becoming more openly celebrated as a source of universal humor. Books setting out to get fun from contrived examples could now assume a general state of knowingness among their audiences, young and old. To return to where we started, anyone today coming fresh to Milne's line "Pooh is poohing in the sun" might no longer be sure whether or not the toy bear was doing exactly what the contemporary slang use of these words implies.

Bibliography

Alderson, Brian. 2010. "The Making of Children's Books." In *The Cambridge Companion to Children's Literature*, edited by M. O. Grenby and Andrea Immel, 35–54. Cambridge: Cambridge University Press.

Ash, Russell. 2010. *It Just Slipped Out . . . A Bulging Encyclopedia of Double Entendres*. London: Headline.

Blake, Stephanie. 2012. *Poo Bum*. Wellington: Gecko Press.

Blyton, Enid. 1940. *The Talking Teapot and Other Tales*. London: J. Coker.

Blyton, Enid. 1942. *Five on a Treasure Island*. London: Hodder and Stoughton.

Blyton, Enid. 1952. *The Queer Adventure*. London: Staples Press.

Brazil, Angela. 1917. *The Madcap of the School*. London: Blackie.

Brent-Dyer, Elinor. 1930. *The School by the River*. London: Burns and Oates.

Brent-Dyer, Elinor. (1950) 1967. *The Chalet School and the Island*. New York: HarperCollins.

Brown, Marlene. 1996. *Cooking with Pooh*. Boston: Little, Brown.

Bruce, Dorita Fairlie. 1937. *Dimsie Intervenes*. Oxford: Oxford University Press.

Bruce, Dorita Fairlie. 1938. *Prefects at Springdale*. Oxford: Oxford University Press.

Chaundler, Christine. 1923. *Jan of the Fourth*. London: James Nisbet.

Cifaldi Brothers. 2012. *Do You Want to Play with My Balls?* Ann Arbor, MI: Bum Bum Books.

Crompton, Richmal. 1924. *William the Fourth*. London: George Newnes.

Festinger, Leon. 1964. *Conflict, Decision and Dissonance*. London: Tavistock.

Fussell, Paul. 1975. *The Great War and Modern Memory*. Oxford: Oxford University Press.

Gaines, Isabel. 1998. *Pooh Gets Stuck*. Glendale, CA: Disney Press.

Geisel, Theodor S. [Dr. Seuss]. 1931a. *Boners*. New York: Viking Press.

Geisel, Theodor S. [Dr. Seuss]. 1931b. *Still More Boners*. New York: Viking Press.

Geisel, Theodor S. [Dr. Seuss]. 1932. *The Pocketbook of Boners*. New York: Viking Press.

Girvin, Brenda. 1912. *Queer Cousin Claude*. London: George Allen.

Gomi, Taro. 2004. *Everybody Poos*. London: Frances Lincoln.

Johns, Captain W. E. 1932. *Biggles: The Camels Are Coming*. London: John Hamilton.

Marchant, Bessie. 1929. *How Nell Scored*. Edinburgh: Thomas Nelson.

Marshall, Arthur. 1974. *Girls Will Be Girls*. London: Hamish Hamilton.

Mencken, H. L. 1919. *The American Language: An Inquiry into the Development of English in the United States*. New York: Alfred A. Knopf.

Milne, A. A. 1926. *Winnie-the-Pooh*. London: Methuen.

Milne, A. A. 1928. *The House at Pooh Corner*. London: Methuen.

Oldham, Wilton. 1961. *The Ismay Line: The Titanic, the White Star Line and the Ismay Family*. Gosport, Hants., England: Journal of Commerce and Shipping.

Oxenham, Elsie. 1950. *Schoolgirl Jen at the Abbey*. Glasgow: Collins.

Oxford English Dictionary (OED). 1893. 1st ed. Oxford: Oxford University Press.

Pemberton, Charles A. 1970. *My Big Book of Pretty Pussies*. London: Egmont.

Pullein-Thompson, Josephine, Diana, and Christine. 1996. *Fair Girls and Grey Horses: Memories of a Country Childhood*. London: Allison and Busby.

Ransome, Arthur. 1930. *Swallows and Amazons*. London: Jonathan Cape.

Rowling, J. K. 2004. *Harry Potter and the Order of the Phoenix*. London: Bloomsbury.

Rutley, Cecily Marianne. 1951. *Little Billy Blue Tit*. London: Frederick Warne.

Smallman, Steve, and Ada Grey. 2015. *Poo in the Zoo*. Wilton, CT: Tiger Tales.

Sweney, Mark. 2018. "ASA Bans Poundland's Lewd Toy Elf Ad Campaign." *Guardian*, February 7. https://www.theguardian.com/business/2018/feb/07/asa-bans-poundlands-lewd-toy-elf-ad-campaign.

Talbot, Ethel. 1925. *Fellow Fags*. London: Sheldon Press.

Thirkell, Angela. 1939. *The Brandons*. London: Hamish Hamilton.

Trease, Geoffrey. 1995. *No Horn at Midnight*. London: Pan Macmillan.

About the Contributors

Megan De Roover is a theater and performance studies scholar with a PhD from Arizona State University (2018). Her research concentrates on environmental agency in the arts and humanities, expressions of Canadian identity and nationalism, and border literature and performance. Most recently she has taught at the University of Waterloo in the Department of Communication Arts. Megan writes from her home country, Canada.

Jennifer Harrison is an instructor of English at East Stroudsburg University, with a PhD in children's literature from Aberystwyth University in the United Kingdom. Jen's current research focuses on ecocriticism, posthumanism, and children's literature and culture. In addition to editing this collection, Jennifer has recently published a monograph exploring posthumanism and the environment in young adult dystopia, as well as articles on Harry Potter, *The Hunger Games*, and Neil Gaiman's *The Ocean at the End of the Lane*. She is an editor for the journal *Jeunesse: Young People, Texts, Cultures* and a reviewer for the *Children's Book Review* website.

Sarah Jackson is a PhD candidate in literature for children and young adults at The Ohio State University. Her dissertation research focuses on preschoolers' engagement with anthropomorphic multicultural books, and some of her other research interests include postmodern picture books, culturally relevant and sustaining education in early childhood, and dramatic learning and inquiry-based education.

Zoe Jaques is senior lecturer in children's literature in the Faculty of Education, Cambridge University, and dean of Homerton College. She is the author of *Children's Literature and the Posthuman* (2015) and coauthor of *Lewis Carroll's Alice's Adventures in Wonderland and Through the Looking-Glass: A Publishing History* (2013). She runs an Arts and Humanities Research Council network on children's literature in US and UK archives and is co–general editor of the forthcoming *Cambridge History of Children's Literature* in three volumes.

Nada Kujundžić is a PhD candidate at the University of Turku (program in folklore studies) and the University of Zagreb (program in comparative literature). Her dissertation examines the structure and role of narrative space in Jacob and Wilhelm Grimm's *Kinder- und Hausmärchen*.

Ivana Milković is assistant professor in the Faculty of Teacher Education, University of Zagreb. Her research interests include children's literature, literature as part of mother tongue and foreign language education, teaching English to young learners, translating children's literature and culture, and translation strategies. She has participated in several research projects and published studies in the areas of comparative children's literature, teaching methodology, and applied linguistics.

Niall Nance-Carroll earned his doctoral degree from Illinois State University; his dissertation focused on Bakhtinian prosaics in literature for children, adolescents, and adults. He has previously published on Milne's Pooh stories, the television series *Glee*, and Antonio Skármeta's *The Composition*. The latter article has been honored with both the Children's Literature in Education Emerging Scholar Award and the Children's Literature Association Emerging Scholar Award. His research interests include ethics, politics, narrative theory, popular culture, and representations of everyday life.

Professor Emeritus of English at the University of Winnipeg, **Perry Nodelman** is the 2015 recipient of the International Brothers Grimm Award for research in children's literature. He has been engaged in research on children's literature for the past four decades and has published four books and a around 150 essays and book chapters on various aspects of it. Much of his work focuses on viewing children's literature through the lens of critical and cultural theory. As a writer of children's fiction, he has published a picture book, four novels of his own, and seven more in collaboration with Carol Matas. He lives in Halifax, Nova Scotia, where he is a volunteer guide and docent for school tours at the Art Gallery of Nova Scotia.

David Rudd was professor of children's literature and director of the National Centre for Research into Children's Literature at the University of Roehampton until 2016, when he retired. He remains an Emeritus Professor at the University of Bolton, where he first introduced children's literature courses for undergraduates in the 1990s, leading later to an MA in children's literature and culture. He has published around one hundred articles and three monographs on children's literature, most recently *Reading the Child in Children's Literature* (2013), which argues for a fresh, more vibrant approach to studying children's literature. He also edited *The Routledge Companion to Children's Literature* (2010), coedits the international journal *Children's Literature in Education*, and was, from 1998 to 2017, list owner of the United Kingdom's Children's Literature discussion list. His 2010 article "Children's Literature and the Return to Rose" was voted article of the year by the Children's Literature Association. He has always been particularly interested in how the discipline has been theoretically and philosophically constituted.

TSANG Chun Ngai, Jonathan earned his MPhil in critical approaches to children's literature at the University of Cambridge. His research interests lie in Disney animation, adaptations (particularly theater), anthropomorphism, and posthumanism. He completed his BA and BEd in language education (English) at the University of Hong Kong and is currently working as a high school teacher of English and music.

Nicholas Tucker was formerly senior lecturer in cultural studies at the University of Sussex. Before that, he was first a teacher and then an educational psychologist. He is the author of nine books about children, childhood, and reading, including *The Child and the Book* (1981 and 1990). He has also written six books for children, broadcasts frequently, and reviews in the *Independent*. Other publications include *Family Fictions: Contemporary Classics of Children's Literature* (coauthored with Nikki Gamble, 2001), *The Rough Guide to Children's Books, 0–5 and 5–11* (2002), *The Rough Guide to Teenage Books* (coauthored with Julia Eccleshare, 2003), and *Darkness Visible: Inside the World of Philip Pullman* (2003 and 2017).

Donna Varga is professor of child and youth study, Mount Saint Vincent University, Halifax, Nova Scotia, teaching in the areas of early childhood and human development. Her research interests include discourses of childhood innocence, the history of ideas in developmental psychology, and sociocultural beliefs about animals and animal-human relationships. She is investigating the life and times of the teddy bear and its iconic status in Western culture as an ideal of adult and childhood innocence as well as its inculcation in racist children's stories.

Tim Wadham has a PhD in comparative literature from the University of Texas at Arlington, with an emphasis in children's literature. His dissertation is a contextual analysis of Susan Cooper's *The Dark Is Rising Sequence*, which examines the connections between Cooper's work and her childhood influences including films, pantomimes, BBC radio plays, and, of course, the books she read as a child. He has also explored connections with symphonic structure in music and visual illustrations. He is currently an online adjunct instructor for Brigham Young University–Idaho and has developed a course for the University of Arizona in the evaluation of children's books. He has published professional books for the school, library, and education market. He has also published a picture book, *The Queen of France*, with Candlewick Press. He has organized and presented a miniconference on the work of Ursula K. Le Guin at Arizona State University in conjunction with her Arbuthnot Lecture there, and has presented at the Southwest Popular Culture Association. He has published articles in the *Horn Book Magazine* and *Children and Libraries*.

Index

CPSIA information can be obtained
at www.ICGtesting.com
Printed in the USA
BVHW031626220521
607915BV00003B/9

9 781496 834119